CHIEF OF STAFF

CHIEF OF STAFF

The Principal Officers
Behind History's Great Commanders

1
VOL

**Napoleonic Wars to
World War I**

Maj. Gen. David T. Zabecki, AUS (Ret.)

NAVAL INSTITUTE PRESS
Annapolis, Maryland

Naval Institute Press
291 Wood Road
Annapolis, MD 21402

This book has been brought to publication with the generous assistance of Marguerite
and Gerry Lenfest and Edward S. and Joyce I. Miller.

Library of Congress Cataloging-in-Publication Data

Zabecki, David T.
    Chief of staff : the principal officers behind history's great commanders. Vol. 1,
Napoleonic Wars to World War I / Maj. Gen. David T. Zabecki, AUS (Ret.).
        p. cm.
    Includes bibliographical references and index.
    ISBN 978-1-59114-990-3 (alk. paper)
    1. Command of troops—Case studies.   2. Leadership—Case studies.   3. Armed
Forces—Officers—Biography.   4. Generals—Biography.   5. Military history—19th
century.   6. World War, 1914–1918.   I. Title.   II. Title: Principal officers behind
history's great commanders.
UB210 .Z26 2008 vol. 1
355.0092'2—dc22

                                                                              2008003391

Printed in the United States of America on acid-free paper ∞
13 12 11 10 09 08   9 8 7 6 5 4 3 2
First printing

Photo Credits: Gneisenau is courtesy of the Library of Congress. Marcy, Ludendorff,
Seeckt, Kuhl, Lawrence, and Harbord are courtesy of the National Archives and Records
Administration. All others are public domain.

To my son, Staff Sergeant Konrad J. T. Zabecki, U.S. Marine Corps.

Not many fathers get to say that their hero is their own son.

Discreet followers and servants help much to reputation. *Omnis fama a domesticis emanate.* [All fame proceeds from servants.]

Francis Bacon
Essays
LV, "Of Honor and Reputation"

Contents

Foreword

by Professor Dennis Showalter

Arguably the distinguishing feature of modern warmaking has been the emergence of the staff system: the institutions and the men who render policies and orders into plans and actions. Most of the existing work focuses on state levels, and such coordinators of public military policy as Helmuth von Moltke, George Marshall, and Colin Powell vie with commanders for pride of place. What has been missing until now is a study of chiefs of staff at the operational, war-fighting level.

The matrix of the position was the "official families" developed by commanders in the early modern era. The family's initial function was personal: providing a nurturing environment for a man under high and constant stress. That pattern persisted well into modern times. John Rawlins did far more as Grant's chief of staff than keep his superior off the bottle—but that was one of his understood functions. A good institutional example of a late-era family might be the headquarters of Stonewall Jackson, with its incongruous mixture of military technicians and spiritual advisors.

During the sixteenth century the family began providing administrative as well as psychological support. As the French Revolution inaugurated the age of mass war and limited the commander's sphere of direct control, an element of planning was added to the mix, most notably in Napoleon's Grande Armée in the person of Marshal Louis-Alexandre Berthier. Berthier had no illusions about his role and no delusions of grandeur. He saw himself from first to last as Napoleon's servant. The "Berthier model" of the chief of staff as facilitator and factotum nevertheless grew increasingly important over the next hundred years.

From its burgeoning bureaucracies to its developing natural sciences, the nineteenth century was an age of classification, of systematization. The sheer proliferation of data periodically swamped existing analytic systems. In that context, to structure phenomena was to understand them. Understanding in turn became a key to maximizing effectiveness and minimizing cost.

Armies, no less than other major public and private institutions, were influenced by this approach. At all levels and in all respects they were characterized by increasingly complex, increasingly systematic organization and articulation. The Napoleonic era's ad hoc orders of battle were replaced by homogeneous establishments. The practice of detailing men as needed from line companies for administrative duties gave way to permanent rear-echelon units. Recruitment was institutionalized on territorial bases. The introduction of rail transportation and electronic communication demanded keeping time not by days and hours but minutes.

Staffs at all levels became increasingly large and increasingly specialized. A Prussian General Staff counting around fifty members in its first half century grew in its German version to 350 by 1914, with five deputy chiefs and eighteen separate departments. Army and corps staffs increased in proportion and complexity. Similar developments took place across the continent, in France, Russia, Austria, and the lesser military powers. The "scientific" officer became an archetype even on the stage. Gilbert and Sullivan's "Modern Major General" is a master of "information vegetable, animal, and mineral." In George Bernard Shaw's *Arms and the Man*, Major Bluntschli furthers his wooing of the heroine by assisting her father in moving soldiers by rail—a task hopelessly beyond that soldier of the old school.

In such contexts it was scarcely remarkable that at corps and army levels a chief of staff who could coordinate administration and data processing was an asset almost beyond price. If his vision extended as well to the realms of planning, like the subjects of this volume, he was even more valuable as whetstone and consigliere. In general, however, even in his developed form the chief of staff remained an attendant lord, implementing and facilitating his chief's decisions. Prussia/Germany's conception as generally understood elsewhere, of a symbiosis between commander and chief, was considered too egalitarian to inspire emulation.

The nineteenth-century chief of staff, however, was far more than an amanuensis. The Revolutionary/Napoleonic period incorporated the developing Romantic perspective in conflating command with leadership, and perceiving the latter as a manifestation of "genius," a particular spark of divine fire that could not be institutionally replicated and therefore required correspondingly high levels of nurturing and support. That concept was part of the subtext of the Military Society founded in Prussia by Gerhard von Scharnhorst in 1801. Its intention was to introduce, a few at a time, a new generation of junior officers with a common intellectual background, an "aristocracy of cultivation," able to advise their superiors through understanding and character developed by the open, systematic exchange of ideas.

Scharnhorst insisted that the "new men" were intended to assist rather than supplant. When in 1813 Hermann von Boyen joined the corps of Friedrich von Bülow as its chief of staff, he was uncertain what to expect from a superior who was both a critic of Scharnhorst and a scion of one of Prussia's greatest military families. Bülow entertained a parallel set of doubts about the whippersnapper assigned to his headquarters. But the two avoided potential wedge issues, listened to each other, and checked the French in front of Berlin in a series of victories that made Bülow into Bülow von Dennewitz and Boyen into Prussia's war minister. The similar relationship between Gebhardt von Blücher and his chief of staff Neithardt von Gneisenau is epitomized by the bon mot credited to Blücher on learning that Oxford proposed to award him an honorary degree. Allegedly the old cavalryman replied that if he was to be a doctor, Gneisenau must be named an apothecary since they always worked together.

Though that affirmative attitude did not universally inevitably prevail after 1815, neither did Prussian generals as a rule regard their senior staff officers as interlopers or outsiders. The "Boyen model" prevailed, and its most common metaphor was of a good marriage: a partnership in which thoughts and deeds harmonized. The metaphor also left no doubt who was ultimately in charge. The familiar image of elderly excellencies and feckless princes under the thumbs of their chiefs of staffs bears less than a marginal relationship to Prussian/German reality. Among nineteenth-century liberalism's most persistent and pernicious legacies is the myth that a hereditary title is the equivalent of a lobotomy. As General Staff officers were regularly rotated to field assignments, so most of the promising line officers served a term attached to the General Staff. Those who reached corps command, the highest level in peacetime, understood the institution well enough not to be mesmerized by it—and in war were able when it seemed necessary to assert authority over the man wearing the carmine trouser stripes. A household, no matter how harmonious, could have only one head.

The ideal consequences were best expressed by British military theorist and writer Sir Ernest Swinton. "The Point of View," published in 1909 in *The Green Curve and Other Stories*, features an army headquarters in a near-future war. Maps and reports show a desperate situation. No one can find the commanding general. At twilight he finally appears, fishing rod and a two-pound trout in hand. He glances at the map and determines the situation to be in fact well in hand. The moral for his stressed-out subordinates—and for Swinton's readers—

is that a commander cannot afford to become enmeshed in details. That is why staffs—and their chiefs—exist.

That was also the model Europe took to war in 1914. The fourteen chapters in this volume offer case studies in its development, application, and modification. They provide general readers a fresh perspective on the changing face of war, and on the human elements that endure at the heart of warmaking. For general officers and their chiefs of staff, the personal was also the professional. Grant and Rawlins, Hindenburg and Ludendorff, Foch and Weygand are case studies in the psychology of relationships as well as the dynamics of planning and command. Historians and military professionals will be engaged as well by the growing significance of imperturbability in an era of expanding force structures with rudimentary communications systems. Between 1789 and 1918, operational command was shaped by incomplete, derivative information to a greater degree than at any time in the history of war. In the process, what Napoleon called "two o'clock in the morning courage" supplanted coup d'oeil and quick reaction as the primary requisite of effectiveness. In this age of instant communication, information saturation, and judgments so flexible as to approach random, it is valuable to be reminded that resolution is also a military virtue—one not to be conflated with stubbornness.

DENNIS SHOWALTER
Professor of History, Colorado College
Past President, Society for Military History

Introduction

C*hief of Staff* examines the history, development, and role of the military duty position of the chief of staff, the principal staff officer in almost all modern military units commanded by a general officer. Many books have studied history's great commanders and the art of command. No book so far has focused exclusively on the chief of staff—that key staff officer responsible for translating the ideas of the commander into practical plans that common soldiers can execute successfully on the battlefield. In some cases, it is almost impossible to think of a certain great commander without also thinking of his chief of staff. Napoleon and Berthier and Hindenburg and Ludendorff are two examples that come immediately to mind.

This two-volume study examines the role and functioning of the chief of staff primarily through profiles of the most significant practitioners of the chief of staff's art. The focus is on the operational-level chiefs of staff—Hoffmann, Harbord, Weygand—rather than on the national-level chiefs of staff—Hindenburg, Robertson, Joffre. Volume 1 examines the nineteenth century and the first part of the twentieth century through World War I, the formative period of the development of the modern military staff. We start with Berthier, who arguably was the first real chief of staff in the modern sense. In keeping with our operational-level focus, we concentrate on the chiefs at the army, army group, and theater echelons of command. Almost half the subjects profiled in both volumes are German officers. As the introductions to both volumes will make clear, the role of the German chief of staff is the most complex, most subtle, and arguably the most successful on the battlefield.

Each profile will examine a particular chief of staff's relationship with his commander; his relationship with subordinate, higher, and lateral commanders; and how he managed and ran the staff. Some of our subjects—Berthier and Lossberg, for example—are known today almost exclusively for their work as a chief of staff. Others—like Seeckt and Ludendorff—are better known for a much wider range of activities.

The Duties and Role of the Chief of Staff

There are two broad types of chiefs of staff in modern military establishments. At the national level of most armies the chief of staff, or the chief of the general staff, is the country's senior military officer. He is not the commander in chief of the army, that role being reserved for a civilian official, be it the head of state, head of government, or minister of defense. The chief of staff's role at this level is to function as the head of the national military staff, coordinating strategy, policy, training, organization, and equipment development and procurement. National-level military staffs once had a direct operational role, but this has become the exception throughout most of the world in the years following World War II (1939–45).

Below the national level, the chief of staff is a position normally found only on the staffs of general officer commanders, usually at the divisional level and above. At the brigade, regimental, and battalion levels, the chief of staff's function in coordinating the staff is performed by the executive officer or the deputy commander in some armies, and by the operations officer in others. The exact role of the unit chief of staff varies somewhat from army to army. Under the American, British, and French systems, he is the principal staff officer and the commander's closest advisor, but he has no direct command authority. Under the Russian/Soviet system, the chief of staff is actually a deputy commander. Under the pre-1945 German system, the chief of staff was almost a co-commander.

The Development of the Military Staff

Staff officers essentially are assistants to the commander. Although staff officers have no direct command authority, they procure information for the commander; prepare the details of his plans; translate his decisions into orders; transmit his orders to subordinate units; and supervise the execution to ensure the commander's intent is achieved. The chief of staff supervises the "general staff," which usually means the functional staff of a general officer commanding a division or larger organization. It also can mean the national level military staff, and in some armies it refers to a specially trained and managed corps of officers. The Germans also use the term "Admiral Staff" (*Admiralstab*) for naval commands headed by an admiral.

The large staff is a relatively modern phenomenon in military history. In the age of small armies and primitive line-of-sight weapons, military commanders did not need a large staff. They were able to control everything personally. As armies grew beyond the size that one man could manage, commanders had to have help. In the army of the Roman republic the command of a legion rotated among six tribunes. The four not currently in command functioned as the staff of the two commanders. The legion staff also included aides-de-camp and personnel whose task it was to gather intelligence. Near the end of the Republican period a legate became commander of a legion, with the six tribunes remaining as his assistants. The first clearly defined staff functions to emerge centered on administration and supply. Those functions were more routine, more predictable, and more easily reduced to set procedures. The operations and intelligence functions emerged later. Those functions were far more general in nature and less easily reduced to set procedures. In smaller armies the operations function was exercised completely by the commander. In larger armies, a council of war among the commanders decided operational matters.

The seventeenth century and the rise of permanently organized military forces marked the beginning of the modern era of military thought and procedure. The growth of special arms, such as artillery and engineers, increased the requirements for officers with special technical training. All modern European staff systems trace their origins to Gustavus Adolphus. His standardized regimental staffs included a colonel, a lieutenant colonel, a major (who was similar to a modern operations officer and adjutant), a chief quartermaster, two chaplains, two judge advocates, four surgeons, four provost marshals, one assistant provost marshal, various clerks, and a hangman. Gustavus' headquarters staff mirrored the regimental staff structure, with the addition of chiefs of the various special arms, including artillery, engineers, and scouts. Gustavus even had a prototype of a chief of staff, Maj. Gen. Dodo von Kniphausen, who actually functioned more like a second in command or the commander of the reserve line.

The French Staff System

In 1639 Cardinal Richelieu took over the remainder of Gustavus' army and it became an elite corps of French army under Bernard of Saxe-Weimar. By the mid-seventeenth century the French army had several officers titled "Maréchal de Camp Général," who handled supply and quartermaster functions and performed some of the functions of the modern chief of staff, serving the Marshal of France. The Maréchal de Camp Général eventually evolved into the Maréchal Général des Logis.

In European military systems up through Napoleon, the position of quartermaster general evolved to something close to the modern chief of staff. That officer's functions included responsibility for reconnaissance, marches, camp layout, and basic supply. In most armies today, the quartermaster is a logistics officer. In the German army, however, the position of quartermaster was associated with operations well into the twentieth century. This can be traced back to the rudimentary staff system used by the Landsknecht in the fifteenth century, where supply, intelligence, and movements all came under a single staff officer. Operations, however, remained the exclusive province of the commander.

Following the heavy officer losses in the Seven Years' War (1756–63), Frederick the Great of Prussia in 1765 established the Academie des Nobles to train young noblemen for the military and diplomatic services. Although he had a small quartermaster general's staff, Frederick essentially remained his own chief of staff and operations officer.

Modern military staffs are a product of the Industrial Revolution. Under Napoleon, the mass armies of the "Nation in Arms" became too large for a single commander to control. Increases in mobility, maneuverability, and firepower complicated the problems of command. Napoleon's solution was to form semiautonomous corps and divisions that conducted parallel movements and converged on a decisive point to give battle. Napoleon still held the reins of command, but he needed a staff to track the movements of the corps and to translate his command decisions into written orders. That staff was managed by Marshal Louis Alexandre Berthier, who became the first version of a chief of staff we would recognize today. By 1796 Berthier had committed to writing his ideas of staff organization and functioning. He stressed the requirement for speed in staff work and accuracy and conciseness in written reports. Berthier's staff still concentrated primarily on logistical and transportation matters, while Napoleon remained his own operations officer.

The nineteenth century saw the rise of national-level general staffs that prepared war plans in peacetime and systematically collected information for use in wartime. The general staffs also assumed the responsibility for the training and intellectual preparation of staff officers. In 1818 French Minister of War Marshal Gouvion Saint-Cyr established a professional Staff Corps. At first the officers rotated between General Staff and troop duties. That practice was abandoned in 1833 and the French Staff Corps became a closed service. The resulting institutional inbreeding contributed to the French defeat in 1870–71.

Following 1871 the French adopted many of the features of the Prussian/ German staff system. They established a true General Staff headed by a chief, the Chef d'État–Major Général de l'Armée. Candidates for the General Staff Corps attended the École Militaire Supérieure, and rotated between staff and troop unit assignments. Around the turn of the century, all French staffs were organized into three principal bureaus:

1st Bureau: Supply and administration
2nd Bureau: Intelligence
3rd Bureau: Operations

The three-bureau structure, however, was based on a model of mobile and intermittent warfare typical of the Napoleonic era or the Franco-Prussian War (1870–71), which featured a relatively low ratio between days of actual combat to the time forces were in the field. World War I (1914–18) was much different, and the French came to recognize the requirement for a staff section to plan and manage supply and transportation. The 4th Bureau for supply was established in 1917, and with it, the logistical aspects of modern warfare achieved full recognition. By the end of the twentieth century the basic French staff model had been adopted by virtually all major Western armies and NATO.

The Prussian/German Staff System

Perhaps no modern military institution has been more studied and less understood than the Prussian/German General Staff. The institution had a profound influence on the development of the staff systems of almost all other countries. Many armies copied to greater or lesser degrees various aspects of the Prussian/German system, but no other country quite managed to make it work the same way.

The Prussian General Staff evolved from Frederick the Great's small Quartermaster General's Staff. By 1785 the General Staff and Quartermaster General's Staff had become virtually synonymous. Following the Prussian defeat at Jena in 1806, the military reformer David Gerhard von Scharnhorst reorganized the Prussian army and with it the General Staff. Scharnhorst established a General Staff Corps, whose officers rotated between general staff and troop unit assignments. Since the higher nobility in Germany had the right to hold senior military commands without having any real military training, Scharnhorst intended to give the dilettante commanders highly professional staffs headed by a strong and capable chief of staff. Poorly qualified noblemen held high command in the German army up through the end of World War I, and over this period the German chief of staff evolved into something approaching an unofficial but very real co-commander. Scharnhorst's concept of the commander/chief of staff relationship was based on his own experiences as Blücher's chief of staff during the retreat to the Danish border after Jena.

In 1810 Scharnhorst established the Allgemeine Kriegsschule (General War School). In 1859 it was renamed the Kriegsakademie (War Academy) and became the primary training institution for General Staff officers. In 1815 the General Staff moved to Berlin and was divided into what was later called the Grossgeneralstab (Great General Staff) and the Truppengeneralstab (General Staff with Troops). The Great General Staff was the national-level staff, and the General Staff with Troops provided trained general staff officers to the field units. The same corps of general staff officers rotated between both elements, which after 1821 came under the direct control of the Chief of the Great General Staff. In contrast to the other great powers of the nineteenth and the first half of the twentieth centuries, the Germans always pursued a policy of building and maintaining the brain of their army before building its body.

The Prussian/German General Staff changed and evolved over time, of course. Throughout most of the nineteenth century the Prussian army was a personal instrument of the king. Until 1821 the chief of the Great General Staff was directly subordinate to the Prussian war minister. After 1821 he became an advisor to the war minister, but not to the king. In the ensuing years there was a constant struggle for the king's ear between the Great General Staff and the Military Cabinet, a situation not unusual in most European armies of the time. Moreover, the Great General Staff essentially was a planning and advisory body, with no operational control over Prussian forces in the field. The status and power of the Great General Staff began to change in 1857 with the appointment of Helmuth von Moltke (the Elder) as chief.

Moltke started out by establishing a good working relationship with the minister of war, Albrecht von Roon, and the Prussian chancellor, Otto von Bismarck. During the 1864 war with Denmark, King Wilhelm I of Prussia took the unusual step of sending Moltke to the field as chief of staff to Prince Friedrich Karl, who replaced General Friedich von Wrangel when it became clear the octogenarian field commander did not understand the plan developed by the Great General Staff.

Moltke's success in turning the situation around enhanced his personal status and earned him direct access to the king. On 2 June 1866 the king granted Moltke the personal authority to issue orders in the name of the king during the Austro-Prussian War. This made Moltke the de facto commander in chief of the Prussian army in the field. During the 1870–71 war with France, Moltke personally conducted operations in the field, assisted by a staff of only thirteen General Staff officers. Moltke's successes in the Austro-Prussian War (1866) and later in the Franco-Prussian War solidified the position of the chief of the Great General Staff through the end of World War I. The Kriegsakademie was placed directly under the chief of the Great General Staff in 1872, and in 1883 Kaiser Wilhelm I granted the chief of the Great General Staff the right of direct access to the throne. This put the chief of the General Staff on the same level as the war minister and the chief of the Military Cabinet.

From Moltke on, the chief of the Great General Staff directed the German field army in the name of the kaiser in wartime. In peacetime he was responsible for war planning and mobilization. He also planned and directed the Annual Kaiser Maneuver. In peacetime he had no power to command or to inspect troops. The War Ministry, not the General Staff, was responsible for troop training, weapons procurement, pay distribution, administration, and military regulations. The chief of the Great General Staff had no influence on the efficiency reports and career development of field commanders, unless they also happened to be General Staff officers. The Military Cabinet remained an independent agency that reported directly to the kaiser.

Even after the establishment of the German empire in 1871, there really was no such thing as a "German General Staff." The kingdoms of Prussia, Saxony, Bavaria, and Württemberg all maintained armies and each had a general staff; but only the Prussian General Staff prepared war plans for the combined German army. In Bavaria the king retained peacetime command authority, although the German kaiser had the right to inspect in peacetime. Bavaria had its own General Staff, and its own Kriegsakademie, whose standards were on a par with Prussia's. Saxony maintained a separate officer corps and a war ministry to administer its army, but the German kaiser exercised peacetime command. The officer corps of Württemberg's army was integrated with that of Prussia's but Württemberg's War Ministry retained control over certain administrative functions. On the eve of World War I Bavaria fielded three of the German army's twenty-five corps; Saxony fielded two, and Württemberg one.

By 1914 the Great General Staff consisted of ten numbered departments and a series of named departments. They further were grouped under the chief of the Great General Staff, one of five Oberquartiermeister (deputy chief of the General Staff), or under the chief of National Survey. The 2nd Department had the leading role, and the Railroad Department had the largest number of assigned personnel.

- *Chief of the Great General Staff*
  Central Department: General Staff personnel, organization, and
      administration
  6th Department: Maneuvers
  Military History Department II: Older Wars
- *Oberquartiermeister I*
  2nd Department: Germany, operations and deployments
  Railroad Department: Movements
  4th Department: Foreign fortifications
- *Oberquartiermeister II*
  3rd Department: France and Morocco; Britain and Egypt; Afghanistan
  9th Department: Belgium, Netherlands, Switzerland, Italy, Spain,
      Portugal, America, and Germany's Colonies
- *Oberquartiermeister III*
  5th Department: Operational studies
  8th Department: Kriegsakademie
- *Oberquartiermeister IV*
  1st Department: Scandinavia, Russia, Persia, Turkey, and East Asia
  10th Department: Austria-Hungary and the Balkans
- *Oberquartiermeister V*
  Military History Department I: Recent wars
  Archives
  Library
- *Chief of National Survey*
  Trigonometric Department
  Topographical Department
  Cartographic Department

Qualified General Staff officers rotated between assignments on the Great General Staff and with field units. Most staff officers in the field units were not General Staff officers. Those who were made up the Truppengeneralstab. The chief of the Great General Staff remained their superior for "professional matters." Both the unit commander and the unit chief of staff (almost always a General Staff officer) wrote efficiency reports on officers posted to the Truppengeneralstab. In matters relating to general staff work, a Truppengeneralstab officer generally reported to the next higher General Staff officer. General Staff officers might supervise routine staff work, but they seldom actually did it. General Staff officers became experts in operations and other areas only so far as they meshed with operations. Technical experts often were assigned to work on the General Staff, but they were not actually members of it.

At the start of World War I, the chief of staff of a field army supervised the other assigned General Staff officers, who dealt primarily with operations. These included:

- Ia: Operations and training
- Ib: Logistics and movements
- Ic: Intelligence
- Id: Artillery and infantry ammunition resupply

The remainder of the field army staff was supervised by an oberquartiermeister, who himself was a General Staff officer. Those sections included:

- II: Administrative and personnel
- III: Judge Advocate General and military police
- IV: Medical and veterinary

At the corps level, generally only the chief of staff and the Ia and Ib were General Staff officers. The division was the lowest echelon to which General Staff officers were assigned. The Ia usually was the only General Staff officer. He normally was a senior captain or a junior major, and he did not supervise the other divisional staff officers.

The pivotal figure in the German system was the chief of staff. In the commander's absence, the chief of staff could make decisions in the commander's name in all matters except legal proceedings. The commander had the final say, but he and his chief of staff discussed matters as almost equals until the final decision was made. It was almost, but not quite, a system of dual command. This peculiar relationship between the commander and his chief of staff was unique to the German army. On purely operational matters, the chief of staff could protest to the next higher-echelon chief of staff the decisions of his commander with which he did not agree. This right, however, was exercised very rarely in the German army. Thus, the chief of staff functioned as both a subordinate of his own commander and as the High Command's liaison to that commander. He was not, however, an all-encompassing chief of staff, as in the American or French armies. A German chief of staff functioned more like a super operations officer. In the twentieth century it became common practice in the German army to replace the chief of staff, but not necessarily the commanding general, if a unit performed poorly in combat.

Until about 1870 it was possible, but not usual, for an officer to become a qualified General Staff officer without attending the Kriegsakademie. Entrance to that august institution was based on a competitive examination that tested military knowledge only. A system of blind numbering on the exams was supposed to eliminate any bias the graders might have in favor of the aristocratic officers from the elite Guards regiments. The Guards officers normally tended to score higher anyway, because being stationed near Berlin most of the time, they had greater military training opportunities. If the entrance examination had been based on broader academic attainment, the officers from the middle class would have done better, as they generally had a better general education than the aristocratic Guards officers. Thus, noblemen were represented disproportionately in the General Staff through the end of World War I. Nonetheless, in 1870 virtually none of the key commanders in the Guard Corps had attended the Kriegsakademie.

Prior to World War I the course at the Kriegsakademie ran three years. Of the 140 to 160 officers who started the program, only about 100 finished. That group faced another competitive examination for General Staff posting, with only about thirty being accepted. That group then underwent a two-year probationary period serving on the Great General Staff, followed by a final selection screening. Only about a half-dozen officers per year made the final cut. Many of those officers who did not make the various cuts, but who were still considered capable of good staff work, became Adjunktantur, working on the General Staff but not doing general staff work proper. Others became instructors in officers' schools, and others still returned to line units. At one time officers who failed to make the final cuts still had an opportunity to be admitted to the General Staff at some point in the future. That practice ended when Helmuth von Moltke (the Younger) was chief of the Great General Staff.

Contrary to the rigid and hierarchical nature of militaries in general, and German society in particular, the German army developed and practiced several innovative and flexible command and staff techniques that many other armies tried to copy, but almost none mastered. Weisungsführung (leadership by directive) allowed great latitude to higher-level subordinate commanders at the army and in some situations at the corps level. Rather than issuing explicit and detailed orders the High Command issued generalized statements of its intentions, which then provided the framework for independent initiative by the subordinate commanders. This technique capitalized on the local commander's superior knowledge of the situation to his direct front, and also compensated for the slow and unreliable communications systems of the late nineteenth century.

Weisungsführung could only work if the commanders and their staffs at all levels operated on the same set of principles and worked through the tactical decisionmaking process with the same set of intellectual tools. The General Staff officers at each echelon provided the common link to ensure that happened. Many critics over the years have dismissed this system as nothing more than "groupthink" on a huge scale, but such an assessment is far too simplistic and misses the main point entirely. The system did not produce perfect solutions every time, but it almost always produced workable solutions. And it produced them more quickly, which gave the Germans a huge tactical advantage over their opponents. As Gen. Friedrich von Bernhardi put it, "Acting with self-reliance in the sense and spirit of General Headquarters, and of the uniform plan of battle known to us, is the decisive factor in modern battle."

Closely allied with Weisungsführung was the concept of Vollmacht, an authority usually delegated to a staff officer to issue orders and shift units without consulting first with the commander. This technique, too, compensated for slow communications, and placed great faith on the staff officer on the spot to make the correct decisions. Vollmacht was an emergency procedure, normally only used in a crisis situation. Most often a staff officer was specifically delegated Vollmacht, but in some rare situations he assumed and exercised it based on the situation. Military historians to this day still debate whether Lt. Col. Richard Hentsch had Vollmacht or if he was just carrying a Weisung (directive) to the First Army during the First Battle of the Marne in 1914. (See chapter 9 on Hermann von Kuhl.)

Another concept that was completely alien to most military hierarchies, and especially to class- and status-conscious German society, was the notion that function overrode rank. The Germans routinely appointed officers to command and staff positions far above their actual rank. Once in the position, however, the officer functioned with the full authority of the position, regardless of the nominal ranks and pay grades of his functional subordinates. Corps chiefs of staff, who may have been lieutenant colonels, routinely passed orders unchallenged to general officers in command of subordinate divisions. During the final German offensives in May through July 1918, Col. Georg Bruchmüller—who was not even a General Staff officer—was designated as the artillery commander of the entire western front, while at the same time the typical army group artillery commander was a lieutenant general. Ludendorff himself never wore more than the equivalent of three stars.

The German General Staff was far from a flawless institution, however. Many historians have pointed out that General Staff training was more narrowing rather than broadening, and the General Staff Corps suffered from overspecialization. General Staff officers were trained to be experts in operations to the exclusion of all else. Before the Wars of German Unification, students at the Kriegsakademie studied leadership and the great military theorists. After the Kriegsakademie came under the direct control of the Great General Staff, the students studied operations and tactics through the case study method. As Herbert Rosinski noted in his book, *The German Army:*

> The average general staff officer was a high-class military technician, excelling in all dispositions dealing with the movement of large masses, their supply, the organization of railway transport. In simple tactical matters his training was far less complete; outside his own field he was helpless. This was particularly conspicuous in all matters pertaining to politics, the ignorance even of outstanding members of the general staff contrasting most strangely with the knowledge of their French and British opposite numbers.

The German General Staff system was never designed to produce officers with broad political and strategic vision, like Napoleon, Ulysses S. Grant, or Ferdinand Foch. As a result, the Germans managed to lose two world wars while simultaneously setting tactical standards on the battlefield that remain unequalled to this day.

At the start of World War I the Germans had a total officer strength of 36,693. Of that number, only 625 were assigned to the General Staff—both the Grossgeneralstab and the Truppengeneralstab combined. Only 352 of that number, however, were actually members of the General Staff Corps. The others were specialist officers attached to the General Staff for specific duties. During World War I the "Chief System" reached the peak of its power and influence. Oberste Heeresleitung (OHL, the German High Command) increasingly held chiefs of staff rather than commanders responsible for tactical and operational failures. Many historians have argued that Ludendorff carried the Chief System to extremes, marginalizing many commanders during the planning of the 1918 offensives.

The Russian Staff System

Russian military staffs also evolved around the expanding duties of the quartermaster. In 1701 Peter the Great appointed Prince A. F. Shakhovskoi as the first Russian army's first quartermaster general. Fascinated with all things European, most of the military reforms under Peter were patterned on Swedish and German models.

In 1769 Gen. Theodore Baur, a trained Hessian staff officer, accepted a commission from Catherine the Great and later served as the quartermaster general of the Russian First Army in the First Russo-Turkish War (1768–63). In 1772 Catherine issued a decree reorganizing the Russian General Staff system based on Baur's recommendations. As in the Prussian army, the Quartermaster General's Staff became virtually synonymous with the General Staff. Tsar Paul I, a student of Frederickian military methods, introduced a wide range of Prussian methods to the Russian army, but he failed to make any significant improvements to the staff system.

In 1813, after a long running dispute with Berthier, Antoine Henri Jomini left French service and joined the Russian army. Jomini had been Marshal Ney's chief of staff, and he would come to have a significant influence on the development of Russian staffs. Two years later Tsar Alexander I established the Headquarters Staff of His Imperial Majesty, the first real Russian General Staff. Based on recommendations from Jomini, Alexander established the Nicholas Academy in 1832. It was Russia's first institution to provide formal training for staff officers. The reforms of 1836 assigned General Staff officers to corps and divisional staffs for the first time.

Following the dismal experience of the Crimean War (1853–56), three successive senior generals deeply influenced the development of professional staff staffs in the Russian Army. The first was Dmitrii Alekseevich Miliutin, who became war minister in 1861. As early as the 1840s and 1850s, while assigned as an instructor at the General Staff Academy, he developed the theories and techniques of what he called military statistics, which evolved into what would be called military intelligence in the twentieth century. Miliutin's protégé, Nikolai Nikolaevich Obruchev, continued to advance his mentor's theories from the 1860s until his own resignation as chief of the Main Staff in 1898. Aleksei Nikolaevich Kuropatkin served as Miliutin's principal aide throughout the 1880s and became war minister himself in 1898. Kuropatkin's work in the General Staff on mobilization planning resulted in Russia's first viable war plan in 1887, making him the "Russian Schlieffen." Kuropatkin also worked hard to eliminate the effects of interference in military operations by aristocratic amateurs, especially those in the tsar's family.

Despite the efforts of Miliutin, Obruchev, and Kuropatkin, Russia's disastrous performance in the Russo-Japanese War (1904–5) still showed that the Russian armies had a chronic blind spot for the logistics function. (Ironically, Kuropatkin himself was the Russian field commander in Manchuria.) Just prior to the war the 1903 *Regulations for the Headquarters Staff* organized the Russian General Staff into five main departments:

- Quartermaster General: Organization, ordnance, supply, quartering, and training
- Quartermaster General II: Intelligence
- Duty General: Administration
- Communications: Transportation
- Topographics: Maps and survey

The quartermaster general was really the chief of staff as we would consider him today. Because of the vastness of Russia and its many sparsely populated areas, the topographic function always played a more important role on Russian military staffs than it did in other European armies. At the corps and divisional levels, there was no staff equivalent to the chief of military communications, which in effect created an institutional disconnect between operational planning and logistics.

In World War I the Russian General Staff was immediately subordinate to the minister of war. The Quartermaster General's staff still functioned as the de facto general staff, and corps and divisional staff structures still were not standardized. By that point, however, a unit's chief of staff had the status of an assistant commander, who automatically assumed command upon the commander's sickness or death. The various staff section chiefs were advisors to the chief of staff, not to the commander. But despite the 1914 regulations, *Status of Field Administration of Troops in Wartime*, overall Russian staff performance in World War I was dismal.

The British Staff System

The earliest formal British military staffs can be traced to Oliver Cromwell's New Model Army, established on 15 February 1645. Cromwell's staff structure was reorganized very closely along the lines of the existing European staffs of the mid-seventeenth century. A staff officer with the title of Sergeant Major General held the position most closely related to the modern chief of staff.

During the period of the duke of Marlborough, the regimental adjutant emerged as an all-purpose staff officer and the principal assistant to the regimental major, who was the operations officer for the regiment. In the higher-level commands the distinction began to emerge between the aides-de-camp and the adjutants. The quartermaster general had the traditional role of selecting and laying out the camp. From Marlborough through the end of the eighteenth century, however, the period was characterized by general disorganization in British military administration.

Under Wellington the British staff system began to take on its modern shape. Wellington stressed efficient supply and transportation systems, which were critical to his operations in the Peninsular War (1808–14). Wellington's staff evolved into three main groups: the commander's personal staff, the Adjutant General's Department, and the Quartermaster General's Department. The Adjutant General's Department primarily handled the operational and intelligence functions, while the Quartermaster General's Department dealt primarily with the administrative and logistics functions. The organization of the staff into two basic functional components negated the requirement for a chief of staff to coordinate. Both departments reported directly to the commander. The same staff organization also existed at the divisional level.

Although the British Staff College was founded in 1858, the British army generally failed to keep pace with Continental military developments of the nineteenth century. British operations in the Crimea and South Africa suffered accordingly. In the 1890s interest in military reform picked up with the publication of Spenser Wilkinson's influential book, *The Brain of an Army,* an incisive analysis of the Prussian military system. The failures in the Boer War (1899–1902) added impetus to the push for military reform. The British General Staff was established in 1906, with an Imperial General Staff established two years later. The *Staff Manual* was published in 1912.

Influenced by the German system, the British added the General Staff as the third section of the staff system that evolved under Wellington. As in the German system, however, the General Staff focused almost exclusively on operations and intelligence. Thus, in World War I and World War II, British staffs at the divisional level and above were organized as follows:

- General Staff (G Branch)
    Intelligence
    Planning
    Operations
- Adjutant General's Staff (A Branch)
    Personnel
    Administration
- Quartermaster General's Staff (Q Branch)
    Supply
    Transportation

As in the German system, the chief of the General Staff essentially was a super operations officer. He coordinated the work of the entire staff, but in collaboration with the chief administrative officer, who supervised both A and Q branches. The chief administrative officer still had direct access to the commander. British General Staff officers of the period held a confusing variety of job titles, which had even more confusing abbreviations:

- General Staff Officer 1 (GSO1), the head of G Branch
- General Staff Officer 2 (GSO2), the head of a staff division, intelligence, operations, etc.
- General Staff Officer 3 (GSO3), an assistant division chief
- Brigade Major, the GSO1 of a brigade
- Brigadier, General Staff (BGS), the senior G Branch officer on corps staff
- Major General, General Staff (MGGS), the senior G Branch officer on army staff

- Assistant Adjutant General or Assistant Quartermaster General (AAG or AQMG), lieutenant colonels, or in some cases colonels, heading sections of the A or Q branches
- Deputy Assistant Adjutant General or Deputy Assistant Quartermaster General (DAAG or DAQMG), majors as assistant section heads of the A or Q branches
- Staff Captain A or Q (SCA or SCQ), captains assigned to the A or Q branches

The American Staff System

During America's earliest days the Continental Army was heavily influenced by British practice. What few trained officers the Americans had, including Washington himself, were products of the British military. On 16 June 1775 the Continental Congress passed legislation detailing the army's staff. The following staff officers were authorized:

- Adjutant General
- Quartermaster General
- Commissary General of Stores and Provisions
- Commissary General of Musters
- Paymaster General
- Chief of Engineers

Additional legislation on 19 July 1775 authorized two additional staff officers:

- Wagon Master
- Commissary of Artillery Stores

Washington's force was not a national army. Each sovereign state had its own military system, and Washington and his meager staff sat on top of and tried to coordinate the operations of a hodgepodge of units supplied by the thirteen colonies. For the most part, the British staff system prevailed at the regimental level, with the principal staff officers being the regimental major, the adjutant, and the quartermaster. As the war progressed, however, the influx of relatively senior-ranking foreign volunteers brought in influences from all the various staff systems of Europe.

Late in 1777 the Continental Congress authorized the establishment of the position of Inspector General, with Thomas Conway appointed on 13 December. Because of his involvement in the "Conway Cabal," Conway did not last long in the position. Conway was replaced as inspector general by Friedrich Wilhelm von Steuben, who was a product of Frederick the Great's staff system. Steuben was the man who brought order out of chaos in the fledgling Continental Army. Being the only trained staff officer on Washington's staff, he really functioned as an all-around staff officer and became Washington's de facto chief of staff. Historians generally agree that von Steuben was the only member of Washington's staff capable of preparing the professional operations order for the Yorktown siege. In every sense of the term, he was the first trained and qualified staff officer in the U.S. Army.

Following the American Revolution (1775–83), the U.S. Army almost disappeared completely, except for one understrength company of artillery left to guard the military stores at West Point. In the closing years of the eighteenth century the force slowly built back up. The Army Legislation of 1796 established a minuscule national level staff for the U.S. Army that consisted of one major general, one brigadier general, one inspector functioning as adjutant general, one quartermaster general, and one paymaster general. Throughout the War of 1812 (1812–15), however, the organization of the regimental staffs was essentially the same as it had been during the Revolution.

In 1855 Secretary of War Jefferson Davis sent a board of three officers to Europe to study and report on the latest advances in military science. Headed by Maj. Richard Delafield, the board also included Capt. George B. McClellan. The Delafield Board spent two years in Europe and then returned to publish their massive report, *The Art of War in Europe*. The Delafield Report detailed all sorts of military equipment used in the European armies, but it did not contain one mention of the Prussian staff system, which arguably was the most significant military innovation of the period.

By the start of the 1860s every general officer with a field command had a staff, sometimes called a General Staff, but more often called a Field Staff. The Field Staff was divided into two major subgroupings. The Special Staff handled supply, transportation, and other technical and specialized functions. The Special Staff officers included the quartermaster general, chief of ordnance, chief of engineers, chief of commissaries, provost marshal, surgeon, and chaplain. The Personal Staff kept the command's records and prepared and distributed the operational orders. By an act of Congress passed on 22 June 1861, a brigade commander was authorized a personal staff of one assistant adjutant general and two aides-de-camp.

Ironically, the lack of a trained staff was one of the biggest headaches General McClellan faced just a few short years after the publication of the Delafield Report, when he assumed command of the Army of the Potomac. In his memoirs McClellan wrote, "One of the greatest defects of our military system is the lack of a thoroughly instructed staff corps, from which should be furnished chiefs of staffs for armies, army corps, and divisions."

McClellan took the first steps to fix that problem with the appointment of his father-in-law, Col. Randolph B. Marcy, as chief of staff of the Army of the Potomac. Marcy thus became the first officer to hold that position officially in the U.S. Army. It was Gen. Ulysses S. Grant, however, who was the most innovative of all the Civil War commanders in how he used his staff. Under the control of his chief of staff, Gen. John A. Rawlins, Grant's staff had genuine input into the commander's decision-making process.

The staffs of the Union Army were nonstandardized and imperfect organs at best, and almost always directly reflected the character of the commander himself. Perhaps the most significant weakness was intelligence, with McClellan relying almost exclusively on the Pinkerton Detective Agency for that function. Some military historians have speculated that Gen. George Meade's lack of a proper staff allowed Lee to disengage without interference after Gettysburg. By the latter part of the Civil War generals commanding independent armies in the field usually had a Personal Staff consisting of a chief of staff, two assistant adjutants general, two military secretaries, an inspector general, and as many as seven aides-de-camp. At the lower echelons, however, the principal staff officer remained the adjutant or the adjutant general. In 1864 a division in the Army of the Potomac had a staff consisting of an adjutant general, an inspector general, a judge advocate, a provost marshal, a quartermaster, commissaries of muster and subsistence, a chief of pioneers (combat engineers), a topographical engineer, an ordnance officer, and a surgeon.

Although the U.S. Army had brigades, divisions, and corps during the Civil War, they were not permanent organizations, and all were disbanded immediately after the war's end. Echelons above the regimental level were again established in April 1898 at the start of the War with Spain, but the war ended that August and within two months the brigades, divisions, and corps were again disbanded. In the years leading up to World War I the U.S. Army conducted various experiments with echelons above the regimental level, but those units existed for the most part on paper only. The U.S. Army's first permanently organized division, today's 1st Infantry Division, was not established until 24 May 1917.

With the highest permanent echelon being the regiment, staff experience and knowledge atrophied in the U.S. Army in the years between the end of the Civil War and America's entry into World War I. In 1867 a commission headed by Lt. Gen. William T. Sherman proposed sweeping staff reforms, but its recommendations were not acted upon. The start of real military reform had to wait until Elihu Root became secretary of war in 1899. A New York lawyer, Root had read and was deeply influenced by Wilkinson's book, *The Brain of an Army*.

Before the Root Reforms of 1903 the U.S. Army had no real General Staff. The army's senior officer, the Commanding General of the U.S. Army, had authority over troops and units, but not over the adjutant general, quartermaster general, chief of engineers, and the other bureau chiefs. The semiautonomous bureau chiefs answered directly to the secretary of war. The obvious lack of ability to coordinate at the highest levels produced disastrous results in the Spanish-American War (1898).

Even before receiving the authority to transform the army, Root laid the groundwork for a solid system of officer education. In 1901 the former Infantry and Cavalry School at Fort Leavenworth became the General Service and Staff College, later renamed the U.S. Army Command and General Staff College. The following year Root established the U.S. Army War College to train future senior officers.

In 1903 Root finally won the authority from Congress to establish a General Staff, despite fierce opposition from the then–commanding general of the U.S. Army, Lt. Gen. Nelson A. Miles. The office of Commanding General of the Army was transformed into the Chief of Staff of the Army. The new General Staff Corps of forty-four officers was manned by rotation, rather than by permanent assignment. By 1908 the U.S. Army General Staff was organized into four sections:

- Mobile Forces
- Training
- Coastal Artillery
- Militia

When America entered World War I the U.S. Army and its staff systems were very much a work in progress. As established by the *Field Service Regulations* of 1905, the staff of a field division consisted of a chief of staff; an adjutant general; an inspector general; a provost marshal; a judge advocate; a surgeon; a quartermaster; and commissary, engineer, signal, ordnance, and muster officers. Except for the addition of the chief of staff, the structure was not very different than that of an American division in 1864.

In 1917 Gen. John J. Pershing studied both the French and the British staff systems. He adopted the simpler and more straightforward four-bureau French model for the American Expeditionary Force (AEF). The Americans added a letter designation to the front of the staff section number to indicate the level of the staff. A staff officer designated as an S-2 or an S-3 would be the intelligence or operations officer of a battalion, regiment, or brigade. The G-2 or G-3 would be their equivalents on divisional staffs and above. The S stood for "staff" and the G stood for "general staff." All general staffs were headed by a chief of staff. Lower command echelons in the U.S. Army, however, had only three staff sections initially, eliminating logistics (S-4). The Americans also added a fifth principal staff section for training at the General Headquarters (GHQ) level. This reflected the realities of having to train a massively expanded mobilization army in the shortest time possible. To provide crash training for 500 General Staff officers, the AEF established a staff college at Langres, France.

Summary

Each of the subjects presented in this study operated within the framework of his own army and its command and staff system of the time. Hence, the purpose of this introduction is to provide the background for the profiles that follow. Although we focus on the operational-level chiefs of staff, this introduction provided an overview of the major national-level staff systems from which they came and under which they operated. In most cases, the national and field-level staff systems evolved together, and staff structures of the field units were smaller versions of the national systems. Following World War I military staffs tended to grow larger and more complex, and the chief of staff's position evolved accordingly. The important post–World War II practitioners of the chief of staff's art will be examined in volume 2.

Selected Bibliography

Bernhardi, Friedrich von. *How Germany Makes War*. New York: George H. Doran, 1914.

Creveld, Martin van. *Command in War*. Cambridge: Harvard University Press, 1985.

Falkenhayn, Erich von. *The General Staff and Its Decisions*. New York: Dodd, Mead, 1920.

Goerlitz, Walter. *History of the German General Staff, 1657–1945*. New York: Praeger, 1953.

Hittle, J. D. *The Military Staff: Its History and Development*. Harrisburg, Pa.: Military Service Publishing, 1949.

Jones, R. Steven. *The Right Hand of Command: Use and Disuse of Personal Staffs in the American Civil War*. Harrisburg, Pa.: Stackpole Books, 2000.

Ludendorff, Erich. *The General Staff and Its Problems*. London: Hutchinson, 1920.

Militärgeschichtliches Forschungsamt. *Die Generalstäbe in Deutschland 1871–1945*. Stuttgart: Deutsche Verlagsanstalt, 1962.

Millotat, Christian O. E. *Das Preussisch-deutsche Generalstabssystem: Wurzeln—Entwicklung—Fortwirken*. Zurich: Hochschulverlag AG, 2000.

————. *Understanding the Prussian-German General Staff System*. Carlisle Barracks, Pa.: Strategic Studies Institute, U.S. Army War College, 1992.

Rich, David Alan. *The Tsar's Colonels: Professionalism, Strategy, and Subversion in Late Imperial Russia*. Cambridge: Harvard University Press, 1998.

Rosinski, Herbert. *The German Army*. Washington, D.C.: The Infantry Journal, 1944.

Wilkinson, Spenser. *The Brain of an Army*. London: A. Constable and Co., 1891.

Wilson, John B. *Maneuver and Firepower: The Evolution of Divisions and Separate Brigades*. Washington, D.C.: U.S. Army Center of Military History, 1998.

Zabecki, David T., and Bruce Condell. *On the German Art of War: Truppenführung*. Boulder, Colo.: Lynne Rienner, 2001.

Great Commanders

Commander	Chief of Staff	Volume
Creighton Abrams	Walter T. Kerwin Jr	2
Friedrich Sixt von Armin	Fritz von Lossberg	1
Claude Auchinleck	Eric Dorman-Smith	2
Hermann Balck	Friedrich-Wilhelm von Mellenthin	2
Fritz von Below	Fritz von Lossberg	1
Gebhardt von Blücher	August Neithardt von Gneisenau	1
Hans von Boehn	Fritz von Lossberg	1
Napoleon Bonaparte	Louis-Alexandre Berthier	1
Karl von Einem	Fritz von Lossberg	1
Dwight D. Eisenhower	Frederick Morgan	2
	Walter Bedell Smith	2
Erich von Falkenhayn	Fritz von Lossberg	1
Ferdinand Foch	Maxime Weygand	1
Friedrich Karl, Prince of Prussia	Helmuth von Moltke (the Elder)	1
Douglas Haig	Launcelot Kiggell	1
	Herbert Lawrence	1
Paul von Hindenburg	Carl Adolf Maximilian Hoffmann	1
	Erich Ludendorff	1
Ulysses S. Grant	John A. Rawlins	1
Albert Kesselring	Siegfried Westphal	2
Alexander Kluck	Hermann von Kuhl	1
Ivan Konev	Vasily D. Sokolovsky	2
Leopold, Prince of Bavaria	Carl Adolf Maximilian Hoffmann	1
Douglas MacArthur	Edward M. Almond	2
George B. McClellan	Randolph B. Marcy	1
August von Mackensen	Hans von Seeckt	1

Commander	Chief of Staff	Volume
Giovanni di Messe	Fritz Bayerlein	2
Bernard Law Montgomery	Francis de Guingand	2
George S. Patton	Hobart R. Gay	2
	Hugh J. Gaffey	2
John J. Pershing	James Guthrie Harbord	2
Erwin Rommel	Fritz Bayerlein	2
	Hans Speidel	2
	Siegfried Westphal	2
Gerd von Rundstedt	Siegfried Westphal	2
Rupprecht, Crown Prince of Bavaria	Hermann von Kuhl	1
Josef Stalin	Aleksei I. Antonov	2
Joachim von Stülpnagel	Hans Speidel	2
Walton H. Walker	Eugene M. Landrum	2
William C. Westmoreland	Walter T. Kerwin Jr.	2
Wilhelm, Crown Prince of Germany	Konstantin Schmidt von Knobelsdorf	1

Part One
The Nineteenth Century

CHRONOLOGY OF LOUIS-ALEXANDRE BERTHIER

20 Nov 1753	Born in Versailles, France.
1 Jan 1766	Entered the French army as a topographical engineer.
1 Mar 1770	Promoted to lieutenant, Legion of Flanders (infantry).
2 Jun 1777	Promoted to captain, Royal Lorraine Dragoons.
26 Apr 1780	Assigned to Soissonnais Infantry Regiment.
Late 1780–81	Served as staff assistant to Marshal Rochambeau in the American Revolution.
2 Dec 1787	Appointed as assistant, General Staff Corps.
1 Jul 1788	Promoted to major.
11 Jul 1789	Promoted to lieutenant colonel.
1 Apr 1791	Promoted to colonel.
22 May 1792	Promoted to brigadier general and appointed chief of staff in Rochambeau's Army of the North.
21 Aug 1792	Suspended from duties by the Assembly; allowed to remain in the army as a private.
2 Mar 1795	Reinstated as a brigadier general and chief of staff to the Armies of the North and Italy.
13 Jun 1795	Promoted to general of division.
5 May 1796	Heroic leadership at the Battle of Lodi.
4 Jan 1797	Heroic leadership at the Battle of Rivoli.
9 Dec 1797	Appointed commander, Army of Italy.
8 Mar 1798	Appointed chief of staff, Army of the Orient.
11 Nov 1799	Appointed minister of war.
2 Apr 1800	Appointed commander, Army of the Reserve.
9 Jun 1800	Heroic service at the Battle of Montebello.
14 Jun 1800	Wounded at the Battle of Marengo.
11 Aug 1800	Appointed Ambassador Extraordinary to Spain.
19 May 1804	Appointed Senior Marshal of Empire.
29 Aug 1805	Appointed chief of staff of the Grand Army.
20 Mar 1806	Made Duke of Valangin and Prince of Neufchatel.
15 Aug 1809	Made Prince of Wagram.
27 Feb 1810	Appointed Ambassador Extraordinary to Vienna.

13 Jun 1810	Appointed colonel general (honorary) of the Swiss.
29 Jan 1814	Wounded at the Battle of Brienne.
1 Jun 1814	Appointed captain, 5th Company, King's Corps Guard.
4 Jun 1814	Elevated to a Peer of France.
1 Jun 1815	Died falling from the Neue Residenz in Bamberg, Bavaria.

Louis-Alexandre Berthier

Samuel J. Doss

Louis-Alexandre Berthier translated his master's strategic visions into practicable operational orders. Napoleon's chief of staff was the quintessential staff officer: tireless, efficient, diligent in the campaigning process, resplendent in uniform and appearance, and a superb intermediary between Bonaparte and his subordinate commanders. Although he was indispensable as chief of staff, Berthier was completely incapable of independent command. Napoleon genuinely liked him and allowed him more familiarity than anyone else, save Marshal Jean Lannes. But Bonaparte worked Berthier relentlessly, and often openly criticized and flew into tirades against him.

Born at Versailles on 20 November 1753, Louis-Alexandre Berthier was the oldest of four sons. His father was Jean Baptiste Berthier. His mother was Marie Françoise l'Huillier de la Serre. As a surveying engineer, his father gained fame by building the magnificent Ministries of Marine, War, and Foreign Affairs at Versailles. Louis XIV rewarded the senior Berthier with a title of nobility, a colonelcy of infantry, an inheritable pension of 12,000 livres, and the title of "Commander in Chief of the Corps of Surveying Engineers," as well as the orders of St. Michael and St. Louis. All the titles were taken from Berthier's family during the French Revolution.[1]

Berthier was not an attractive man. However, his ability as a staff officer was unmatched, his endurance second to none, and he was renowned for his capacity to write clear and concise orders for hours on end. At any hour on the clock he appeared fully dressed, ready for intense labor, and knowledgeable of the exact whereabouts of each subordinate commander, unit strength, and to what location he should send their next orders. But whenever his mind was not consumed by work, his life's love, the beautiful Madame Guiseppina de Visconti, was the only thing on his mind. Berthier was head-over-heels in love with her, and never for a moment swayed from this devotion.[2]

Berthier initially followed his father, becoming a topographical engineer in 1776. Commissioned a lieutenant in 1770, he first served with the Legion of Flanders. In 1777 he became a captain in the Royal Lorraine Dragoons, and then he transferred to the 2nd Chasseurs-à-Cheval in 1779.[3]

Berthier is the only marshal of France to have served in the American War of Independence, the French revolutionary wars, and the wars of Napoleon, serving in the direct presence of both George Washington and Napoleon Bonaparte. Berthier came to North America to fight in the American Revolution, arriving with the Soissonnais Infantry Regiment. He later became one of the Comte de Rochambeau's close staff officers—an aide to the quartermaster general. As such, Berthier participated in the planning by Washington and Rochambeau at many locations on the east coast of America. His planning skill and cartographic wizardry exerted considerable influence in keeping the American and French armies well provisioned during the march from Rhode Island to Virginia. Berthier also proved to be an able assistant during the siege of British Lord Cornwallis' forces at Yorktown in the fall of 1781. In all likelihood, the future marshal of France worked closely with Alexander Hamilton, the Marquis de Lafayette, and a score of other distinguished soldiers during the campaign. Berthier left North America for a brief period of duty in the Caribbean, and finally arrived back in France at Brest in June 1783.[4]

Berthier was promoted to lieutenant colonel in 1789 and became chief of staff to Gen. Pierre Victoire de Besenval, who commanded the troops around Paris. Shortly after, the king of France appointed Berthier to command the National Guard of Versailles. Berthier survived the bloodbaths of 1789–90, but he fell out of favor with the revolutionaries by aiding in the escape of Louis XVI's aunts. He managed to retain his high rank, and he successively served as chief of staff to such varied personalities as Ronsin in the Vendée, the ex-aristocrat Biron, and Rossignol. On 22 May 1792 Berthier became a brigadier general and chief of staff to Rochambeau's Army of the North. Berthier avoided the Terror for two years, but the Assembly required his destitution on 21 August 1792. Berthier was allowed to remain a private in the army.[5]

The Republican armies were revamped in 1795. Lazare Carnot, the minister of war, reinstated Berthier as General de Brigade in early 1795. Then he was posted as chief of staff to the elderly General François-Christophe Kellerman (the victor of Valmy) in the Army of the Alps. In June Berthier was promoted to General de Division.[6]

Berthier developed his own staff system, with "divisions" taking specific duties. The first division was responsible for actions requiring Berthier's immediate attention; the second provided equipment of many sorts; the third division provided inspections for forage and food, reconnaissance, and intelligence; and the fourth was tasked with liaison responsibilities, quartering the troops, and provost marshal matters.[7]

In 1796 Berthier became Napoleon's chief of staff during the first Italian campaign. He continued his ever humble and obedient service to Napoleon until 1814 on every campaign save Waterloo. On 27 March 1796 Berthier, Joachim Murat, and August-Frédéric-Louis Marmont arrived in Nice with Napoleon, and their long eighteen-year association began. During this campaign, as he would later, Berthier often proved his courage in combat. He led a cavalry charge at the Battle of Rivoli and a direct infantry attack at the Battle of Lodi.[8]

Berthier was sixteen years older than Napoleon, but this did not seem to cause difficulties. He had an incredible knack for overcoming Napoleon's comparatively poor Corsican French and his horrible handwriting. Berthier's greatest brilliance was perhaps in overcoming his boss's penchant for broad-brush concepts, and creating detailed, logical orders to execute Napoleon's intent. When he received a written order from Napoleon, Berthier read the order and then passed it to one of his four adjutants general, whose department was responsible for the matter. If necessary, the order was passed to multiple departments, with Berthier giving the necessary guidance.[9]

Berthier was always immaculately dressed. Many reported finding him dressed at all hours of the night, somehow in clean uniforms, despite everyone around him being filthy. Louis-Alexandre is said to have set the "fashion scene" among the officers in Napoleon's army. Others, such as Murat, were too outlandish. According to David Chandler, Berthier was also the most decorated of all the marshals, accumulating at least thirteen orders (including the Grand Eagle) in just more than three years.[10]

Berthier oversaw both a personal staff and a military staff. In some ways a reflection of Napoleon himself, Berthier had his own large personal staff, including a personal secretary, a cashier, and a small accounts department. Each of Berthier's secretaries had a staff and establishment of his own. Similar to Napoleon's private secretaries, Berthier's private secretaries also had staffs who were civilians rather than military or retired military. Their mutual opinion on this subject was that active-duty officers could not be spared for what was essentially sedentary work; active-duty officers were better suited for work with troops.[11]

In 1796 Berthier wrote his treatise on the functioning of the staff, *Document sur le Service de L'État-Major Général à l'Armée des Alpes*. This document, and Berthier's example in practice, established the pattern of staff functioning throughout the Napoleonic Wars. Many of Berthier's principles apply to today's modern armies.

According to Berthier, the chief of staff "is the central pivot of all [staff] operations," and "speed is the most important thing in general staff work." In some ways Berthier's adjutants general were similar to modern staff sections, but Berthier had overlaps in duties that would completely confuse the modern staff officer. In some cases he allocated both administrative and operational functions to the same adjutant general. As described by J. D. Hittle, "There was a constant tendency to fail to distinguish between operational, intelligence, and administrative functions, as, for instance, Berthier placed troop movements in the first section, which was also concerned with staff records and organization." Hittle also noted, "In another instance he grouped the postal service under the same section that was charged with intelligence. By placing reconnaissance, marching, and plans under the same section, he failed to demonstrate that he realized the basic difference between the operational and intelligence function." Curiously, neither Napoleon's nor Berthier's staffs were mirrored in the French army's many subordinate corps headquarters staffs. In contrast, the corps staffs varied in size and function. And, unlike Berthier, the corps chiefs of staff in most cases exercised significant control over tactical operations and planning.[12]

As a general rule, Berthier directly accompanied Napoleon, as did the Master of the Horse, the Marshal of the Palace, a large and able group of aides-de-camp, several diligent secretaries, and Napoleon's personal bodyguard. Napoleon was often angry at Berthier for one reason or another. According to C. Brian Kelly, Napoleon once referred to his chief of staff as a "chief clerk," who was "just a gosling transmuted by me into some kind of eagle." On rare occasions Napoleon physically assaulted Berthier, once slamming his head into a stone wall.[13]

Berthier never presumed to be more than a servant to his master, striving for perfection in his staff and advisory duties rather than striving for his own command. On those few occasions when Berthier exercised command, he performed poorly. According to F. Loraine Petre:

> He had an unrivaled knowledge of detail and a most intimate acquaintance with Napoleon's methods of work and command, which makes it all the

more remarkable that he should have shown himself so incompetent to play, even temporarily, the master's part. He was an illusion of the evil of Napoleon's system of suppression of all independence on the part of his subordinates. . . . His methods of command excluded them [the marshals] from the sphere of higher strategy.[14]

Upon Napoleon's departure from Italy, Berthier was placed in command of the Army of Italy on 9 December 1797. Only two months later he handed over this command to another future marshal of France, André Massena.[15] When Napoleon began reorganizing his army for the expedition at Toulon in 1798, he selected generals who were generally younger, men who had shown energy and promise. But he retained Berthier as his chief of staff.[16]

During the Egyptian campaign Berthier was designated as chief of staff to the Army of the Orient on 8 March 1798. The expedition brought success initially, but as the months dragged by, Berthier's duty performance declined precipitously. He missed his mistress, Madame Visconti, who was still in Italy. He hated Egypt and slipped ever deeper into depression. Berthier begged Napoleon to let him risk the English blockade and leave the burning sands of Egypt.[17]

Relations between the two became chilly, for Napoleon did not like groveling. To Gen. Jean Batiste Kleber, Napoleon said, "Look at Berthier . . . pouting and grumbling, and that is the man with his old woman's temper, whose flatterers call him my mentor. If I ever get into power, I'll put him so high that everyone will see his mediocrity."[18] Napoleon finally consented to Berthier's departure, but when Berthier learned that Napoleon had plans to set off for Asia, he decided to remain and the two quickly reconciled. On 24 August 1799 Napoleon departed Egypt for France. With him were Berthier, Murat, Jean Lannes, and a few others. Napoleon left Kleber in charge of the army in Egypt, and ultimately that army met disaster.[19]

Berthier was with Napoleon on 9 November 1799 during the coup d'état of 18 Brumaire. Berthier's part in the coup itself was somewhat passive. A few days later Berthier was appointed minister of war, a position he technically held until 1807. Berthier then immediately had the enormous task of reorganizing and refitting the French armies.[20]

The second Italian campaign began in the spring of 1800. Napoleon sent Berthier ahead to assemble 60,000 troops near the Alpine passes, in the vicinity of Dijon. Berthier organized this army and made special preparations for winter clothing and equipment. In this capacity, he technically commanded the Army of the Reserve. As First Consul, Napoleon was not constitutionally allowed to command an individual army. This piece of information was openly publicized by Napoleon as a ruse to his enemies. In practice, however, Napoleon was most certainly in command. When he arrived in April, the army was ready to campaign. During the campaign Berthier was wounded at Marengo on 14 June 1800.[21]

From Italy Berthier was posted to Spain as an ambassador-extraordinary. In accordance with guidance received from Foreign Minister Charles-Maurice de Talleyrand, he hammered out the secretive Treaty of San Ildefonso. He then resumed his post as chief of staff to the Grand Armée that would assemble near Boulogne.[22]

Napoleon was proclaimed emperor on 18 May 1804. The next day he established the Marshalate. Berthier was the first marshal on the list of fourteen, thus becoming the senior Maréchal d'Empire. At the time he was fifty-one years of age. On 24 August Napoleon also gave Berthier another title he was to retain until the end of his services. As chief of the General Staff, Berthier's official title was now Major General de l'Armée. It was thereafter to Berthier's personal cabinet that Bonaparte would come to examine campaign maps and make war plans. General Louis Desaix had devised a system of colored pins to represent the location of friendly and enemy formations, and Berthier perfected the technique. The Austerlitz campaign the following year was perhaps the best example of Berthier's most exceptional and studied staff work.[23]

On 30 March 1806 Napoleon named Berthier Duke of Valangin and Prince of Neufchatel. It appears he never even visited the principality, although many of its taxes went into his personal account.

Prussia had sided with the allies of the Third Coalition in 1805, but Napoleon's quick victories at Ulm and Austerlitz gave King Frederick of Prussia no time to mobilize and commit troops. After the Austerlitz campaign, much of the French army was still in Bavaria, rested, fit, and trained to the peak of its fighting skill. In September 1806 the emperor placed Berthier in charge of the army in Germany. Then, apparently forgetting, Napoleon also gave that job to Murat. Both marshals began to issue orders, in some cases contrary to one another. Napoleon subsequently went to Mainz to sort out the confusion. Napoleon spent the following days in a frenzy of writing orders for concentrating his army in Franconia, Bavaria. It turned out to be a brilliant campaign plan, with precisely designated routes of march for each of the army's corps.[24]

Berthier joined Napoleon shortly thereafter, and dutifully executed his master's plans. The results were Napoleon's 14 October victory at Jena and Marshal Louis Davout's even more impressive victory twelve miles away at Auerstaedt that same day. The subsequent relentless pursuit to the sea almost destroyed the entire Prussian army. As always, Berthier issued orders and followed the movements of the emperor's dispersed corps. But a quick end to the war eluded Napoleon, and the campaign continued throughout the cold harsh winter of 1806–7. The bloody battles of Eylau and Friedland concluded the campaign in the spring of 1807.[25]

Despite Berthier's undying affections for Guiseppina Visconti, Napoleon forced him into a marriage of political value. On 9 March 1808 Berthier wed Princess Maria Elizabeth of Pfalz-Zweibrücken-Birkenfeld. His new wife understood the importance of the arrangement and apparently even made allowances for Berthier to see Madame Visconti.[26]

That same year, Berthier served as chief of staff to the Army of Spain and then became Major General of the Grand Armée. Spain was not to Napoleon's liking, however. Soon he and Berthier departed the Iberian Peninsula, leaving the fighting to other marshals, most of whom demonstrated poor generalship in Spain and Portugal. Eventual British victory on the Iberian Peninsula, although never a decisive theater of the Napoleonic Wars, was an irreparable crack in the concrete of Napoleon's once-solid empire.

Napoleon was absent at the beginning of the 1809 campaign. During the early stages, Berthier's awful handling of the troops in Bavaria almost spelled disaster. Marshal Davout had been reporting from Warsaw and Breslau that the Austrians were mobilizing as early as September 1808. Without any formal announcement of their intent to go to war, the Austrians began moving up the Danube Valley in February 1809 and overran a series of small French outposts. Rushing down from the north, Davout understood the enemy threat and the scope and sequence of operations necessary to deal with the situation. The "Hand of Iron" (Davout) began concentrating French forces at Ratisbon (modern-day Regensburg).[27]

Unfortunately for the French, it was not Napoleon who next arrived, but Berthier. By being first on the 19 May 1804 list of the Marshalate, Berthier was senior to Davout. He thus took overall command of the French armies in Germany on 13 April. Berthier's first actions were to issue orders canceling Davout's orders to concentrate at Ratisbon. As described by A. G. MacDonell:

> It was now thirteen years since Berthier had begun to work at the side of the greatest military genius in the world, and he had played an intimate part in every single one of the sensational and wonderful victories of those thirteen years. But during all that time he had not even grasped the vaguest elements of Napoleonic strategy.[28]

Davout protested vigorously, but to no avail. Receiving orders and counterorders, the army was thrown into disarray. Napoleon arrived on 17 April and immediately sent a note to Berthier, stating, "What you have done appears so strange, that if I was not aware of your friendship, I should think that you were betraying me. Davout is at this moment more completely at the Archduke's [Charles] disposal than at my own." All the emperor's genius and Davout's tactical skill were needed to redeem the situation. Victory in the Battle of Eckmuehl (Eggmuehl) —by Davout and Massena—and the capture of Ratisbon—by Lannes—ended the crisis.[29]

After that campaign Napoleon's attitude clearly cooled toward his devoted chief of staff. Nonetheless, on 14 August 1809 Napoleon rewarded Berthier with the title of Prince of Wagram. An annual sum of 250,000 francs derived from this additional title raised his total endowments to more than 1.3 million francs per year.[30]

From the 1809 campaign onward, Napoleon seems to have given Berthier less discretion with operational orders, retaining the function of operations officer himself. Perhaps Napoleon's actions grew less from reluctance to delegate authority, as J. D. Hittle has suggested, but more from his lack of faith in Berthier's tactical ability.[31]

Except in Spain and on the high seas, Europe was at peace in 1810. The years 1811 and 1812, however, were to bring more political intrigue, international alliances, economic competition, and bickering among the generals. Napoleon could hardly communicate with some of them. By 1812 Napoleon was so angry with Murat, whom he had made the king of Naples, that he rarely communicated with him unless by official correspondence through Berthier, or through Napoleon's sister, Caroline. War with Russia seemed necessary, so the emperor put Berthier to work formulating plans. Massing for his invasion of Russia, Napoleon reinforced his allies in eastern Germany and Poland. On 1 February 1812 Berthier took charge as chief of staff. But because Napoleon was not to arrive until May Berthier was the de facto commander.[32]

By the opening of the Russian campaign, Berthier and Davout were in open conflict with each other. They had not met since 1809, when Berthier's dispositions of the army nearly led to disaster at Ratisbon. They quarreled incessantly. Now Berthier was with the emperor in the headquarters and had Napoleon's ear. Davout, of course, was with his troops, and being so distant left him at a distinct disadvantage. Unfairly, Napoleon became chilly and distant to Davout.[33] Another of Berthier's archenemies among the marshals, Bernadotte, was gone, having become crown prince of Sweden.

By 1812 both Napoleon's and Berthier's staffs become larger and more lavish. The closely located tent complexes required several acres, and much time, to set up. An entire transport battalion was needed to move the tents and equipment.[34]

The Russia campaign proceeded successfully enough at first, but the Russian countryside could not support so large a force as the Grand Armée. Berthier's degree of responsibility in the disastrous campaign is difficult to evaluate. He has been criticized for his failure to provide enough horses and adequate forage for the existing horses. With few exceptions (such as Davout), most generals seemed to disregard the requirements for keeping the horses healthy. This was especially true of Murat, the commander of the huge Cavalry Reserve. Murat cared for his men little better than his horses.

On 17 October Napoleon ordered his staff and commanders to prepare for a strategic withdrawal via Smolensk. Berthier organized the evacuation of every possible man who could not walk on his own. He even included the French population of Moscow, or at least those willing to come. Complications and Russian countermeasures mounted. At Ghorodnia on 24 October, Berthier stood with Jean-Batiste Bessiéres and Murat, waiting for Napoleon's orders; but none were forthcoming as the emperor was at his wit's end. The next day Berthier and Napoleon were temporarily surrounded by a group of Cossacks, even drawing their swords to defend themselves. An aide-de-camp to Berthier was wounded in the ensuing fight, before the Guard Cavalry dispersed the Cossacks.[35]

Berthier became more and more depressed as the Russia campaign wore on. He was on the verge of a nervous collapse as a result of the carnage and exhaustion. During the retreat Napoleon decided to leave the army behind and return to France. Berthier begged to go with his master, but to no avail. The emperor departed on 5 December, and his chief of staff dutifully served under Murat for the remainder of the retreat.[36]

In 1813 the Allies resolved to defeat the "Tyrant of Europe" through sustained and unified action. In late August and September the French and Allied armies were locked in several engagements in Silesia and around Dresden. There were several days in late September in which Berthier was sick, creating a further handicap for the emperor.[37]

Berthier was strongly jealous of Marshal Ney's chief of staff, General the Baron Antoine Henri Jomini (1779–1869), who had considerable authority under Ney. After the Battle of Bautzen in 1813, Napoleon had recommended Jomini for divisional command. Berthier blocked the promotion, ordering Jomini's arrest and accusing him of "neglect of duty." Jomini left the French army, eventually to become a general in the Russian army, thus introducing modern French practices into Russian military thought.[38]

On 30 March 1814, during the retreat to Paris, Napoleon left the exhausted army under command of Berthier, then raced ahead toward Fontainebleau with a small escort. Berthier was drawing to the end of his tether. On 14 April Berthier was in the room with Napoleon at Fontainebleau when in strode marshals Ney, Bon Adrien Moncey, and François-Joseph Lefebvre. The trio demanded both an end to the war and Napoleon's abdication. The emperor described a bold new stroke he was planning to rescue the dire situation. None, including the old chief of staff, offered a word of agreement. Napoleon raised his tone, shouting, "The Army will obey me!"

Ney retorted, "The Army will obey its generals." Napoleon looked to Berthier for support, but none was forthcoming. That night the emperor signed his abdication.[39]

Berthier supported a return of the Bourbon monarchy under the rotund and puffing King Louis XVIII, who effectively made Berthier the commander of his personal bodyguard. His title was Capitaine des 5eme Cie. Du Garde du Corps Royale. On 4 June Berthier was made a peer of France; in September he became a Commander of the Order of Saint Louis.[40]

Upon news of Napoleon's escape from Elba, Berthier did not openly support his old master. Despite Berthier's position as Captain of the Royal Bodyguard, Louis XVIII still did not trust him. Nonetheless, the king feared for his life and decided to leave Paris. Berthier departed Paris with King Louis XVIII on 19 March 1815 and accompanied him into exile as far as Ghent. There Berthier assured Marshal Jacques MacDonald that he would return to France with his family. He traveled to Bamberg, Bavaria, to the home of his wife's father. But upon arrival Berthier was thrown deep into thought. He was old and tired. Berthier had lost his will to fight, and he decided not to return to Paris.[41]

On 1 June 1815, from the high third-floor window of the Neue Residenz, the sixty-one-year-old Berthier watched the march of Russian troops through the city, and on the street just below. Then, he was either pushed, or fell, or deliberately jumped to his death on the cobblestone street below. The details of his death are and will remain a mystery. Who was in the room with him at the time and what had been discussed? Perhaps Berthier—known to imbibe in good drink—had had a bit too much, leaned out too far, and lost his balance. Perhaps he received a strong shove from an enemy in the room. It is unlikely, however, that the old brave soldier would have killed himself. After all, he had come to Bamberg to look after the safety of his family.[42]

Of Berthier, Napoleon later remarked on St. Helena, "There was in the world a no better chief of staff; that is where his true talent lay, for he was not capable of commanding 500 men."[43]

Notes

1. A. G. MacDonell, *Napoleon and His Marshals* (New York: Macmillan, 1934; reprint, London: Prion, 1990), 8. See also Charles Raeuber, "Duty and Discipline—Berthier," in *Napoleon's Marshals*, ed. David G. Chandler (New York: Macmillan, 1987), 42, 44.
2. MacDonell, *Napoleon and His Marshals*. See also Georges Blond, *La Grande Armée*, trans. Marshal May (reprint, London: Arms and Armour Press, 1997), 91–92; and Raeuber, "Duty and Discipline," 46.
3. Raeuber, "Duty and Discipline," 42, 44. See also MacDonell, *Napoleon and His Marshals*, 8.
4. Raeuber, "Duty and Discipline," 42, 44.
5. Ibid., 42, 45–46. See also MacDonell, *Napoleon and His Marshals*, 8–9.
6. Raeuber, "Duty and Discipline," 42, 45.
7. J. D. Hittle, *The Military Staff: Its History and Development* (Harrisburg, Pa.: Military Service Publishing, 1949), 87–89.
8. Owen Connelly, *Blundering to Glory: Napoleon's Military Campaigns* (Wilmington, Del.: Scholarly Resources, 1987), 24–25, 73.
9. Hittle, *Military Staff*, 87–89.
10. David G. Chandler, *Jena 1806: Napoleon Destroys Prussia*, Osprey Military Campaign 20 (London: Osprey Publishing, 1993), 25–26.
11. F. Loraine Petre, *Napoleon's Conquest of Prussia—1806* (reprint, New York: Hippocrene Books, 1977), 34.
12. Hittle, *Military Staff*, 87–89, 92, 100–101.
13. C. Brian Kelly, "Costly Retreat from Moscow," *Great Battles: The Age of Napoleon* 9, no. 1 (Summer 1998): 74. See also Raeuber, "Duty and Discipline," 46.
14. Petre, *Napoleon's Conquest*, 33–34.
15. Raeuber, "Duty and Discipline," 46.
16. Connelly, *Blundering to Glory*, 52.
17. MacDonell, *Napoleon and His Marshals*, 31–32.
18. Connelly, *Blundering to Glory*, 52.
19. Ibid., 60.
20. Ibid., 57; Raeuber, "Duty and Discipline," 47–48; and Chandler, *Jena 1806*, 26.
21. Connelly, *Blundering to Glory*, 63–64; Raeuber, "Duty and Discipline," 46.
22. Raeuber, "Duty and Discipline," 46–47.
23. Ibid., 46. For the best account of the Ulm-Austerlitz Campaign, see Scott Bowden, *Napoleon at Austerlitz* (Chicago: Emperor's Press, 1997).
24. MacDonell, *Napoleon and His Marshals*, 105–7. See also Connelly, *Blundering to Glory*, 95–96; Guenther Steiger, *Die Schlacht bei Jena und Auerstedt 1806* (Cospeda, Germany: Gedenkstaette 1806, 1981).

25. Connelly, *Blundering to Glory*, 107–16. See also Chandler, *Jena 1806*, and Steiger, *Die Schlacht bei Jena und Auerstedt 1806*.

26. Raeuber, "Duty and Discipline," 48.

27. MacDonell, *Napoleon and His Marshals*, 162. See also David G. Chandler, *Aspern and Wagram* (New York: Macmillan, 1994), 24–25.

28. MacDonell, *Napoleon and His Marshals*, 162–63.

29. Ibid., and Hittle, *Military Staff*, 100. See also Chandler, *Aspern and Wagram*, 12–13, 24–25; and Ian Castle, *Aspern and Wagram 1809: Mighty Clash of Empires*, Osprey Military Campaign 33 (London: Osprey Publishing, 1994; reprint, 1997).

30. Raeuber, "Duty and Discipline," 48–49.

31. Hittle, *Military Staff*, 100.

32. David Johnson, *Napoleon's Cavalry and Its Leaders* (New York: H&M Publishers, 1978), 107.

33. MacDonell, *Napoleon and His Marshals*, 208.

34. Connelly, *Blundering to Glory*, 158.

35. Ibid., 174–75, and Johnson, *Napoleon's Cavalry*, 107–8.

36. Johnson, *Napoleon's Cavalry*, 121.

37. Connelly, *Blundering to Glory*, 192.

38. Hittle, *Military Staff*, 101–2.

39. Connelly, *Blundering to Glory*, 198, and MacDonell, *Napoleon and His Marshals*, 254–55.

40. Raeuber, "Duty and Discipline," 42, 49.

41. MacDonell, *Napoleon and His Marshals*, 267, 271. See also Connelly, *Blundering to Glory*, 206, and Kelly, "Costly Retreat from Moscow," 74.

42. MacDonell, *Napoleon and His Marshals*, 271–72. See also David Chandler, *Waterloo*, Osprey Military Campaign 18 (London: Osprey Publishing, 1993), 11, and Kelly, "Costly Retreat from Moscow," 74.

43. *Court and Camp of Bonaparte* (London, 1831), 242, quoted in Philip J. Haythornthwaite, *The Napoleonic Source Book* (New York: Facts on File Books, 1990), 327.

CHRONOLOGY OF AUGUST NEITHARDT VON GNEISENAU

27 Oct 1760	Born in Schildau bei Torgau, Saxony (now Schildau, Gneisenaustadt, Germany).
1778	Entered Austrian military service.
1780	Assigned to a Jäger battalion in the army of Ansbach Bayreuth.
1782	Promoted to lieutenant.
1782-1783	Served in Canada during the American War of Independence.
Feb 1786	Joined the Prussian army. Promoted to senior lieutenant.
Jun 1790	Promoted to staff captain.
1793-1794	Assigned to 15th Fusiliers Battalion.
Nov 1795	Promoted to captain. Assigned as company commander in the Fusilier Battalion Rabenau.
1796	Married Caroline von Kottwitz. The marriage produced two sons and four daughters over the next ten years.
14 Oct 1806	Wounded at Battle of Jena-Auerstadt.
Dec 1806	Promoted to major.
1807	Assigned as commander of the Fortress Kolberg. Appointed to the Military Reorganization Commission under Scharnhorst. Promoted to lieutenant colonel.
1808	Appointed inspector of fortifications.
Sep 1808	Appointed to chief of the Engineers Corps.
1809	Served in the Department of Artillery and Engineering in the Prussian Ministry of War.
Mar 1809	Promoted to colonel.
Jul 1811	Appointed to the Prussian Staatsrat.
1812	Resigned from the Staatsrat and the military and undertook a diplomatic mission to Austria.
1813	Promoted to major general and appointed second quartermaster general of the Silesian Army under Gen. Gebhardt Leberecht von Blücher.
Jun 1813	Replaced Scharnhorst as Prussian chief of staff under Blücher.
16-19 Oct 1813	Battle of Leipzig.

Dec 1813	Promoted to lieutenant general.
18 Jun 1815	Battle of Waterloo.
Dec 1815	Promoted to general of the infantry and assumed command of the Generalkommando on the Rhine.
May 1816	Resigned from the army citing reasons of health.
1817	Appointed to the newly constituted Staatsrat.
9 Sep 1818	Appointed governor of Berlin.
1825	Appointed chief of the Supreme Military Examinations Commission. Promoted to general field marshal.
Mar 1831	Returned to military service during the Polish insurrection and appointed supreme commander of the I, II, V and VI Army Corps.
23 Aug 1831	Died of cholera in Posen.

August Neithardt von Gneisenau

Steven B. Rogers

Augst Wilhelm Anton Graf Neithardt von Gneisenau was one of Prussia's leading military strategists and reformers. He was born the son of a junior artillery officer in Schildau, near Torgau, in Saxony on 27 October 1760. Although he came from an impoverished noble family with no long-established military tradition, von Gneisenau joined the Austrian army in 1778 after a brief attempt at university life in Erfurt, and he served for two years in an Austrian cavalry regiment. Von Gneisenau offered his services to the tiny principality of Ansbach in 1780, and in 1782 he was seconded to the British army in Canada during the American Revolution. The war was over by the time he reached Halifax, but he remained in Canada until 1783 before returning to Ansbach.[1]

Von Gneisenau realized that military service in Ansbach offered him little chance of advancement, and in 1785 he sent a direct appeal to King Friedrich II for a commission in the Prussian army. Following a personal audience with the Prussian king, von Gneisenau entered the Prussian army as a career soldier in February 1786 and was quickly promoted to senior lieutenant. For the next thirty years, until his resignation in 1816, he slowly rose through the ranks, serving almost twenty years in obscure military posts in Silesia before finally distinguishing himself in battle against the French armies under Napoleon.[2]

Von Gneisenau was promoted to the rank of staff captain in June 1790 and remained at his post in Silesia until 1793, when he was assigned to the 15th Fusiliers Battalion. In 1794 he participated in events that led up to the Third Partition of Poland the following year.

Von Gneisenau's abilities as a military theorist and planner came to the attention of his superiors when, following the French defeat of the Austrian and Russian armies at the Battle of Austerlitz in December 1805, Prussia abandoned its neutrality in 1806 and entered the Third Coalition War against France. Von Gneisenau finally had a chance to test his abilities in combat, beginning with a military engagement at Saalfeld on 10 October 1806. As a staff officer serving under Gen. Friedrich Ludwig, Prince of Hohenlohe, who commanded the left flank of Field Marshall Gebhardt von Blücher's army, von Gneisenau experienced the disastrous defeat of the Prussian army at Jena-Auerstadt on 14 October 1806 during which he was wounded.[3] Although the fate of the Prussian army looked bleak in the months following the defeat at Jena, von Gneisenau saw action against the French in Lithuania, and he continued to distinguish himself as commandant of the Kolberg fortress where he directed its successful defense against superior French forces between April and July 1807. The Prussian army was ultimately defeated and Prussia was forced to accept an unpopular alliance with France under the humiliating terms of the Peace of Tilsit on 9 July 1807. Von Gneisenau was awarded the Pour le Mérite and promoted to lieutenant colonel.

The Prussian defeat at Jena served as the catalyst for the reorganization and modernization of the Prussian army. Hanoverian General Gerhard von Scharnhorst enlisted von Gneisenau and other reform-minded officers to serve on the Immediat-Kommission (the Military Reorganization Commission), which proposed the introduction of universal military service, a reduction in the number of foreign mercenaries serving in the Prussian army, the creation of a reserve militia, admission of nonnobles into the officer corps, and the revision of the code of military discipline based on corporal punishment.[4] The king, however, opposed reform of the traditional military establishment.[5] Friedrich Wilhelm III eventually realized that reform and reorganization of the Prussian army were necessary if the rump Prussian kingdom was to reclaim its role as a dominant European power. The Treaty of Tilsit limited the Prussian army to a maximum strength of 42,000 men, yet through the annual forced retirement of trained regulars and their replacement by new recruits, Scharnhorst's Krumpfersystem managed to almost double the number of available trained troops.[6]

Scharnhorst, with the aid of von Gneisenau, also called for the establishment of a General Staff, a "collective genius" necessary to implement the new reforms of the Prussian army. The impetus behind this initiative occurred during the Battle at Jena when Scharnhorst became separated from the Prussian headquarters. When he encountered Blücher in the field, the Prussian commander appointed him to serve as his military advisor for the remainder of the campaign, thereby permitting him to develop and implement new strategies in the field where the tide of battle was constantly in flux.[7] Scharnhorst believed that the General Staff would serve as the Prussian army's principal instrument for coordinated military planning to insure that the army always stood at optimum military readiness, even during peacetime. It would monitor the army's preparations for war, as well as those of any potential enemies, and prepare strategies for mobilization and combat logistics. The General Staff also would coordinate and supervise the planning and operational readiness of the various corps and divisions so they could perform their missions as efficiently as possible. Scharnhorst, and later von Gneisenau, believed that the General Staff should never interfere with the operations of these large army units as long as they were operating at peak efficiency. General Staff officers could, however, assume direct command of any formation or unit that failed to measure up to expectations.[8]

In 1808 von Gneisenau was first appointed inspector of fortifications until September, when he was appointed chief of engineers. He was promoted to colonel in March 1809 and served in the Department of Artillery and Engineering in the Prussian Ministry of War until 1 July, when he resigned to protest Prussian continued neutrality in Austria's war against France. He secretly traveled to England in August 1809, hoping to garner support for the creation of a coalition against Napoleonic hegemony in Europe. He returned home in July 1810, only to visit Austria, Sweden, Finland, and Russia to seek support for an anti-French coalition. Appointed to the Prussian Staatsrat in July 1811, he was charged with the preparation of a popular revolt against the French. Von Gneisenau, however, continued to distance himself from the Prussian military following his resignation in 1809.

Scharnhorst was appointed the first chief of the General Staff under Field Marshall Blucher that year, and from this position he was slowly able to introduce additional technical reforms within the ranks of the Prussian army.[9] Forced into a military alliance with France after Tilsit, Prussia permitted its army to join the French invasion of Russia in 1812. In the wake of Napoleon's defeat at Moscow and his forced retreat westward across Germany, Prussia saw an opportunity to ally itself with Russia on 27 February 1813 and to declare war on France on 17 March 1813. A new sense of patriotism swelled the ranks of the Prussian army to 280,000 men willing to fight in the new Wars of Liberation, as they are known in Germany.[10] Von Gneisenau returned to active military service and was promoted to major general and appointed second quartermaster general on the General Staff for the newly reorganized Prussian army.

Although growing in strength and full of patriotism, the inexperienced Prussian army was defeated by the French at Gross-Goerschen (Luetzen) and at Bautzen on 2 May 1813, but using strategies prepared by the General Staff led by Scharnhorst (who was seriously wounded at Gross-Goerschen) and von Gneisenau, it made an orderly retreat from Saxony into Silesia.[11] But those were only tactical victories for Napoleon, whose armies suffered heavy casualties as the Prussians, Russians, and Swedes took turns attacking the French rear and forcing Napoleon to withdraw farther westward to protect his supply and communication lines to the Rhine. Ignoring his wounds, Scharnhorst went to Prague, where he successfully convinced Austria to join the alliance against Napoleon, and it was there that he died on 26 June 1813 after failing to get proper medical treatment.[12]

Von Gneisenau succeeded Scharnhorst as chief of the General Staff. With the military strategists he and Scharnhorst had assembled for the General Staff, Blücher and von Gneisenau led the Prussian Army of Silesia against a considerably weakened French army south of the Elbe River. Blücher and von Gneisenau together would become the model command entity for those who would follow in their footsteps—Blücher as commander in chief with battlefield savvy to inspire the men under his command, and von Gneisenau as chief of staff with the tactical and operational genius to plan, direct, and supervise the combined order of battle.[13] In doing so, von Gneisenau continued to refine and adapt the structure of the Prussian General Staff as envisioned by Scharnhorst. Using his own relationship with Blücher, however, von Gneisenau initiated a new practice, whereby the chief of staff for each major formation—army, corps, and divisions—was to share command responsibility with the commander of that formation.[14]

The Prussian army under Blücher and von Gneisenau, with approximately 98,000 troops at their command, defeated the French at Grossbeeren on 23 August 1813, thereby thwarting a French attempt to capture Berlin and further raising the morale of the Prussian army, which had not beaten the French since 1806. Von Gneisenau took no time to prove his mettle on the battlefield.

The French managed an empty victory at Dresden on 26–27 August, owing in large part to the Allies' failure to take decisive action against a French force, whose morale was fortified by the arrival of Napoleon taking direct command of his army. But superior Prussian, Russian, and Austrian forces, executing a plan designed by von Gneisenau, which called for the four

Allied armies to advance on the French army simultaneously from several different directions, obliged Napoleon to withdraw to Leipzig for what the Allies hoped would be a final and decisive battle to defeat Napoleon and lift French hegemony in central Europe.

What followed was the longest battle of the Wars of Liberation, the Battle of Nations at Leipzig on 16–19 October 1813. With Napoleon withdrawing to new defensive positions in and around Leipzig, Blücher and von Gneisenau began to deploy the Prussian Army of Silesia (150,000 men) north and northwest of the city. The Swedish Army of the North (110,000 men), commanded by Prince Jean Bernadotte, and the Austrian Army of Bohemia (255,000 men), commanded by Prince Carl zu Schwarzenberg, advanced on Leipzig from the south and southeast. The Allied armies kept constant pressure on Napoleon's flanks as he withdrew toward Leipzig. The Prussians gained another minor but important victory over the French at Dennewitz on 6 September but von Gneisenau saw a chance to tighten the noose around the French. He knew he had the upper hand.

On 15 October Napoleon deployed almost 140,000 troops in and around Leipzig with several thousand more on the way to bolster French defensive positions. The Austrian Army of Bohemia under Schwarzenberg, consisting of four main corps and one reserve corps, advanced on the city from the direction of Dresden to the south with approximately 180,000 troops. It was followed by a combined Russian force commanded by General of Infantry Count Mikhail Bogdanovich Barclay de Tolly. Schwarzenberg hoped to engage the French while moving around the city to link up with Blücher to the north and west. Napoleon, knowing neither the exact location of Blücher's forces and von Gneisenau's intentions, nor the location of the Swedish army under Bernadotte, assumed that they were somewhere to the east, between Leipzig and Dresden. He therefore prepared to meet the immediate threat of the Austro-Russian forces advancing on the city from the south, while holding enough troops in reserve and spreading them around the city.

Little did Napoleon know that Blücher and the Prussian army, with approximately 60,000 troops, were advancing on Leipzig from Halle, north and west of the French positions, and threatening to cut off his retreat route to the Rhine and France. That fact that would become readily and painfully apparent to Napoleon the following day. Von Gneisenau's plan appeared to be working. Bernadotte's army sat on Blücher's left flank, but too far away to immediately engage the French. Both Blücher and von Gneisenau were self-assured as they prepared to meet the French in a fateful battle the following day. Ernst Moritz Arndt, a Prussian artillery major who knew both men, visited Blücher's headquarters on 15 October. He described von Gneisenau as "confident that the great decision would be achieved in the next few days." Blücher "laughed and chatted as if we were going on an exercise in peacetime and not into a fight for life and death with Napoleon, the greatest commander of all time." When asked about the coming campaign, Blücher answered: "The young scamp [von Gneisenau] understands everything. You'll have to ask Gneisenau, he knows best how it should be done because he's the cleverest of our crew here."[15]

On 16 October, the first day of the battle, Napoleon counterattacked Schwarzenberg's advancing Austrian army and forced it back to its original position south of Leipzig. He also managed to fend off Blücher, whose army marched from the north against a resolute French defense and came within a mile of the city gate. Von Gneisenau had still not shown his hand, however. The second day of the battle, 17 October, was a stalemate with only very minor engagements. The remaining French troops managed to withdraw into Leipzig to strengthen Napoleon's defensive line, but the delay also allowed the Swedish Army of the North, which up until this point seemed determined to hold its position despite pressure from von Gneisenau to join the Prussian attack in the north, to begin its advance. Meanwhile, roughly 25,000 Russian troops of the Reserve Army of Poland, commanded by General of the Cavalry Count Levin August Gottleib (Leontii Leontievich) von Bennigsen, also began to advance on Leipzig from the north to join forces with Blücher. Schwarzenberg's Army of Bohemia awaited important reinforcements moving up from Dresden.

On 18 October Bernadotte moved the Swedish Army into the fray with the Prussians and the Russo-Austrian force on either flank, and a combined Allied force of approximately 350,000 troops advanced on a numerically inferior French force. When Napoleon's Saxon allies quit the battle and went over to the other side, he quickly realized that his position at Leipzig could no longer be defended. He was impelled to withdraw in the direction of Erfurt. Adding to this defeat, the premature blowing up of the lone escape bridge over the Elster River stranded several thousand French soldiers in Leipzig, many of whom died in an attempt to swim to freedom. Von Gneisenau's strategy and planning had worked, and the Prussian army and its allies won a battle, "the like of which has scarcely been seen in the history of the world. . . . This battle will decide the fate of Europe."[16] Writing to his wife on 19 October, von Gneisenau confessed: "The great battle is won; the victory is decisive. . . . It was a spectacle such as has not been seen for thousands of years. . . . All measures have been taken to pursue the enemy as hard as possible. We want to destroy the remnants of his army."[17] Von Gneisenau would repeat this sentiment two years later when he once again faced a French army in retreat at Waterloo.

With the French defeat at Leipzig, the Army of Silesia and its allies finally forced Napoleon to quit German territory and withdraw across the Rhine. Several Allied leaders counseled against an invasion of France, thereby permitting Napoleon to remain on the French throne and to rebuild his army. Von Gneisenau, who was promoted to lieutenant general in December 1813, urged them to attack while Napoleon was too weak to defend even France's fortresses along the Rhine. Napoleon refused all Allied peace offers which would have kept France behind more traditional borders—the Rhine, the Alps, and the Pyrenees—and forced it to forego any claims to Belgium and other foreign territories. Blücher once again agreed with his chief of staff, and the Prussian army spearheaded an Allied invasion of France across the Rhine on 1 January 1814. Simultaneously, an independent Prussian corps advanced into the Netherlands in the north.

Blücher and von Gneisenau marched almost 30,000 battle-tested Prussian troops westward across France and finally encountered a French army made up mostly of recruits at Brienne on 29 January. Nevertheless, the French managed to win the day and almost succeeded in capturing both Blücher and von Gneisenau before leaving the field to reorganize at La Rothière. Napoleon planned to attack the Prussians there, but an Allied force of several thousand troops was not far away and Napoleon decided to consider other options. Blücher, despite von Gneisenau's words of caution, was always anxious to engage the French, and he forced Napoleon's hand at La Rothière on 1 February in a battle that ended up a virtual stalemate.

The French engaged and defeated a Russian corps at Champaubert and Montmirail on 10–11 February, before Blücher and von Gneisenau could deploy reinforcements to support them. These engagements were followed by a French attack on Gen. Johann Yorck's Prussian Corps at Château-Thierry on the Marne on 12 February, subjecting it to a rather ignominious defeat. Napoleon pursued Yorck's corps in the hope that he might engage the Prussian forces under Blücher's direct command. The Prussian army, spearheaded by a second Prussian corps commanded by Gen. Friedrich Kleist, advanced to Vauchamp to reinforce Yorck. There the two Prussian corps engaged the French on 14 February. Once again Napoleon was able to win the day, forcing Blücher and von Gneisenau to withdraw with heavy losses in the face of a larger French force. At Monterau on 17 February, Napoleon with fewer than

60,000 troops forced an Allied army twice that size to retreat once again. Von Gneisenau realized that a new strategy was necessary if he was going to defeat the French on their home territory.

In the meantime, the Allies had initiated a peace conference at Chatillon on 3 February, hoping Napoleon might sue for peace in order to save Paris from attack and occupation. Napoleon, encouraged by his recent victories, gambled that the Allied coalition would break apart before it could threaten Paris. But Schwarzenberg's Army of Bohemia was advancing on the French capital. Napoleon turned his attention away from the Prussians to face this new threat, marching his army south to Monterau and allowing Blücher and von Gneisenau to lick their wounds. Sensing the futility of the Chatillon negotiations, von Gneisenau developed a plan similar to the one that was so successful at Leipzig. The Allies must attack the French from several directions and force Napoleon to divide his forces. It was hoped that this plan would reinvigorate the Allied advance. Von Gneisenau immediately recommended that Blücher march the Prussian army north to link up with the independent Prussian corps in the Netherlands.

By early March 1814 the Army of Silesia had regained its footing and once again began to threaten the French northern flank. Napoleon pushed the Allies back over the Aube River and Blücher moved to counterattack. The French met the superior Prussian force at Craonne on 7 March and despite heavy losses managed to outflank Blücher and halt his advance. Two days later Napoleon hoped to repeat this success with another flanking movement at Laon. Outnumbered almost two to one, Napoleon divided his forces to launch an unsuccessful assault against Blücher's left flank. This maneuver failed and Napoleon was forced to withdraw.

Following the Prussian defeat of the French at Laon, the Allies resumed their advance on Paris. Napoleon attempted one final gambit. A French force of 28,000 assaulted 80,000 troops of the Army of Bohemia and forced them to abandon Arcis-sur-Aube on 20 March. The Austrians eventually prevailed the next day, however, and Napoleon and the French army were forced to retreat for a final defense of Paris against a growing Allies threat. All was for naught. France surrendered and Paris was occupied on 31 March. Napoleon was forced to abdicate and went into exile on the island of Elba on 11 April. Von Gneisenau's policy that the chiefs of staff share command responsibility with the army, corps, and divisional commanders they served had been put to the test again during the campaigns of 1813–14. Once again it proved successful.[18]

With Napoleon defeated and the Bourbon monarchy back on the French throne, the Allies convened in Vienna to decide how to divide the spoils of war. During the winter of 1814–15 the Prussian army returned home and underwent a period of downsizing and reorganization for peacetime. Although Scharnhorst before his death in 1813 was able to get Friedrich Wilhelm III to agree to provisional compulsory military service, the Prussian king did not agree to universal compulsory military service until 1814, as the war with France was approaching its end.[19] Now von Gneisenau had an opportunity to enact many of the other reforms envisioned years earlier by Scharnhorst. Militia and volunteers units, which had been a mainstay of the army, were disbanded, while units of regular troops were reorganized and often renamed. Von Gneisenau hoped to create a more efficient and mobile field army based on Scharnhorst's earlier recommendations.[20]

Blücher and von Gneisenau had shown that they could work well together. Despite his effectiveness, however, von Gneisenau was not respected in all quarters. Even the Prussian king had been lukewarm to von Gneisenau's accomplishments. Writing to his wife following the victory at Leipzig in 1813, von Gneisenau complained that Friedrich Wilhelm III had expressed to him "rather cold but friendly words of his satisfaction with the army. . . . Nothing of me personally. I have still heard not one word of satisfaction about our crossing the Elbe or the developments in the campaign following it. . . . But you can see how deep-rooted is the king's rejection of all those who do not share his political opinions." Furthermore, von Gneisenau made a promise. "As soon as this holy war is over, I will resign from his army; I would sooner eat crust than serve this unfriendly monarch."[21]

But the war was not over and von Gneisenau would have yet another opportunity to test his abilities. While the diplomats argued at the Congress of Vienna, Napoleon escaped from Elba, returned to France in March 1815, and took command of an army that quickly grew to approximately 150,000 regular soldiers. The newly reorganized Army of the Lower Rhine, as the Prussian army was now called, was under the command of General of Infantry Friedrich Heinrich Kleist Graf von Nollendorf; the aging Blücher had returned home to Silesia after Napoleon's defeat in 1814. But with Napoleon once again a threat, Friedrich Wilhelm III decided that the command of his army should remain in tried and trusted hands. He ordered Blücher to return to his post. Despite his earlier threat to quit, von Gneisenau returned as chief of the General Staff and rushed to Mainz to help put the army on a war footing.

General Yorck, one of the most capable Prussian corps commanders and a key to the Prussian successes since Leipzig, refused to serve under Blücher and von Gneisenau again. Two other senior corps commanders who outranked von Gneisenau, Generals Kleist and Friedrich von Bülow, also saw their power reduced as von Gneisenau consolidated his own.[22] Von Gneisenau knew he must have the authority to assume command should the commander in chief be killed or otherwise incapacitated. The Prussian king also knew this. As a result, von Gneisenau restructured the Army of the Lower Rhine by the creation of seven permanent army corps, four of which would be commanded by generals Hans Ernst von Ziethen, von Borstel, Johann Adolf Freiherr von Thielemann, and von Bülow. These four corps constituted the main frontline of the Prussian army. The remaining three corps were to be held in reserve for home defense. As before, von Gneisenau and his General Staff were responsible for overall planning and operational authority. Once again each army and corps command was assigned a chief of staff and the necessary subordinate staff to assist in the execution of strategic planning. Each infantry brigade and cavalry command had trained general staff officers assigned to their commands.[23] The basic role of the General Staff remained the same on all levels—to receive and implement troop dispositions, operational orders and other more routine daily orders, and to draft daily reports and maintain unit war diaries.[24]

Within two months of Napoleon's return his army grew to more than 200,000 frontline troops. The Congress of Vienna called on the Allied armies to meet the new French threat, and the duke of Wellington (Arthur Wellesley), in command of a joint Anglo-Dutch army, along with von Gneisenau arrived in Belgium in early April 1815 to begin preparations for a new invasion of France. Both Wellington and von Gneisenau were suspicious of the other's intentions. Wellington hoped to minimize Prussia's role in a post-Napoleon Europe, while von Gneisenau wanted to strengthen Prussia's hand in Vienna. Von Gneisenau's plan called for three Allied armies to invade France through Belgium and across the middle and upper Rhine, with a strong reserve held in the rear. Each of the invading armies would reach Paris at the same time. The idea was to force a numerically inferior French army to split its forces and to confront three widely scattered Allied armies. While Napoleon's attention focused on one invading army, the other two would continue toward Paris, the ultimate goal of von Gneisenau's plan. Wellington agreed with von Gneisenau's general strategy of attacking France with overwhelming force, but he simply wanted to defeat Napoleon. The capture of Paris seemed unnecessary to accomplish that goal.[25]

But Napoleon remained confident. As his army grew in strength he vowed to invade Belgium and to destroy individually the Anglo-Dutch Army, numbering 107,000 men and commanded by Wellington, and the Army of the Lower Rhine, with 128,000 men commanded by his old Prussian nemesis Blücher, before they could join forces and before the Austrian and Russian armies invading across the Rhine could come to their aid and require Napoleon to further divide his smaller army. Friedrich Wilhelm III put his faith and trust in von Gneisenau. In appointing him chief of the General Staff of the Army of the Lower Rhine, the Prussian king charged him with full authority to reorganize the army . . . and more. His Order-in-Cabinet of 29 March 1815 reads:

> I cannot, in view of the distance from the area of operation, give you any definite orders as to how you should act in case of unforeseen events, but I must leave it to you to make such arrangements with the Duke of Wellington as suit the circumstances and to act in agreement with him in all things. While I empower you to do so and assure you of my fullest confidence in you, I also make you responsible for acting with all prudence and the most careful consideration in every matter affecting the future of Europe.[26]

Napoleon made good on his promise. He crossed into central Belgium on 11 June with an army numbering 128,000, but he quickly split his army to advance against Wellington and Blücher separately. Blücher's Army of the Lower Rhine was deployed along a lengthy front on Wellington's left flank. Von Gneisenau appointed General Baron Karl von Müffling to serve as his liaison officer with Wellington's headquarters, so that they might better coordinate their preparations for battle. Despite his king's order to cooperate with Wellington in every way to ensure victory, von Gneisenau was suspicious of the British field marshal's actions and intentions and warned Müffling to be on his guard. Wellington and von Gneisenau continued to disagree on the best way to confront the French threat. Von Gneisenau suspected that the French would first attack the Austrians under Schwarzenberg in the hope of forcing them to quit the war before becoming fully engaged in the conflict. Such was not the case. Napoleon's true intentions became evident when French units engaged Lieutenant General von Ziethen's I Corps on 15 June near Charleroi in Belgium. Blücher and von Gneisenau grew anxious because Wellington's army was not yet fully prepared to fend off an imminent French attack.[27]

The problems von Gneisenau had experienced with the senior corps commanders during the period of reorganization came back to haunt him. Bülow's IV Corps was supposed to be positioned to support the three other

Prussian corps. Bülow, who outranked von Gneisenau, was not obliged to take orders from him—the chief of staff could only suggest that the corps commander do what was asked of him—and apparently von Gneisenau had not impressed upon Bülow the importance of his mission.[28]

On 16 June Napoleon led part of his army against the Prussians at Ligny, northeast of Charleroi. The French crushed the center of the Prussian line and forced Blücher, who was disabled and almost killed in the battle, and von Gneisenau, who briefly assumed command of the Army of the Lower Rhine, to retreat to Wavre, only eight miles from Waterloo, south of Brussels. Wellington's disorganized army was defeated by the French the same day at Quatre Bras, a strategic crossroads between Brussels and Charleroi. Two years earlier Napoleon had been forced to retreat to Leipzig to await the Allied attack that would follow. Now Wellington was forced to retreat to the farmland around Mont Sainte-Jean, just south of the village of Waterloo, to await Napoleon's next move on 18 June.

Von Gneisenau, still distrusting Wellington and believing he had failed to come to the aid of his Prussian allies at Ligny, urged Blücher, despite the Prussian king's explicit orders to the contrary, not to go to Wellington's aid at Waterloo and to consider a strategic retreat in the direction of the Rhine. Blücher, who had recovered from his injuries, and Gen. Karl Wilhelm Georg Grolman, the Prussian quartermaster general, convinced von Gneisenau to drop his objections. Blücher sent word to Wellington that he hoped to soon join him at Waterloo the following day. While acquiescing to Blücher and Grolman, von Gneisenau nevertheless made certain that the Army of the Lower Rhine advanced cautiously so that it could retreat in orderly fashion should circumstances warrant.[29] Most certainly the efficiency of von Gneisenau's General Staff had facilitated an orderly withdrawal to Wavre, thus enabling the Army of the Lower Rhine to regroup and prepare to engage the French at Waterloo the following day.[30] Von Gneisenau also was taking into consideration the possibility that he would assume command of the Prussian army should something happen to the seventy-two-year-old Blücher. In the meantime, Napoleon made a critical mistake assuming that he had forced the Prussians to quit the conflict and that he would only have to deal with Wellington in the north.

Wellington and Blücher were separated by eight miles on 17 June as the Army of the Lower Rhine prepared to join forces with Wellington near Waterloo the following day. Unfortunately, heavy rains and poor roads prevented the Prussians from reaching Wellington until late in the afternoon on 18 June, well after the beginning of the initial French attack around midday. The Prussians contributed some artillery support on their flank, but it was Wellington's army that was required to fend off the French attacks, counterattacks, and flanking movements. Finally, late in the day, Blücher, von Gneisenau, and the main body of the Prussian army arrived on the field of battle and took up positions on Wellington's left flank. Suddenly, Napoleon's position grew desperate, as he failed to break through the center of the Allied line. He now had to fight them combined or retreat. He chose the latter.

Following the battle, Wellington and Blücher had to decide whether to await the arrival of the Austrian and Russian armies, or to pursue Napoleon on their own. Von Gneisenau, who at first was hesitant to provide assistance to the Anglo-Dutch Army at Waterloo, now counseled Wellington and Blücher to pursue the retreating French and to defeat them decisively, just as they had tried to do in the days following Leipzig. Recalling Friedrich Wilhelm III's faith in his ability to make important decisions when the fate of Europe rested in the balance, von Gneisenau reminded Wellington and Blücher that it was the aggressiveness and independent actions of the French commanders that had led to Napoleon's victorious campaigns in 1806–7, particularly their pursuit of the defeated enemy following the Battle of Jena-Auerstadt.[31] Prussian corps and divisional commanders showed little interest in pursuing the French. It was von Gneisenau and Blücher who urged them on, and who often took direct command of the Prussian columns moving against the retreating French army. Because of their quick judgment, they prevented Napoleon and the remnants of his army from taking up defensive positions around Paris.[32]

After the final defeat of Napoleon, von Gneisenau assumed command of Prussian forces in the west, but he eventually resigned from the army in May 1816 citing poor health, although political considerations certainly played a major role in his decision. He returned to his estate in Silesia, if only briefly. He was appointed to a newly constituted Staatsrat in 1817, and on 9 September 1818 he was appointed governor of Berlin to succeed Kalhreuth. He was named chief of the Supreme Military Examinations Commission and promoted to the rank of general field marshall in 1825. He returned to military service in March 1831 during the Polish insurrection and was named supreme commander of the Army of Observation along the Polish frontier. He fell ill with cholera and died in Posen on 23 August 1831.

Notes

1. T. N. Dupuy, *A Genius for War: The German Army and General Staff, 1807–1945* (Englewood Cliffs, N.J.: Prentice-Hall, 1977), 21.
2. Ibid., 21.
3. Gebhardt Leberecht von Blücher (1742–1819) commanded the Prussian army during its ill-fated 1806 campaign against the French under Napoleon. He would later win brilliant victories against the French, including the defeat of Napoleon at Leipzig in 1813, during the French campaign in the winter of 1813–14, and in the Waterloo campaign of 1815. Friedrich Ludwig, the prince of Hohenlohe (1746–1818), was one of Blücher's most trusted generals prior to the defeat at Jena.
4. Gerhard Johann David von Scharnhorst (1755–1813) is primarily recognized for his reorganizing of the Prussian army beginning in 1807 following the defeat at Jena-Auerstadt. He later served as chief of staff to Field Marshal Blücher until his death in 1813 when he was succeeded by von Gneisenau.
5. Klaus Epstein, *The Genesis of German Conservatism* (Princeton, N.J.: Princeton University Press, 1966), 392. William O. Shanahan, *Prussian Military Reforms, 1786–1813* (New York: AMS Press, 1966). Peter Paret, *Yorck and the Era of Prussian Reform, 1807–1815* (Princeton, N.J.: Princeton University Press, 1966). Early recommendations of the Immediat-Kommission ran contrary to French restrictions placed on the Prussian military by the Treaty of Tilsit. Realizing that only a full mobilization of the Prussian army could free Prussia from French domination, Scharnhorst, with the support of von Gneisenau, recommended the introduction of universal military service regardless of class, and the creation of a reserve militia. This new popular army would help generate a sense of patriotism for Prussia. The Prussian king, Friedrich Wilhelm III, was troubled by these recommendations and opposed reform that called into question the dominance of the Prussian aristocracy. Scharnhorst and his reformers nevertheless managed to initiate a change in the military code of discipline based on honor rather than the threat of brutal corporal punishment. The officer corps and the army schools were completely reorganized to permit entry of any soldier who demonstrated the proper intelligence and sense of duty. Perhaps the most important reform instituted by Scharnhorst and von Gneisenau was the establishment of a General Staff, a collective military planning team subordinate to the Prussian Ministry of War yet responsible for long-range strategic command planning.
6. Michael Broers, *Europe Under Napoleon, 1799–1815* (New York: Hodder Arnold, 1996), 238.
7. Peter Hofschröer, *1815: The Waterloo Campaign—Wellington, His German Allies and the Battles of Ligny and Quatre Bras* (London: Greenhill Books, 1998), 61.
8. Dupuy, *Genius for War*, 46–47; for a detailed discussion of the establishment of the Prussian General Staff and Scharnhorst's tenure as the first chief of the General Staff see 17–32.
9. Hajo Holborn, *A History of Modern Germany, 1648–1840* (New York: Knopf, 1973), 417–20.

10. Ibid., 423.
11. Often distraught by Prussian defeats on the battlefield, Blücher relied heavily on Scharnhorst and applauded his reforms. For more information on this relationship, see Roger Parkinson, *The Hussar General: The Life of Bluecher, Man of Waterloo* (London: P. Davies, 1975).
12. Dupuy, *Genius for War*, 32–33.
13. Hofschröer, *1815*, 61.
14. Dupuy, *Genius for War*, 33.
15. Digby Smith, *1813: Leipzig— Napoleon and the Battle of the Nations* (London: Greenhill Books, 2001), 66. This is an excellent reference book, which goes into great detail in its description of both sides' preparations for the battle, as well its outcome and geopolitical implications.
16. Ibid., 174.
17. Ibid., 293.
18. Dupuy, *Genius for War*, 34.
19. Hofschröer, *1815*, 61.
20. Dupuy, *Genius for War*, 34–35.
21. Smith, *1813*, 294.
22. Hofschröer, *1815*, 99–101. Ironically, Bülow outranked von Gneisenau and therefore the Prussian chief of staff could only suggest that a subordinate corps commander carry out his orders.
23. Hofschröer, *1815*, 62–67; E. Kaulbach, "The Prussians," in *Waterloo: Battle of Three Armies*, ed. Lord Chalfont (New York: Knopf, 1980), 54–55.
24. Hofschröer, *1815*, 62.
25. Ibid., 105–7.
26. Kaulbach, "The Prussians," 53
27. Hofschröer, *1815*, 220.
28. Ibid., 220–22.
29. See G. H. Pertz, *Das Leben des Feldmarschalls Grafen Neithardt von Gneisenaus*, vols. 1–3 (Berlin: Reimer, 1864–69).
30. Kaulbach, "The Prussians," 55.
31. Dupuy, *Genius for War*, 35–36.
32. Militärgeschichtliches Forschungsamt, *Rückzug und Verfolgung: Zwei Kampfarten, 1757–1944* (Stuttgart: Deutsche Verlags-Anstalt, 1960), 235–36.

CHRONOLOGY OF RANDOLPH B. MARCY

9 Apr 1812	Born in Greenwich, Massachusetts.
1 Jul 1832	Graduated from the U.S. Military Academy and assigned as a brevet second lieutenant to the 5th Infantry. Marcy served mainly on the Michigan and Wisconsin frontier until outbreak of Mexican-American War.
1833	Married Mary A. Mann.
25 Nov 1835	Promoted to second lieutenant.
22 Jun 1837	Promoted to first lieutenant.
1846	Served briefly in the Mexican-American War.
18 May 1846	Promoted to captain.
1847–54	Performed escorts through and conducted explorations of the Southwest.
1852	Led the Red River expedition with George B. McClellan as his second-in-command.
1857	Served in Florida during the Third Seminole War.
1857–58	Directed an intrepid winter march through the Rocky Mountains during the Mormon War.
1859	Published *The Prairie Traveler*.
11 Aug 1859	Promoted to major and appointed paymaster.
20 May 1860	Daughter Mary Ellen ("Nelly") married George B. McClellan.
May 1861	Appointed George B. McClellan's chief of staff in the Department of the Ohio.
9 Aug 1861	Promoted to colonel and appointed inspector general.
23 Sep 1861	Promoted to brigadier general of volunteers as chief of staff of the Army of the Potomac.
Mar–Aug 1862	Participated in the Peninsula campaign.
Sep–Nov 1862	Participated in the western Maryland campaign.
14 Sep 1862	Engaged in his only field action of the Civil War at South Mountain.
9 Nov 1862	Stepped down as chief of staff, Army of the Potomac, upon the relief of George B. McClellan.
1863–78	Served in the inspector general's department.

13 Mar 1865	Received brevet promotions to brigadier general and to major general.
1866	Published *Thirty Years of Army Life on the Border*.
1872	Published *Border Reminiscences*.
12 Dec 1878	Appointed inspector general of the U.S. Army with the substantive rank of brigadier general.
1878	Wife Mary died.
2 Jan 1881	Retired from the U.S. Army and settled in West Orange, New Jersey.
1885	Traveled in the West with George B. McClellan just prior to McClellan's death from a heart attack.
1885–86	Last journey to the Rocky Mountains.
22 Nov 1887	Died, West Orange, New Jersey.

Randolph B. Marcy

David S. Heidler and Jeanne T. Heidler

O n the first day of June 1861, Maj. Gen. George B. McClellan wrote to President Abraham Lincoln: "You will double my efficiency if you can find it possible to place Major Marcy in the position I refer to."[1] The position McClellan was referring to was chief of staff, and although McClellan wanted Randolph Barnes Marcy at this point only for a regional command in what was then called the West—the Shenandoah Valley of western Virginia—Marcy would soon follow McClellan to a higher station. Thus would Randolph Marcy become the first operational chief of staff for the U.S. Army.[2]

The U.S. Army had not needed a chief of staff until the Civil War. The army's size during the Early Republic and antebellum periods had simply made the post unnecessary. When the American Revolution ended, the army was so reduced that its muster rolls would not have consumed more than a few pages to list both officers and rank and file. The country instead persistently relied on militia as the principal line of national defense and domestic enforcement. Experience in subsequent conflicts, such as the War of 1812, impressed the military with the need for a more reliable armed force, but Congress would not alter its habit of depending on citizen soldiers. That custom resulted from frugality as much as it did from philosophy.[3]

Neither Indian wars, especially in Florida, nor the Mexican-American War impinged on this political thinking. Even in the Civil War dependence on so-called volunteer forces endured throughout the conflict. In some profoundly fundamental ways, however, the Civil War changed virtually everything about the American military. The conflict's vast scope provided architects of military organization the chance to revise principles that had guided policy since the Revolution. Certainly, European innovations were not previously unknown to Americans, nor had they been completely omitted in practice, but employment of European techniques had been infrequent and at best unsystematic. The rejection of Calhoun's Expansible Army project in the early 1820s had set the pattern. Forty years later, European models, especially borrowed from the French and to some extent the Prussians, at last appeared on American landscapes, including the appointment of an operational chief of staff.[4]

When Maj. Gen. George B. McClellan set about to create the first operational chief of staff in the U.S. Army, he secured the services of Randolph B. Marcy. Marcy was born on 9 April 1812 in Greenwich, Massachusetts, to a family of old stock in that state and whose connections stretched from the professions to politics. Marcy made a career of the army, starting with attendance at the U.S. Military Academy. His performance at West Point was adequate, yet in the main undistinguished, placing him twenty-sixth in a class of forty-five upon his graduation in 1832. Marcy was not without talent, however. An intuitive ability to move through unblazed wilderness was evident in, for one thing, his life-long love of hunting. Fragile health sometimes afflicted him, a problem that troubled him throughout his life and occasionally interfered with his work.[5] Yet, even this misfortune had felicitous consequences. Fresh out of West Point, a recuperating Marcy met Mary Mann during a furlough required by illness. He married her in 1833.

Marcy served in the 5th Infantry on the Old Northwest frontier of Michigan and Wisconsin Territory for more than a decade after graduating from West Point. He was briefly detached twice to the East as a recruiting officer. Meanwhile, he plodded upward in rank at the slow pace customary to the peacetime army of this period, finally becoming a captain on the eve of the Mexican-American War. His service in that conflict was slight. He was with Zachary Taylor's army in the earliest stages at Palo Alto and Resaca de la Palma, but his activities were so routine they drew little notice. For the remainder of the war, he performed recruiting duty in Pennsylvania.

Marcy's most significant achievements came after the Mexican-American War. For a dozen years, he traveled, explored, and mapped the vast expanses beyond the Great Plains (dubbed the Great American Desert at the time), reaching into the Rocky Mountains and the arid Southwest. During the 1850s he conveyed pioneers to Santa Fe, escorted dignitaries on inspection tours, and directed important exploratory missions. He was in Florida briefly during the Third Seminole War in 1857, but it was in the Mormon War immediately afterward that he proved most resourceful, conducting an epic trek through the Rocky Mountains during the winter of 1857–58. Both the official records of these journeys and the popular accounts of them reveal Marcy as capable, stolid, and resolute, possessing admirable qualities that inspired men to follow him even under the most adverse conditions.[6]

Marcy's ability to inspire men to endure hardship with relative optimism was contagious. It must have served him well when, later, as chief of staff of the Army of the Potomac, he would confront some days as seemingly hopeless as those had been at Fort Bridger during the brutal winter in the Rockies. While serving in the West, Marcy also attended to an affair closer to his home. He exerted considerable pressure on his daughter to discourage her courtship with a young West Point graduate named Ambrose Powell Hill. He wrote to Mary Ellen—affectionately called "Nelly"—to catalogue the misfortunes of an officer's wife and make apparent that in Hill she was casting her sights much too low. He declared that he would regard it as a personal affront for her to continue the relationship and an irredeemable breach for her to take it to the altar. Marcy's campaign was successful. When Nelly broke off the flirtation in 1856, Marcy was delighted because it opened the way for other suitors, one of whom was George B. McClellan, coincidentally Hill's roommate during their West Point days. Although she was at first cool, McClellan persisted and finally won Nelly's hand. Marcy was most pleased.[7]

George B. McClellan was the rising young man defined. The son of a celebrated ophthalmologist, McClellan graduated second in the West Point class of 1846, a class full of luminaries destined for acclaim in the American Civil War.[8] He served in Mexico, where his exploits gained high praise and earned him three brevets. When he left the army in 1857, he already had made captain, a pace of promotion that was noteworthy but nonetheless too slow for this young man in a hurry. He elected to pursue a more financially rewarding career with the Illinois Central Railroad, soon becoming its vice-president.

McClellan and Marcy knew one another as members of that close-knit fraternity that was the peacetime service. In 1852 McClellan had served as second-in-command in Marcy's seventy-five-man expedition to find the source of the Red River. The party traveled from the Brazos River in Texas at Fort Belknap through the Comanche territory to Fort Arbuckle. It was on this occasion that McClellan first saw his future wife, Mary Ellen Marcy, although only in a photograph.[9] The girl's image impressed him at the time, as did the girl's father. During a trip made famous by rumors claiming the party had been annihilated, McClellan served the forty-year-old Marcy with enthusiasm and an uncharacteristic sense of subordination. Yet, he bristled when he heard that Marcy's report would mention him only in a diminished role. This also was nothing more than rumor, but McClellan did not discover that until he had petulantly predicted that "one of these days I may have the gentleman serving under me."[10] By the time the Civil War had begun and circumstances made that prediction prophetic, Marcy had become George McClellan's father-in-law.[11]

As for McClellan himself, the Union's woefully undermanned army reached out to experienced personnel, and the young railroad executive soon found himself back in uniform with an impressive rank. Within weeks of the attack on Fort Sumter, he was a major general of volunteers and regulars and in command of the Department of Ohio. At the end of April, McClellan wrote to Commanding General Winfield Scott requesting additions to his staff, specifically that Maj. Fitz John Porter be made his adjutant general and Capt. John H. Dickerson his quartermaster. He also requested that Major Marcy be made his department's paymaster. Marcy at the time was attached to the paymaster general's office. Scott denied all of McClellan's requests except for the assignment of Marcy. Scott's adjutant Lt. Col. E. D. Townshend counseled McClellan to "do as well as you can with the talent and zeal you can find in your command."[12]

Doubtless the familial association reinforced McClellan's already substantial respect for his former commanding officer. In his original request for Marcy's appointment, he had noted "that my intimate personal & official relations with him show him to be possessed of precisely those qualities that I need in my advisor & chief of staff."[13] McClellan relied on his father-in-law for companionship and sought to elevate his station in his official family. When Joseph K. Mansfield was promoted and given command of the Department of Washington, McClellan on 1 June asked President Lincoln to appoint Marcy to the post of inspector general. Accordingly, on 9 August 1861 Marcy was promoted to colonel in the regular army. By then, the main Union Army had been shattered at First Bull Run, and McClellan had been summoned from western Virginia to assume command of what would become officially on 20 August the Army of the Potomac. These were big changes, and they came so rapidly they would have dazed anyone.

A week before the disaster at Bull Run, McClellan had been sharing a large tent with Marcy pitched under a tree on a quiet field outside of Buckhannon, Virginia.[14] Now he was the toast of Washington and the hope of the country. Marcy had vaulted from a job in the Paymaster Department to become the Army of the Potomac's chief of staff (4 September 1861) and then a brigadier general of volunteers (23 September 1861).[15] What all this change meant was cloaked in uncertainty. Marcy's duties were not only new to him but also a novelty for the army, and they remained unsettled most importantly in the mind and habits of the army's commanding officer. At least McClellan's previous experience in the military had made him aware of the emerging drive for professionalism. In 1855 he also had traveled abroad with majors Richard Delafield and Alfred Mordecai as the third member of a commission to observe the French and British armies during the Crimean War. Just how educational this experience was for McClellan is in dispute; perhaps it provided, as some have said, nothing more tangible than new ways to pitch a tent or rig a hammock.[16] Although McClellan learned much from his inspection of European military organizations, he was curiously heedless about organizational innovations in command structures.[17]

Nobody disputes that McClellan effectively refurbished the Union Army that returned smashed from First Bull Run in July 1861. To the rabble that had limped back from Manassas Junction he brought order, restored pride, and created cohesion ranging from the lowest ranks to the highest echelons of command. Yet for all that, his most striking innovation was to make the army a reflection of his personality, which was orderly, prideful, and remarkably cohesive (some would have said overbearing) for one so young. The Army of the Potomac, like McClellan, became more competent in appearance than it was in practice. The idiosyncrasy carried over into McClellan's organizational innovations. His changes in command structure and the delegation of duties were theoretically creative but remained largely unrealized practically. For instance, when McClellan took command of all the armies after Winfield Scott's retirement in November 1861, he did not significantly alter the organization of the Potomac army, and he did not merge the headquarters of it and the regular army at large. "Thus Gen. Marcy, the chief of staff of the Army of the Potomac," McClellan later explained, "had nothing to do with the headquarters of the Army of the United States."[18]

In fact, McClellan kept two staffs with two adjutant generals, one for the Army of the Potomac and another for the overall U.S. Army. Even as he enlarged his staff, he did little to delegate duties, reflecting an unshakable distrust that any subordinate could do a job as well as he could. So he did create the position of operational chief of staff—before McClellan there was no such thing in the U.S. Army—yet, he made it essentially meaningless in execution. Randolph B. Marcy was never given any important role in strategic planning or the execution of command. McClellan, in fact, resisted reorganizing the army into corps so that he would be better able to command the army personally, maintaining a belief that an army of ten divisions could be managed by one person. That one person was always to be George McClellan.[19]

That Marcy was also McClellan's father-in-law was not lost on some observers, even during a time accustomed to familial patronage.[20] "McClellan makes his father-in-law, a man of very secondary capacity, the chief of staff of the army," Adam Gurowski noted in his diary. "It seems that McClellan ignores what a highly responsible position it is, and what a special transcendent capacity must be that of a chief-of-staff—the more so when of an army of several hundreds of thousands. I do not look for a Berthier, a Gneisenau, a Diebitsch, or a Gortschakoff, but a Marcy will not do."[21]

Given such criticism and low expectations, it is a tribute to McClellan's force of personality that he did as well as he did, and it is a testament to Marcy's professionalism that he remained in his post throughout McClellan's tenure in command. These men would conduct two major campaigns in the spring and fall of 1862, the first on the Virginia peninsula and the second in western Maryland, superintending a vast army across widely varied and unfamiliar terrain. In helping to direct the army, Marcy became a mixture of "executive secretary, courier, public information officer, and liaison" between the sensitive McClellan, the newspapers, the political class in Washington, and his increasingly disillusioned civilian superiors in the Lincoln administration.[22]

Actually, Marcy sometimes performed little other service than to absorb the administration's anger at McClellan's missteps. Just prior to the Urbana campaign in early 1862, McClellan was attempting to clear the upper Potomac region of the Confederate presence. The army's own engineers foiled an attempt to bring canal boats down the Chesapeake and Ohio Canal to serve as part of a bridge at Harper's Ferry. They had neglected to measure a lift lock, so after much effort it was discovered that the canal boats were too wide to pass into the Potomac from the canal. Stanton was livid, and Lincoln nearly as much so. Marcy bore the brunt of the president's wrath in an uncomfortable interview. Called in from headquarters, he was lectured by Lincoln and unable to mollify the president with assurances that McClellan would be able to clarify the situation. Indeed, Lincoln was so furious about the pontoon boat episode— "a hell of a rage," in Marcy's estimation—it was in the following week (8 March 1862) that Lincoln and Secretary of War Edwin Stanton finally forced the reorganization of the Potomac army into corps. The president himself designated the officers to command these new corps.[23]

On 11 March Marcy sent McClellan a telegram alerting him of the need to come to Washington because former Ohio governor John Dennison wanted to see him immediately. Dennison was the one who was going to tell McClellan that he was being relieved as general in chief to command only the Army of the Potomac while in the field. McClellan, however, would not come, claiming that he was too tired. "Besides," he said, "I think the less I see of Washington the better."[24] It was an attitude he took to heart because whenever possible he always sent Marcy to Washington instead.

McClellan's habit of ranging away from headquarters to manage matters himself in the field frustrated his superiors in Washington. In what became a common event, Marcy assumed the role of courier. When popular impatience and Lincoln's corresponding insistence finally forced McClellan to move the Army of the Potomac in the direction of Richmond, McClellan hoped to avoid another direct confrontation with the Confederates with a vast, amphibious flanking maneuver to the York Peninsula. On his way to Fort Monroe to begin this Peninsula campaign, McClellan dispatched Marcy to explain arrangements for the capital's defenses.[25] He also entrusted Marcy with the important job of bringing in mortars and siege guns to Fort Monroe as a preparation for the assault on Yorktown, as well as Richmond, where he expected to "find earthworks heavily garrisoned."[26] It was a rare delegation of operational power, and for Marcy it was a brief one.

Once on the peninsula, McClellan made Fitz John Porter "Director of the Siege" outside of Yorktown. It was, he said, "a novel title but made necessary by the circumstances of the case." McClellan intended to manage the siege through Porter, thus supplanting Marcy, even as chief of staff "for that portion of the work." McClellan explained, "It not being M[arcy]'s specialty he cannot assist me in siege operations." Indeed, according to McClellan, an inspection of siege lines the previous day had revealed "so many blunders committed that I was very thankful to put Porter on duty at once."[27] It was hardly a vote of confidence in the operational abilities of his operational chief of staff.

Usually McClellan made Marcy little more than an extension of his own fretful attention to minute detail. Slogging up the peninsula to the environs of Richmond, McClellan was the victim, albeit a willing one, of faulty intelligence regarding Confederate strengths and hampered, he said, by the anxieties of the administration in Washington. On the evening of the Battle of Fair Oaks, he nervously instructed Marcy to get everybody fed, rested, and ready for a fight. He fussed over the condition of bridges across the swollen creeks and rivers outside Richmond as well as the safety of his baggage trains.

"If the bridges cannot be built tonight, commit the work to Porter & Franklin. I am sure Duane can do it. If they cannot, the sooner we get rid of the Corps of Engineers the better—communicate this to Barnard."[28]

Marcy's main roles remained those of courier, messenger, and booster, this last especially when needed, and when the campaign on the peninsula first stalled and then went sour, McClellan needed as many champions as he could muster. To help bolster McClellan's image, Marcy fed stories to newspaper reporters, making sure that they put the best light on pressing concerns and McClellan's way of meeting them. And as Marcy continued to run interference with the administration while laboring to keep up his chief's fragile spirits, he also found himself coping with Lincoln's exhausted patience. When the newly named Confederate Army of Northern Virginia, now under Robert E. Lee, began a pounding, weeklong assault on McClellan, it nearly drove him from the peninsula. After the Union retreat from Malvern Hill at the close of the Seven Days' Battles, Marcy went to Washington and reported to the president. He said that the army was in such sorry shape that if it were attacked again, it would have to "capitulate." When Lincoln exploded about both the word and the sentiment that prompted it, Marcy insisted he was only talking in the hypothetical, and Lincoln calmed down a little. "The President and Secretary [of War Edwin Stanton]," he assured McClellan, "speak very kindly of you and find no fault."[29]

Nonetheless brooding at Harrison's Landing, McClellan sought to reorganize his officer corps with dismissals and transfers. Marcy dutifully took the list to Washington and advised that these changes be made as gradually as possible to prevent too much dissension both within and without the army.[30] Stanton, however, had already far advanced his plans to replace McClellan with the western general John Pope. At the end of July, when McClellan was ordered to press Richmond to determine if Lee was moving north to fight Pope, McClellan told Marcy to inform the War Department that he would need reinforcements to carry out the job. Marcy brashly telegraphed the War Department something that McClellan had not said, but which appeared to carry the general's attitude: that reinforcements would put the Army of the Potomac in Richmond in less than a week. At that point, it did not seem a bad idea to embellish McClellan's belligerence toward the enemy, especially when it was unlikely that it would ever be tested.[31]

When John Pope led his newly created Army of Virginia to disaster at Second Bull Run in August 1862, McClellan again found himself in command of the main federal army, once more the Army of the Potomac. Marcy had remained its chief of staff during that army's brief eclipse by Pope's forces, and he continued in that role during the army's final campaign under McClellan that would conclude on the banks of Antietam Creek in September 1862. General Robert E. Lee's Army of Northern Virginia had moved across the Potomac River into western Maryland after Second Manassas, scattering across the countryside behind the shelter of the Blue Ridge. McClellan cautiously shadowed the Confederates as they trudged northward until chance handed him Lee's plans.[32]

As the Army of the Potomac suddenly and uncharacteristically abandoned its slow prudence to race through the passes of the Blue Ridge and pounce upon Lee's scattered Confederates, Marcy had his only recorded experience in the war of directing operations in the field. At South Mountain, responding to a request for reinforcements at the rear of the pass there, McClellan put Joseph Hooker to the task and Marcy accompanied him. McClellan later remarked that he thought Marcy had done most of the direction of this movement, but counted Marcy's modesty as the reason "he could say little or nothing about it."[33]

Whatever the case, once through the passes, McClellan's old wariness returned, and he gave Lee enough time to cobble together a force that would survive the furious battle at Antietam Creek on 17 September 1862. The failure to destroy the Confederates at this battle or to harry them with any enthusiasm as they retreated across the Potomac finally cost McClellan his job and, with it, Marcy's as well. Thus the service of the first chief of staff in the U.S. Army ended as equivocally as it had begun, a circumstance occasioned by the vagaries of its creator, George McClellan, and his unique relationship to its first designee, his father-in-law Randolph B. Marcy.

Others would follow Marcy, and the post would mature under the practices of different commanders and the personalities of their chiefs of staff, for the stark necessities of commanding vast armies dictated greater and more refined forms of delegation. Commanders more inclined to entrust subordinates with the routine business of putting into execution larger strategic and specific tactical plans would follow McClellan's model without restricting it with McClellan's habits. Thus George Leonard Andrews would more successfully serve as chief of staff for both Nathaniel Prentiss Banks and E. R. S. Canby. Canby had observed the talented George W. Cullum, Halleck's chief, firsthand in Washington, D.C. And Daniel Butterfield would follow in Marcy's footsteps with the Army of the Potomac to serve under both Joseph Hooker and George Gordon Meade with greater efficiency and effectiveness.

Marcy was the first, however, and correspondingly he suffered the fate of many forerunners who feel their way along imperfectly but best they can. Doubtless his difficulties almost completely stemmed from the unique flaws McClellan brought to command, but Marcy remained loyal to the commander who was his son-in-law as well as his chieftain, serving as his champion as well as his factotum. McClellan made mistakes both serious and small in his time as commander of the Army of the Potomac. Randolph Marcy was not one of them. Marcy continued in the service after leaving the Army of the Potomac, but he was never again attached to an active field command. Instead, he was placed in the Inspector General's department and went on missions related to that duty for the remainder of the war. In spite of having earned the dislike of Stanton, doubtless for his unavoidably continued association with McClellan (he served as an unofficial advisor during McClellan's Democratic presidential bid in 1864), Marcy would remain in the service for almost another two decades, finally retiring in 1881.[34]

Brevetted twice at the end of the Civil War, he became a brigadier general in 1878 upon his appointment as inspector general of the army, the rank he held at the end of his career. His wife Mary died in 1878, and upon his retirement he settled in West Orange, New Jersey, to be near George, Nelly, and his grandchildren. He remained active until his death by taking yearly hunting trips in the West, one with his son-in-law and former commanding officer in 1885 just before McClellan died of a heart attack. After one more such excursion to the Rockies, Marcy himself returned to New Jersey, fatigued and ailing. He died in West Orange on 22 November 1887.

Notes

1. McClellan to Abraham Lincoln, 1 June 1861, in *The Civil War Papers of George B. McClellan: Selected Correspondence, 1860–1865*, ed. Stephen W. Sears (New York: Da Capo Press, 1992), 29–30, hereafter cited as Sears, ed., *McClellan Correspondence.*

2. Technically Marcy ranks as the first official chief of staff, although necessity usually thrust such duties unofficially upon the ranking officer of any staff. Archer Jones and Herman Hattaway explain that "the senior officer on any staff had taken the title [of chief of staff] while still continuing in his other functions." See Hattaway and Jones, *How the North Won: A Military History of the Civil War* (Urbana: University of Illinois Press, 1983), 107. While Marcy was indeed the first chief of staff with his commission dating from August 1861, George Washington Cullum also would serve as chief of staff in Henry Wager Halleck's command of the Department of Missouri and Mississippi starting in November 1861. Cullum went to Washington with Halleck

in July 1862 when Halleck became general in chief. Cullum served as chief in Halleck's staff of twenty-three officers in the War Department with the task of coordinating logistical and operational activities, including information gathering. When Ulysses S. Grant became general in chief in 1864, Halleck himself in turn became chief of staff.

3. The War of 1812 produced a cadre of young officers who ever afterward saw themselves as professional military men. Alexander Macomb, Edmund Pendleton Gaines, and Winfield Scott had entered the army before the War of 1812, had determined upon a military career, and chafed at the incompetence of the amateur army after the war started. When Maj. Gen. Jacob Brown gave Scott the task of establishing a training camp at Buffalo, New York, Scott did so by integrating a French system of infantry tactics from an untranslated copy he owned. See William B. Skelton, *An American Profession of Arms: The Army Officer Corps, 1784–1861* (Lawrence: University Press of Kansas, 1992), 110–11, and Winfield Scott, *Memoirs of Lieut.-General Scott, LL.D., Written by Himself*, 2 vols. (New York: Sheldon and Company, 1864), 1:188–89.

4. More than a score of American officers traveled in Europe during the Early Republic, including Maj. William McRee and Capt. Sylvanus Thayer, whose Corps of Engineers training would be enhanced by study in French military academies. They brought to West Point manuals, books, and other instructional aids. Thayer admired the emphasis on engineering in France's military schools, so West Point emphasized engineering accordingly. In 1816 Claudius Crozet, formally trained in France and having served under Napoleon, became professor of engineering at the Academy. See Skelton, *An American Profession of Arms*, 115, for American officers abroad during the period; also see Edward Coffman, *The Old Army: A Portrait of the American Army in Peacetime, 1784–1898* (Oxford: Oxford University Press, 1986), 43, 47, 49; and Lester A. Webb, *Captain Alden Partridge and the United States Military Academy, 1806–1833* (Northport, Ala.: American Southern, 1965), 49; and Roger J. Spiller, "Calhoun's Expansible Army: The History of a Military Idea," *South Atlantic Quarterly* 79 (Spring 1980): 196, 200. Even so, the first Union field commander in the East, Irvin McDowell, was forced to perform for himself many duties usually relegated to a chief of staff. When he herded the army to Manassas in July 1861, he finally had a staff of sorts, but it was woefully undermanned and very unpracticed. See Archer Jones, *Civil War Command and Strategy: The Process of Victory and Defeat* (New York: Free Press, 1992), 41.

5. Marcy apparently suffered from acute asthma. See W. Eugene Hollon, *Beyond the Cross Timbers: The Travels of Randolph B. Marcy, 1812–1887* (Norman: University of Oklahoma Press, 1955), 22.

6. Marcy's reports appear in Senate Executive Documents, no. 64 (31st Cong, 1st sess.), no. 54 (32nd Cong., 1st sess.), and no. 60 (34th Cong., 1st sess.). In 1854 he published *The Prairies Traveler* under the auspices of the War Department as a practical guidebook for pioneers. After the Civil War, he published his memoirs recounting his career in the West. *Thirty Years of Army Life on the Border* appeared in 1866 (Lansing: Scholarly Publishing Office, University of Michigan Library, 2006) and *Border Reminiscences* in 1872 (Whitefish, Mont.: Kessinger, 2007).

7. The story of Mary Ellen Marcy and Hill is ably related in William Woods Hassler, *A. P. Hill: Lee's Forgotten General* (Richmond, Va.: Garrett and Massie, 1962; reprint, Chapel

Hill: University of North Carolina Press, 1988), 16–22. The anecdote has been told often of how Hill's failed romance with and McClellan's successful courtship of Ellen Marcy became part of the Army of Potomac's lore. On one occasion, it was said, as A. P. Hill's division conducted an especially furious assault against McClellan's forces, one Yankee was heard to lament, "My God, Nelly! Why didn't you marry him?" The story, which McClellan doubted, is told in Henry Kyd Douglas, *I Rode with Stonewall, Being Chiefly the War Experiences of the Youngest Member of Jackson's Staff from the John Brown Raid to the Hanging of Mrs. Surratt* (Chapel Hill: University of North Carolina Press, 1940), 178.

8. In addition to Hill, McClellan's classmates included Thomas Jonathan Jackson, later to be known as "Stonewall" Jackson.

9. Some writers have mistakenly had the two meeting, but Ellen Marcy was attending school back east. See H. J. Eckenrode and Bryan Conrad, *George B. McClellan: The Man Who Saved the Union* (Chapel Hill: University of North Carolina Press, 1941), 11–12; also see Stephen W. Sears, *George B. McClellan: The Young Napoleon* (New York: Ticknor and Fields, 1988), 33.

10. Sears, *McClellan*, 34.

11. Ellen Marcy and McClellan were married on 22 May 1860 in New York City.

12. McClellan to Scott, 23 April 1861, in *McClellan Correspondence*, ed. Sears, 8; *Official Records of the War of the Rebellion*, ser. 1, 1:342–43.

13. McClellan to Lincoln, 1 June 1861, in *McClellan Correspondence*, ed. Sears, 29–30.

14. McClellan to Mary Ellen McClellan, 7 July 1861, in ibid., 49–50.

15. Marcy would hold the brigadier rank until 4 March 1863.

16. Herman Hattaway cites historian J. D. Little for this charge. See Hattaway, *Shades of Blue and Gray: An Introductory Military History of the Civil War* (Columbia: University of Missouri Press, 1997), 21; yet Hattaway himself disagrees and regards the Delafield Commission's observations as useful. See p. 55. McClellan's most thorough biographer, Stephen W. Sears, also regards the journey as valuable, to a point. He attributes McClellan's caution outside Yorktown to his recollection of the siege at Sevastopol. See Sears, *McClellan*, 46. Also see Matthew Moten, "The Delafield Commission and the American Military Profession," Ph.D. diss., Rice University, Houston, 1996.

17. Sears, *McClellan*, 48.

18. McClellan to Ulysses S. Grant, 26 December 1866, in George B. McClellan, *McClellan's Own Story: The War for the Union, the Soldiers Who Fought It, the Civilians Who Directed It, and His Relations to It and to Them* (New York: Charles L. Webster and Company, 1887), 219.

19. Sears, *McClellan*, 111–12. "McClellan," notes Marcy's biographer, "delegated little responsibility to his subordinates, his father-in-law included." See Hollon, *Beyond the Cross Timbers*, 242. "In heaven's name," McClellan had moaned in the summer of 1861, "give me some General Officers who understand their profession. I give orders & find some who cannot execute them unless I stand by them. Unless I command every picket & lead every column, I cannot be sure of success. Give me such men as Marcy . . . etc & I will answer for it with my life that I meet with no disaster." See McClellan to Col. E. D. Townshend, 19 July 1861 (telegram), *McClellan Correspondence*, ed. Sears, 61. Yet when McClellan fell ill with typhoid fever on 20 December 1861, and Marcy ostensibly

took over the day-to-day routine of the army, according to Eckenrode and Conrad, he simply "did not know what to do in his [McClellan's] absence." See Eckenrode and Conrad, *George B. McClellan*, 37. McClellan was back at headquarters on 13 January. The same season of typhoid that felled McClellan also assailed Marcy who was in January under the care of his brother Dr. Erastus E. Marcy who had just previously been attending to McClellan. See McClellan to Mary M. Marcy, 23 Jan 1862, in *McClellan Correspondence*, ed. Sears, 155.

20. William H. Seward and Charles Francis Adams were among those who regarded offices in their power as apprenticeships for sons.

21. Adam Gurowski, diary from 4 March 1861 to 12 November 1862, quoted in Hollon, *Beyond the Cross Timbers*, 242. Gurowski was referring in part to Alexandre Berthier, Napoleon's chief of staff, who was noted for an animus against Antoine Henri Jomini that drove Jomini from the French army. In any event, Marcy was not the only relative on McClellan's staff. Family surrounded him. "Marcy & Arthur are for the present living with me," he noted in the fall of 1861. Arthur, a captain on McClellan's staff, was also his brother. See McClellan to Elizabeth B. McClellan, 9 November 1861, *McClellan Correspondence*, ed. Sears, 129.

22. Hollon, *Beyond the Cross Timbers*, 241. McClellan's staff for the Army of the Potomac consisted of the following: Brig. Gen. Randolph B. Marcy, Chief, assisted by Capt. E. A. Raymond; Brig. Gen. Seth Williams, Adjutant General, assisted by Lt. Col. James A. Hardie and Capts. Richard B. Irwin, Joseph Kirkland, Arthur McClellan, M. T. Mahon, William P. Mason Jr., and William F. Biddle; Col. T. T. Gantt, Judge Advocate General, succeeded by Col. Thomas M. Key; Col. D. B. Sackett, Inspector General, with two aides-de-camp; Brig. Gen. John G. Barnard, Engineers, with fourteen subordinates; Lt. Col. John Macomb, Topographical Engineers, succeeded by Brig. Gen. A. A. Humphreys, with four subordinates; Surgeon Charles S. Tripler, Medical Department, succeeded in July 1862 by Surgeon Jonathan Letterman; Brig. Gen. Stewart Van Vliet, Quartermaster, succeeded in July 1862 by Lt. Col. R. Ingalls; Col. Henry F. Clarke, Commissary, with eight subordinates; Col. C. P. Kingsbury, Ordnance, succeeded in July 1862 by Thomas G. Baylor; Brig. Gen. Andrew Porter, Provost Marshal; Albert J. Myer, Signal Corps; Maj. Thomas T. Eckert, Telegraphic Operations; and Prof. Thaddeus Lowe, Balloons. Additional aides-de-camp included Lt. Cols. Abner V. Colburn, N. B. Sweitzer, Edward McK. Hudson, Paul von Radowitz, Majors H. von Hammerstein, and W. W. Russell. Several foreign observers accompanied the army's staff during the early stages of the Peninsula Campaign including members of the French deposed House of Orléans, such as the Duc de Chartres and the pretender to the French throne, the Comte de Paris. After the Peninsula Campaign, McClellan consolidated the Engineer and Topographical Engineers and placed the new department under J. C. Duane. It functioned thusly during the campaign in western Maryland. See McClellan, *McClellan's Own Story*, 125–35.

23. Sears, *McClellan*, 156–57; also see Benjamin P. Thomas and Harold M. Hyman, *Stanton: The Life and Times of Lincoln's Secretary of War* (New York: Knopf, 1962), 177–78.

24. McClellan to Marcy, 11 March 1862, in *McClellan Correspondence*, ed. Sears, 201. McClellan was relieved of overall command of the federal armies on 11 March 1862. See Dyer's *Compendium*, pt. 1, 254.

25. Warren W. Hassler Jr., *General George B. McClellan: Shield of the Union* (Baton Rouge: Louisiana State University Press, 1957), 81. Marcy met with Ethan Allen Hitchcock and thus initiated what would become one of the great controversies of the war. Lincoln and Stanton grew so anxious over McClellan's proposed protection of the capital that they held back units from his Peninsula Campaign. McClellan would always claim that the absence of these forces doomed his efforts on the Peninsula.

26. McClellan to Marcy, 22 March 1862, in *McClellan Correspondence*, 216.

27. McClellan to Mary Ellen McClellan, 27 April 1862, in ibid., 250.

28. McClellan to Marcy, 31 May 1862, in ibid., 284. Later at the end of the campaign, McClellan would still occasionally order the positioning of individual artillery pieces: "De Russy's two guns should at once be drawn behind the entrenchments," read one instruction to his chief of staff, 25 June 1862, telegram, ibid., 311. As Stephen Sears notes, "The lessons of the campaign did not convince him of the need for an operational staff." See Sears, *McClellan*, 238.

29. Sears, *McClellan*, 181, 226; Marcy to McClellan, 4 July 1862, quoted in Hassler, *General George B. McClellan*, 175.

30. A measure of McClellan's mood can be taken from his note to his wife written from Harrison's Landing while shells came in from Union gunboats in the James River. "Marcy & I have just been discussing (another [shell passes overhead]) people in Washn & conclude that they are 'a mighty trifling set.'" McClellan to Mary Ellen McClellan, 31 July 1862, in *McClellan Correspondence*, ed. Sears, 380.

31. Hassler, *General George B. McClellan*, 176; Sears, *McClellan*, 243.

32. Lee's famous "Lost Order" that detailed the disposition and lines of march for his entire army was discovered wrapped around several cigars by Union soldiers who promptly sent the document on its way to McClellan's headquarters.

33. McClellan, *McClellan's Own Story*, 583.

34. McClellan to Elizabeth B. McClellan, 6 December 1863, and McClellan to Samuel L. M. Barlow, 21 September 1864, *McClellan Correspondence*, ed. Sears, 563, 601.

CHRONOLOGY OF JOHN A. RAWLINS

13 Feb 1831	Born, Galena, Illinois.
1854	Admitted to Illinois State Bar.
30 Aug 1861	Appointed captain and assistant adjutant general of volunteers on Grant's staff.
14 May 1862	Promoted to major of volunteers.
1 Nov 1862	Promoted to lieutenant colonel U.S. Army and assigned as Grant's chief of staff.
11 Aug 1863	Promoted to brigadier general of volunteers.
3 Mar 1865	Promoted to brigadier general in the regular U.S. Army.
9 Apr 1865	Promoted to major general, U.S. Army.
11 Mar 1869	Appointed secretary of war.
12 Mar 1869	Resigned commission in U.S. Army.
6 Sep 1869	Died, Washington, D.C.

John A. Rawlins

Steven E. Woodworth

John Aaron Rawlins was born in Galena, Illinois, 13 February 1831, the second child in a family of ten children. His father, James, had farmed in Missouri and Illinois before becoming a charcoal burner, supplying charcoal for the extensive lead-smelting industry based on the mines in northwestern Illinois. Unfortunately, James Rawlins was also a drunk, and his son John had the traumatic experience of observing how alcohol had destroyed his father and impoverished the family. Young John became a life-long enemy of beverage alcohol and determined never to partake of it. When he was eighteen years old, his father went west in the California Gold Rush, leaving John to take over the charcoal-burning business and support the family. Despite this heavy workload, Rawlins strove to educate himself by reading books in his spare time. In 1853 he began studying law with Galena lawyer Isaac P. Stevens. The following year he became Stevens' partner, and in 1855 he took over the practice. Rawlins excelled as a lawyer because of his exceptional skills in forceful and impassioned oratory.[1]

Ulysses S. Grant came to Galena in 1860 after a difficult decade. After graduating from West Point in 1843, Grant had served capably as a junior officer in the Mexican War. After the war he married Julia Dent, but then he was transferred to a post in California and could not bring his family with him. Depressed, Grant turned to drink and eventually had to leave the army. Civilian employment turned out little better for Grant, who lacked business acumen, and he was finally forced to accept a job working in the Galena leather goods store of his often-critical father, Jesse Grant. It was a tacit admission that he could not succeed on his own in business and pained Ulysses deeply. Still he served capably in Galena, operating the store and collecting outstanding bills. Although Jesse Grant was one of Rawlins' clients, Grant had, at most, only a passing acquaintance with the lawyer.[2]

A thousand miles away, Rebel artillery opened fire on Fort Sumter on 12 April 1861. The U.S. garrison in the fort surrendered thirty-four hours later. On 15 April Pres. Abraham Lincoln issued a proclamation declaring that an insurrection existed and calling on the states to provide 75,000 troops to suppress it, the first of what would be many calls for troops. Response in the northern states was immediate and enthusiastic. In Galena, citizens held a mass meeting the day after Lincoln's proclamation, but Mayor Robert Brand created an uproar by expressing opposition to the war. After the enraged citizenry had shouted down the mayor, a series of speakers took the stand one after another to give rousing patriotic speeches in favor of the Union and the war. Though local congressman Elihu B. Washburne was among the speakers, the man who made the biggest impression was John Rawlins, and among those impressed by his performance was Ulysses Grant. The meeting adjourned with a call for another gathering two days later, specifically for the purpose of raising troops in response to the president's call.

When that meeting convened, those present elected Grant to fill the chair. Rawlins and others again supported the cause with fiery speeches, and the result of the evening's work was the decision to recruit a company of troops. Grant, Rawlins, and others worked hard to obtain the necessary number of recruits in the surrounding counties, and Grant helped drill the new troops. He declined, however, to serve as captain of the company, believing himself qualified for higher rank.[3]

He was right. That summer he received a commission as colonel of the 21st Illinois regiment and in August received promotion to the rank of brigadier general. In selecting his original staff, Grant was governed more by personal than by professional considerations. He wanted above all men he could trust, and he tended to select those with whom he felt comfortable or who had stood by him in one way or another during his hardscrabble years out of the army. Aide-de-camp Capt. William S. Hillyer was a St. Louis lawyer who had befriended Grant during his difficult times in that city. Clark B. Lagow, with a similar appointment, had been a lieutenant in the 21st, Grant's springboard to success. Grant also chose Rawlins, a representative of his recently adopted hometown, and asked him to serve as his assistant adjutant general, though he still did not know the Galena lawyer well enough to spell his name correctly and wrote in a letter to Julia that he had invited "Mr. Rollins" to join his staff.[4]

Rawlins responded with a cordial letter accepting the appointment but explaining that he could not assume his duties immediately due to personal considerations. His wife was dying of tuberculosis at the home of her father in Goshen, New York. After her death on 30 August, he had to arrange for the care of his three children, all under the age of five. Some of Rawlins' friends and political supporters in Galena feared that the delay would prompt Grant to withdraw his offer and wrote Grant to urge him not to. Grant replied, this time spelling Rawlins' name correctly and assuring them that his offer stood. Finally in mid-September Rawlins arrived at Grant's headquarters ready to go to work. By that time Grant had been transferred from his small command in southern Missouri to a more important assignment at Cairo, Illinois, junction of the Ohio and Mississippi rivers and gateway to the lower Mississippi Valley.[5]

Rawlins arrived at an opportune time, for routine administrative work had been keeping Grant busy in his headquarters until two or three o'clock every morning and then up and back to work again before dawn. Rawlins' arrival immediately helped relieve Grant of this crushing workload.[6] Rawlins' chief duties consisted of distributing orders and handling other routine paperwork. Orders from headquarters began to appear over his signature, including the order that brought on Grant's first battle as a commander, the November 1861 Battle of Belmont.[7] During that battle, Rawlins stayed close to Grant under heavy enemy fire and was alongside his commander when Grant's horse was shot.[8] Fortunately for both men's chances of surviving the war, Grant's duties in subsequent battles usually did not bring him under the sort of hot fire he endured at Belmont.

Another of Rawlins' principal duties on Grant's staff was to protect Grant against charges of drunkenness—and perhaps against drunkenness itself. The officer corps of the prewar U.S. Army had been small enough that gossip traveled ubiquitously. All of Grant's fellow officers knew of the drinking problem he had had in California nearly a decade before. Some of those who became jealous of Grant, or desired to destroy his career for various reasons of their own, were quick to use his reputation against him by spreading false charges that he had been drinking again. By February 1862 Grant's own commanding officer, Henry W. Halleck, was deliberately initiating false reports of Grant's drinking. Rawlins felt especially qualified to combat such slanders. Against some of the earliest accusations, Rawlins responded with a letter to his fellow townsman and Grant's congressional patron, Elihu Washburne, assuring the congressman that Grant had taken only an occasional drink and had not been intoxicated since Rawlins had been serving with him. "I regard his interest as my interest," Rawlins wrote of Grant. "I love him as a father; I respect him because I have studied him well, and the more I know him the more I respect and love him." It was a telling statement coming from the son of the besotted James Rawlins. Here at last was a man John Rawlins could look up to and respect, and this time he meant to see to it that alcohol did not take that away from him.[9]

During the course of the war, Rawlins took it upon himself to keep Grant on the wagon. When in November 1862 Lt. James H. Wilson reported for duty on Grant's staff, then–Chief of Staff Rawlins showed him an abstinence pledge that he had persuaded the general to sign. Grant, he told Wilson, would lead them to victory, "if his friends could stay him from falling."[10] Rawlins clearly gloried in his role as the guardian of Grant's sobriety. If Grant was the man who would save the country, then Rawlins, in his own mind, was the man who would save Grant and the only one who could.

Once during the Vicksburg siege and again during operations around Chattanooga in the fall of 1863, Rawlins wrote lengthy letters to Grant taking his commander to task for renewed consumption of alcohol. "The great solicitude I feel for the safety of this army leads me to mention, what I hoped never again to do, the subject of your drinking," Rawlins wrote Grant in the June letter. Grant, he asserted, had pledged earlier that spring not to partake of any liquor during the remainder of the war, but now, he continued, "I find you where the wine bottle has just been emptied, in company with those who drink and urge you to do likewise." If Grant would not stop drinking, Rawlins said he wanted to be relieved from the staff. In the case of the second letter, Rawlins decided to pocket it and discuss the matter with Grant instead. In both cases, the chief of staff endorsed his copy of the letters with a notation that Grant's response had been satisfactory. He then filed the missives away for posterity. Historians are unanimous, however, in believing that Rawlins exaggerated his own role in keeping Grant sober. Undoubtedly he helped, but ultimately Grant restrained himself.[11]

Rawlins' duty as Grant's self-appointed sobriety policeman would not have been possible had he not established a very close personal relationship with his commander. Rawlins became Grant's closest friend, aside from his wife, Julia, who of course usually could not accompany the army. To Rawlins Grant confided much that he did not share with other officers. As Grant and Rawlins stood on the deck of a steamboat pulling away from Paducah, Kentucky, at the beginning of Grant's first major Civil War campaign, Grant clapped Rawlins on the shoulder, a gesture of friendship the taciturn general rarely displayed, and said, "Now we seem to be safe, beyond recall" by irresolute superiors. "We will succeed, Rawlins," Grant added. "We must succeed."[12]

Useful as he may have been to Grant in many respects, Rawlins, like most other Civil War officers, was at the outset still a civilian in uniform who had to learn on the job. On 15 February 1862 the Confederates made a surprise sortie from Fort Donelson to attack Grant's besieging force. Grant was several miles away conferring with Andrew H. Foote, the wounded commander of the cooperating naval squadron. Before leaving for the conference, Grant had issued orders, written by Rawlins, directing his three division commanders to hold their positions and initiate no action during his absence without further orders.[13] During the crucial hours of battle before Grant's return, neither Rawlins nor then–Chief of Staff Joseph Webster had—or took—the authority to issue the necessary orders for the 2nd and 3rd Divisions to reinforce the hard-pressed 1st Division. Apparently, they did not urge the senior division commander, the old Regular Charles F. Smith, to do so either. Rawlins did ride to the 3rd Division's sector and confer with its commander, Brig. Gen. Lew Wallace. Wallace recalled that he had to stop Rawlins from shooting a panicked officer who rode by on his way to the rear shrieking, "We're cut to pieces!" Ultimately, Wallace decided to send the needed reinforcements on his own responsibility. If he made that decision at Rawlins' urging, he gave the staff officer no credit for it in his postwar memoirs.[14]

Rawlins learned much from his experience at Fort Donelson, though he never reached the point at which he would likely have issued necessary orders in Grant's absence. Still, he continued to improve rapidly as a staff officer. On 21 March 1862 he issued General Order No. 21, probably at Grant's direction, carefully defining the duties of each member of the staff. In Rawlins' definition, which was probably Grant's, the duty of the chief of staff, Joseph Webster, was to serve as "the advisor of the general commanding," and "give his attention to any portion of duties that may not receive proper attention."[15]

On 6 April 1862 Confederate forces launched a powerful surprise attack against Grant's army encamped at Pittsburg Landing, Tennessee. Hurrying to the battlefield with his staff, Grant quickly decided that the situation warranted bringing up Maj. Gen. Lew Wallace's detached 3rd Division, encamped five miles away at Crump's Landing. Grant instructed Rawlins to go back to the river and send Capt. Algernon S. Baxter, the assistant quartermaster on Grant's staff, back up the river aboard the steamboat *Tigress* to Crump's Landing to tell Wallace to come at once.[16] Back at the landing,

Baxter asked Rawlins for a written order, so Rawlins hurriedly went aboard *Tigress* in search of writing materials. He found a tobacco-stained, boot-marked piece of paper lying on the floor of the cabin and scrawled the order in pencil before handing it to Baxter.[17]

That piece of paper—and what Rawlins wrote on it—became the fulcrum of the controversy over why Wallace's badly needed division did not appear on the battlefield until some twelve hours later. Rawlins claimed he had directed Wallace to take the River Road. Wallace insisted that no road was specified but that the order directed him to come up on the right flank of William T. Sherman's 5th Division, for which purpose the Shunpike, rather than the River Road, was the natural route. Wallace marched his division up the Shunpike and reached the outskirts of the battlefield, only to find that he was far behind enemy lines. He turned the division's head and retraced the march until he could gain the River Road and use it to approach the battlefield from the proper direction, far too late to participate in the first day's fighting. The exact wording of the disputed order remained a matter of conflicting testimony, since Wallace's assistant adjutant general lost the original.[18] Grant blamed Wallace rather than Rawlins for the mistake.

Rawlins accompanied Grant on the battlefield of Pittsburg Landing, or Shiloh, during much of the day and was again under heavy enemy fire along with his chief. Late in the afternoon, impatient for the arrival of the 3rd Division, Grant dispatched Rawlins to hurry Wallace along, and the fiery staff officer came very near placing Wallace under arrest for his stubborn refusal to push his men at a fast pace.[19]

After the Battle of Shiloh, Grant's confidence in Rawlins continued to grow steadily. "Rawlins had become thoroughly acquainted with the routine of the office and takes off my hands the examination of most all papers," Grant wrote in a letter to Julia the month after the battle. "I think he is one of the best men I ever knew." He even went so far as to predict that if the country got into another war, Rawlins would be a great general. "He unites talent with energy, and great honesty," Grant continued.[20]

That summer Grant assigned Webster to supervising the construction of fortifications on the south side of Memphis. It was a curious duty for a chief of staff, but Grant had never really used Webster as a chief of staff but rather as a sort of all-purpose utility staff officer. His talents were more suited to the new assignment than to serving as a true chief of staff. Rawlins had to be absent from the army on sick leave for several weeks that summer, but after his return that fall, Grant appointed him to serve as both chief of staff and assistant adjutant general, with the new rank of lieutenant colonel.[21]

A fellow staff officer wrote that Rawlins "made it his practice to see that everyone else performed the services assigned him." When they would not do their jobs, they quickly incurred the hostility of the new chief of staff. James H. Wilson wrote of Rawlins, "He appeared to know instinctively a worthless or vicious man, and to abhor his example and influence." Rawlins had no sooner assumed his new authority than he began a quiet campaign to rid Grant's staff of officers whom he deemed to be lazy, inefficient, and worst of all, constant threats to Grant's sobriety. Colonels Clark Lagow, John Riggins, and William Hillyer drank hard and frequently, and Rawlins feared that their ways might become a temptation to Grant. Yet Rawlins did not have the power to sack these men, and Grant proved too tenderhearted to do so. He was dissatisfied with many of the officers on his staff, at one time during the spring of 1863 writing that Rawlins and Theodore Bowers were the only "indispensable" officers on the staff—with the strong implication that he could very well dispense with all of the others. He did not, however, because of his strong sense of personal loyalty to anyone who had shown kindness to him. For the time being, Rawlins simply had to put up with the inadequate staff officers.[22]

During the early months of 1863, as Grant prepared to implement his daring plan against Vicksburg, Rawlins performed another valuable service for his chief. Jealous fellow officers and sensation-seeking newsmen continued to purvey the image of Grant as a failed general and hopeless drunk. Seeking to learn the truth about Grant, Secretary of War Edwin M. Stanton dispatched former newspaper editor, now assistant secretary of war, Charles A. Dana on an extended fact-finding mission to Grant's Army of the Tennessee. A negative report from Dana could have ended Grant's career before he ever got a chance to carry out his plans to take Vicksburg. With Grant's full approval, Rawlins received Dana warmly and made him a virtual member of the general's staff, insuring that Dana's perspective on events in the Mississippi Valley was that of Grant and his staff. Rawlins' charm offensive with the assistant secretary was as successful as Grant's own campaign against the Rebels holding Vicksburg. Long before the river fortress fell, Dana's dispatches read like communiqués from Grant's own staff—as indeed they sometimes were. When his eyes were sore from too much writing by candlelight, Dana sometimes had Lieutenant Wilson write his messages to the secretary of war.[23]

A fellow staff member later recalled that Rawlins "always had the courage of his convictions, and was capable of stating them with great force." Grant, by contrast, was usually very taciturn. In the discussions during the winter encampment before Vicksburg, Rawlins vigorously advocated the plan Grant finally adopted for getting his army ashore on the east bank of the Mississippi south of Vicksburg—so much so that Lieutenant Wilson later thought it was Rawlins' idea. About that, however, the lieutenant was mistaken, for the plan was definitely Grant's own. Rawlins' role in reality was that of encouraging his chief to move forward with a daring scheme.[24]

With the Vicksburg campaign underway, Rawlins performed several functions. As usual, the most significant was as a transmitter and distributor of Grant's orders. These, however, were orders that Grant wrote himself. Curiously, although Rawlins was the more facile orator, Grant could write far more clearly, quickly, and precisely than his chief of staff. Years later, Sherman stated that he possessed many letters and notes in Grant's own handwriting, "prescribing the routes of march for divisions and detachments, specifying even the amount of food and tools to be carried along. Many persons," Sherman noted, "gave his adjutant-general, Rawlins, the credit for these things, but they were in error; for no commanding general of an army ever gave more of his personal attention to details, or wrote so many of his own orders, reports, and letters, as General Grant." Rawlins' task was merely to see to it that the order was copied, if necessary, and distributed to all of the proper recipients. Rawlins also took a more active role in the campaign. He rode with the lead elements of the army during the rapid advance through the state of Mississippi and personally supervised the reconstruction of burned bridges over the north and south forks of Bayou Pierre, aggressively pushing the work to completion.[25]

After the fall of Vicksburg, Grant sent Rawlins to deliver his report and the rolls of paroled Confederate prisoners to the adjutant general's office in Washington. Grant also wanted Rawlins to meet with Lincoln and explain the campaign that had just closed, particularly the fact that Grant had seen fit to dismiss from his army the president's old political associate, Maj. Gen. John A. McClernand. In this Rawlins was successful, winning over both president and cabinet. Secretary of the Navy Gideon Welles noted that "though the president feels kindly toward McClernand, Grant evidently hates him, and Rawlins is imbued with the feelings of his chief."[26]

That summer Grant wangled for Rawlins a promotion to brigadier general, effective 11 August. In his recommendation of Rawlins, Grant stated that his chief of staff "would make a good corps commander." Modern historians are inclined to think that Grant was exaggerating, for Rawlins in fact had no experience at all in actual command of troops. Grant, however, showed his sincerity by leaving Rawlins temporarily in command of the entire Army of the Tennessee when for several days during September 1863 Grant had to travel to New Orleans to confer with Gen. Nathaniel P. Banks. At the time, of course, the army was encamped and neither planning nor expecting any active operations, and Rawlins carefully refrained from taking any important actions without consulting Sherman, the senior corps commander.[27]

In the cold, damp weather of the fall 1863 Chattanooga campaign, Rawlins began to show the first symptoms of the tuberculosis that had killed his first wife and would take his life as well. He continued to function capably as Grant's chief of staff, however, ably handling the larger and much more capable staff that served Grant as commander of all Union armies. Over the last half of 1863 and first few months of 1864, the inefficient staff officers whom Rawlins had long wanted to oust gradually moved off the staff by attrition, and Grant replaced them with bright, highly qualified professional military men who had proven themselves in active service during the war. Ironically, Rawlins was not always pleased with these new men, not because they lacked ability but rather because they had so much of it. The chief of staff sometimes felt threatened by Grant's reliance on the advice of other officers and could occasionally be as protective of his exclusive relationship with Grant as he habitually was of the general himself.[28]

In October 1864 Grant entrusted Rawlins with a mission of great responsibility. Grant believed that Maj. Gen. William S. Rosecrans, commanding Union forces west of the Mississippi River, had far more troops in his department than were justified by any strategic purpose. Yet getting Rosecrans to release those troops would be difficult. Rosecrans was notoriously testy and was unusually susceptible to the common error of believing that his own department was both the most important and the most seriously threatened and therefore the most in need of additional troops. To make matters worse, there had been bad blood between Rosecrans and Grant for the past two years. Grant assigned Rawlins to travel to Rosecrans's headquarters in St. Louis, assess the situation in that department, and decide which of Rosecrans's troops could be spared and where they should go. For this purpose, Grant invested Rawlins with full authority to issue orders in Grant's name. As it turned out, Rosecrans proved shockingly cooperative, and all Rawlins had to do when he got to St. Louis was see to the arrangements for transportation of the troops that would be heading east.[29]

During this trip, however, Rawlins committed one of his rare acts of disloyalty to Grant. Sherman had been lobbying Grant to allow him to take his army on a march through Georgia from Atlanta to the sea. Grant had become convinced that the move would be a good idea. Rawlins had not. Indeed, in frequent, lengthy, and sometimes rather loud discussions with other staff officers, Rawlins had roundly denounced the plan. During his October trip, Rawlins stopped off in Washington, D.C., and shared his misgivings with Lincoln, temporarily jeopardizing the implementation of the plan.[30]

Back at Grant's side, Rawlins continued to serve as a capable administrator to the general in chief through the final winter of the war. In the Appomattox campaign, Rawlins the lawyer was able to give Grant good advice on how to handle the correspondence with Lee leading up to the surrender of the Army of Northern Virginia. Rawlins astutely alerted Grant to an attempt by Lee to draw the exchange away from discussion of the surrender of an army and toward the negotiation of a general peace agreement that would be something less than a complete Union victory. Advised by Rawlins, Grant steered the exchange of notes back into its proper course. Grant may not have needed a lawyer's advice in order to avoid this pitfall, but by contrast, Sherman attempting to secure the surrender of the Confederacy's other major army nine days later, fell into exactly the same trap against which Rawlins had warned Grant.[31]

After the war Rawlins was appointed a brigadier general in the Regular Army and assigned to fill the newly created post of chief of staff to the commanding general of the army. His tuberculosis continued to worsen, however, despite a trip to the arid West. When Grant was elected president, he appointed Rawlins secretary of war. It was a post he was destined to fill for only six months, as he died of tuberculosis on 6 September at the age of thirty-eight.[32]

With a few exceptions, Rawlins' service to Grant was almost exclusively administrative, along with the moral support of his friendship. Though the lawyer from Galena did his best to learn military matters, he nevertheless remained far behind Grant, both because of Grant's head start in training and experience and because of Grant's exceptional ability. It is questionable whether Rawlins was truly able to give Grant much operational advice of any value. Staff officer Horace Porter once noted that Grant "paid but little attention to the opinions of others upon a purely military question about the advisability of which he really had no doubt in his own mind." Nevertheless, as Porter also noted, Rawlins was "frank, honest, and resolute, and loyally devoted to his chief." Furthermore, "he possessed natural executive ability of a high order." All of these qualities made Rawlins, as Grant himself said, "indispensable."[33]

Notes

1. James Harrison Wilson, *The Life of John A. Rawlins* (New York: Neale, 1916), 23; E. B. Long, "John A. Rawlins: Staff Officer Par Excellence," *Civil War Times Illustrated* 12, no. 9 (1974): 6; R. Steven Jones, *The Right Hand of Command: Use and Disuse of Personal Staffs in the Civil War* (Mechanicsburg, Pa.: Stackpole Books, 2000), 67–68.

2. Brooks D. Simpson, *Ulysses S. Grant: Triumph over Adversity, 1822–1865* (Boston: Houghton Mifflin, 2000), 18–76; Long, "John A. Rawlins," 7.

3. Wilson, *Life of John A. Rawlins*, 46–49; Augustus Chetlain, *Recollections of Seventy Years* (Galena, Ill.: Gazette Publishing, 1899), 69–80.

4. Jones, *Right Hand of Command*, 66–68; John Y. Simon, ed., *The Papers of Ulysses S. Grant*, 24 vols. (Carbondale: Southern Illinois University Press, 1969–), 2:96–97, 117, 126–27.

5. Wilson, *Life of John A. Rawlins*, 53–56; Jones, *Right Hand of Command*, 68–69; Simon, ed., *Papers of Ulysses S. Grant*, 2:160–61, 182, 238.

6. Simon, ed., *Papers of Ulysses S. Grant*, 2:238; Simpson, *Ulysses S. Grant*, 89–90; Bruce Catton, *Grant Moves South* (Indianapolis: Little, Brown, 1960), 67–69.

7. U.S. War Department, *The War of the Rebellion: Official Records of the Union and Confederate Armies*, 128 vols. (Washington, D.C.: Government Printing Office, 1881–1901), ser. 1, vol. 3, p. 270 (hereafter cited as *OR*; all references are to ser. 1).

8. Wilson, *Life of John A. Rawlins*, 64–67; Jones, *Right Hand of Command*, 71–72.

9. Simpson, *Ulysses S. Grant*, 107.

10. Wilson, *Life of John A. Rawlins*, 99–100; Jones, *Right Hand of Command*, 100.

11. Simon, ed., *Papers of Ulysses S. Grant*, 9:475–76; Long, "John A. Rawlins," 44.

12. Jean Edward Smith, *Grant* (New York: Simon and Schuster, 2002), 141; Simpson, *Ulysses S. Grant*, 111.

13. Ulysses S. Grant, *Personal Memoirs of Ulysses S. Grant*, 2 vols. (New York: Charles L. Webster and Company, 1885), 1:304.

14. Lew Wallace, *Smoke, Sound, and Fury: The Civil War Memoirs of Major-General Lew Wallace, U.S. Volunteers*, ed. Jim Leeke (Portland, Ore.: Strawberry Hill Press, 1998), 79–82.

15. Jones, *Right Hand of Command*, 78–79; *OR* 10, pt. 2, p. 41.

16. Douglas Putnam Jr., "Reminiscences of the Battle of Shiloh," *Papers of the Military Order of the Loyal Legion of the United States*, 56 vols. (Wilmington, N.C.: Broadfoot, 1994), 2:198–207; *OR* 10, pt. 1, pp. 180, 185; Smith, *Grant*, 191.

17. *OR* 10, pt. 1, p. 185; Wallace, *Smoke, Sound, and Fury*, 113.

18. *OR* 10, pt. 1, pp. 174–75, 185; Wallace, *Smoke, Sound, and Fury*, 113; Grant, *Personal Memoirs*, 1:336; William Tecumseh Sherman, *Memoirs of General W. T. Sherman* (New York: Library of America, 1990), 266; Allen, "'If He Had Less Rank,'" 73–74.

19. *OR* 10, pt. 1, pp. 180–81, 187; Wallace, *Smoke, Sound, and Fury*, 117.

20. Simon, ed., *Papers of Ulysses S. Grant*, 5:130, 140; Jones, *Right Hand of Command*, 89–90.

21. Jones, *Right Hand of Command*, 98.

22. Wilson, *Life of John A. Rawlins*, 61; Long, "John A. Rawlins," 8; Simpson, *Ulysses S. Grant*, 166–67; Jones, *Right Hand of Command*, 98–106.

23. Wilson, *Life of John A. Rawlins*, 120–22; Simpson, *Ulysses S. Grant*, 184; Jones, *Right Hand of Command*, 106–7.

24. Wilson, *Life of John A. Rawlins*, 114–15; Horace Porter, *Campaigning with Grant* (New York: Bonanza Books, 1961), 32; Jones, *Right Hand of Command*, 106.

25. Wilson, *Life of John A. Rawlins*, 125–27; Jones, *Right Hand of Command*, 111–12; Sherman, *Memoirs*, 359.

26. Simpson, *Ulysses S. Grant*, 218–19; Porter, *Campaigning with Grant*, 273; Jones, *Right Hand of Command*, 120.

27. Long, "John A. Rawlins," 9; Jones, *Right Hand of Command*, 178.

28. Simpson, *Ulysses S. Grant*, 234, 279; Jones, *Right Hand of Command*, 176–205.

29. Porter, *Campaigning with Grant*, 318; Jones, *Right Hand of Command*, 207.

30. Simpson, *Ulysses S. Grant*, 390; Porter, *Campaigning with Grant*, 314–16, 318.

31. Wilson, *Life of John A. Rawlins*, 318–24; Jones, *Right Hand of Command*, 211.

32. Sherman, *Memoirs*, 933; Long, "John A. Rawlins," 9.

33. Porter, *Campaigning with Grant*, 32, 316.

CHRONOLOGY OF HELMUTH CARL BERNARD GRAF VON MOLTKE

26 Oct 1800	Born, Parchim, Mecklenburg.
22 Jan 1818	Danish cadet and page to the Danish king.
1 Jan 1819	Appointed lieutenant in Danish Infantry Regiment Oldenburg.
12 Mar 1822	Appointed second lieutenant in Prussian Infantry Regiment 8.
1 Oct 1823	Student, General War School.
4 May 1828	Candidate in the Topographical Bureau.
30 Mar 1832	Candidate member of the Great General Staff.
30 Mar 1833	Promoted to first lieutenant in the General Staff.
30 Mar 1835	Promoted to captain.
20 Sep 1835	Seconded to Turkey as military advisor to Sultan Mahomet.
1 Aug 1839	Assigned to Great General Staff.
10 Apr 1840	Assigned to General Staff, IV Army Corps.
12 Apr 1842	Promoted to major.
21 Oct 1843	Elevated to the title of baron (*Freiherr*).
18 Oct 1845	Appointed adjutant to Prince Heinrich of Prussia.
24 Dec 1846	Assigned to General Staff, VIII Army Corps.
16 May 1848	Appointed department chief, Great General Staff.
22 Aug 1848	Appointed chief of staff, IV Army Corps
26 Sep 1850	Promoted to lieutenant colonel.
2 Dec 1851	Promoted to colonel.
1 Sep 1855	Appointed first adjutant to Prince Friedrich Wilhelm of Prussia.
9 Aug 1856	Promoted to major general.
29 Oct 1857	Assigned as acting chief of the Great General Staff.
18 Sep 1858	Appointed chief of the Great General Staff.
31 May 1859	Promoted to lieutenant general.
30 Apr 1864	Appointed chief of staff of the Combined Army in Schleswig-Holstein.
2 Jun 1866	Appointed war commander of the Prussian Army.
8 Jun 1866	Promoted to general of infantry.
20 Sep 1866	Appointed colonel in chief, Grenadier Regiment 9.

20 July 1870	Appointed chief of the General Staff at the headquarters of the King of Prussia.
29 Oct 1870	Elevated to the title of count (*Graf*).
16 Jun 1871	Promoted to field marshal.
3 Nov 1872	Appointed colonel in chief, Russian 69th Infantry Regiment.
1 Sep 1873	Fort II in Strassburg renamed Fort Moltke.
10 Aug 1888	Retired and appointed head of the Prussian Defense Commission.
24 Apr 1891	Died, Berlin.

Helmuth Carl Bernard Graf von Moltke

Antulio J. Echevarria II

Best known for his part as both composer and conductor of the brilliant campaigns against Denmark, Austria, and France that contributed to the unification of Germany and the creation of the Second Reich, Count Helmuth von Moltke was arguably the most important chief of staff of the nineteenth century.[1] He served first as chief of the Prussian General Staff from 1857 to 1871, then as chief of the German General Staff from 1871 to 1888—a total of more than thirty years at the head of Europe's premiere war-planning organization. During that time he exerted a profound influence upon modern German military thought, establishing enduring paradigms—many of which are still in effect today—for tactical, operational, and strategic thinking.[2]

One cannot separate Moltke's service as chief of the General Staff from his accomplishments as a field chief of staff. Except for a brief period in Turkey (1838–39), where his position as military advisor to Gen. Hafiz Pasha bore some resemblance to the role of a chief of staff, he never served as a wartime field chief of staff without simultaneously serving as chief of the General Staff. As explained in the introduction to this volume, the Prussian General Staff system was designed so that experience in the one complemented the other and vice versa. Moltke's case, however, went one step farther. Serving simultaneously as a field chief of staff and chief of the General Staff gave Moltke access to all the intelligence gathering, analytical, and war-planning capacities of the General Staff—a benefit that other field chiefs of staff, such as Fritz von Lossberg, did not enjoy.

One must also remember that Moltke benefited from a number of years of experience as chief of the General Staff before fighting the campaigns that made him famous. He had seven years' experience as chief of the Prussian General Staff before the campaign in Denmark, a total of ten years before the conflict with Austria, and more than thirteen years before the war against France. In fact, by the end of his career, he not only had more experience as chief of staff than any other officer in this volume, he had more than most of them combined.

Perhaps more important, these years of experience gave Moltke the advantage of a reservoir of foreknowledge before each campaign. As historian Arden Bucholz has pointed out, one of the primary functions of the Prussian General Staff during Moltke's era was to conduct campaign planning for future wars.[3] This planning included not only the customary march plans and mobilization timetables generally considered the stock-in-trade of staff work, but extensive wargaming of possible campaign scenarios. The war against Denmark, for example, was war-gamed at length over the eighteen months before it began. Similarly, in the campaigns against Austria and France, numerous scenarios were developed and tested in advance, all incorporating such factors as terrain and transportation networks, mobilization schedules and initial deployments, and variations in subsequent movements. In other words, Moltke went into the campaigns of 1864, 1866, and 1870–71, not entirely with an ad hoc—or wait-and-react—approach to strategy, as is so often claimed. One might easily draw this conclusion based on what Moltke himself said about strategy being an "*ad hoc* system of expedients."[4] Instead of developing his strategy on the fly as this statement might imply, Moltke ran and reran numerous scenarios until he entered each of those conflicts with a clear sense of the opportunities and pitfalls that awaited the combatants once battle was joined, and of how he might respond if certain situations developed.

This foreknowledge resembles the way in which a chess grand master tests numerous variations from the initial opening moves to the middle or end game. Chess masters do not rely solely on being able to think ahead twenty or thirty moves during each turn, as commonly supposed. Instead, they study in advance which combinations will and will not succeed under certain circumstances. Then, pattern recognition—and memory recall—take over during the game. The master's skill comes into play when he correctly recognizes a pattern from an otherwise complex, and perhaps chaotic, melee of pieces of different ranges and capabilities, and makes the right move. The experience and foreknowledge Moltke gained as chief of the General Staff thus contributed directly to his success as a field chief of staff.

Without such an ability to recognize patterns, Moltke might have remained an obscure chief of staff. As his penchant for architectural drawing and cartography reveals, however, he appears to have had an innate talent for conceptual—visionary—thinking, which goes hand-in-hand with pattern recognition. Moltke drew many architectural sketches and mapped a great deal of terrain. While in Turkey he completed topographical surveys of Constantinople, the Bosporus, and the Dardanelles. He also completed maps of several towns and cities, including Rome.[5] Architectural drawing and cartography require the ability to convert concrete three-dimensional, spatial relationships and perspectives (patterns) into a convincing, two-dimensional representation on paper that preserves the integrity of the original. This skill, in turn, closely resembles that which is necessary to convert one's conceptual intent for a campaign or a battle into concrete, executable schemes of maneuver. Ironically, Moltke's training in topography honed his innate conceptual ability. The training was part of the preparation for his assignment to the topographical division of the General Staff, an assignment that occurred virtually by default since Moltke could not afford a horse, a prerequisite for service in the other divisions.[6]

Moltke was born to an impoverished family on 26 October 1800 in the town of Parchim in the Duchy of Mecklenburg. His father, Friedrich Philip, was a minor noble who had retired from the Danish army at the rank of lieutenant general. Unfortunately, Friedrich lost his estates through a variety of misfortunes and had only a paltry pension from which to provide for a family of six. Because of the family's straitened circumstances, Moltke's father sent him to a boarding school at the age of nine, then to the Royal Danish Academy of Cadets in Copenhagen two years later. Moltke finished his training as a cadet in 1818 and entered military service in the Royal Danish Oldenburg Infantry Regiment. After three years, he requested and received permission to enter the Prussian army, where the pay and opportunities for promotion seemed better. After passing the entrance examination, he became a second lieutenant in the 8th Infantry Regiment stationed at Frankfort-on-Oder. The following year he passed the qualification examination for the General War School (Allgemeine Kriegsschule), later called the War Academy (Kriegsakademie), from which he graduated with distinction in 1826. Carl von Clausewitz was serving as the War Academy's director at the time. Yet, the two had little, if any, interaction, since Clausewitz performed an administrative role and, despite having a strong desire to do so, was unable to influence the curriculum in any substantial way.[7]

Moltke cut a tall, lean figure and, while not handsome, was at least not homely. Biographers have said that he possessed a reserved and taciturn nature, being "silent in seven languages." Yet, among members of the Prussian royal family, Moltke was actually an engaging conversationalist. Two political essays, "Holland and Belgium in Their Mutual Relations" and "An Account of the Internal Circumstances and Social Conditions of Poland," published in 1831 and 1832, respectively, demonstrate that he was well informed about the political issues of his day.[8] In 1827 he published a short romance entitled *The Two Friends*, which shows that he was well-read enough to imitate some of the popular literary styles of his day.[9] The story takes place during the Seven Years' War with two Prussian officers—Ernest and Gustavus—apparently having fallen in love with the same woman. Moltke's novelette does not, of course, compare to a work of literature as sublime as Goethe's *Sorrows of Young Werther*; it does, however, employ parallelism on multiple levels: the woman turns out to be two women, so the friendship between Ernest and Gustavus is preserved; the Prussian officers themselves appear to represent conflicting natures—one Teutonic and the other Latin (a familiar theme in German literature)—but as the two are the best of friends, one underlying message is that these two opposite natures can get along; and the Prussian officers seem to have the same sense of honor and nobility as their Austrian foes, making them more like comrades-in-arms separated by politics, rather than true enemies. The work also reveals Moltke's deeply romantic view of war and soldiering, attitudes which, as his famous letter to Dr. Bluntschli reveals, never left him.[10] Moltke thus brought together a piercing intellect and an unassuming personality, a combination that endeared him to ruling elites who desired stimulation, but were put off by intimidation.

In 1832 Moltke was posted to the General Staff; he was promoted to first lieutenant the following year, and to captain two years later. In 1835, he obtained six months' leave to travel through southeastern Europe. When he arrived in Constantinople, however, Sultan Mahomet requested that Moltke stay on as military advisor. Berlin approved, and Moltke remained in Turkey for the next four years, advising the sultan on matters ranging from fortifications and the employment of artillery to the building of new roads and waterways. While Moltke's advice was graciously accepted on the surface, the Turks evidently made little effort to implement his recommendations.

In 1838 Mehemet Ali, a former Albanian soldier who had risen to power in the Ottoman province of Egypt, began to challenge the authority of Constantinople with a semimodern army based on the French model. The sultan ordered General Hafiz Pasha to put down the revolt and sent Moltke to serve as his military adviser—essentially a field chief of staff.

When Moltke arrived at Hafiz's headquarters in March 1838, he found the Turkish army in dreadful shape. Dispersed over too great an area, it occupied poorly sited defensive positions, lacked adequate artillery support, and appeared undisciplined and badly trained, and wanted for sound supply and sanitation measures. Moltke at once set to conducting a full reconnaissance of the terrain and assembling a detailed status of each of the Turkish units. Appalled by what he saw, Moltke nonetheless began developing operational plans for his commander, Hafiz. He decided that, with the abysmal condition of the Turkish army and what he perceived as the Muslim inclination toward passivity, defense was the best course of action. He settled on a plan that concentrated some of the Turkish forces in a formidable defensive position at the city of Biradschik along the Euphrates River with a larger concentration of force held in reserve near the town of Ufra.

Preparations for the campaign extended into the winter of 1838–39, which proved particularly brutal; some 30–50 percent of the Turkish forces either deserted or fell ill. Nonetheless, when spring came, the Turkish army doggedly made its way through difficult mountain passes still covered in ice and snow and marched over rough plains in driving wind and rain to reach their designated defensive positions. Hafiz had about 30,000 men and 110 guns at his disposal. In accordance with Moltke's advice, he deployed some of them in a forward position near the frontier town of Nezib.[11] The rest he deployed in and around Biradschik. Moltke advised against building bridges across the Euphrates, believing that men without a way to retreat would fight harder. In the end, however, the lack of bridges would not matter.

On 28 May Mehemet Ali crossed the frontier with an army of 40,000 men and 160 guns.[12] In march-column with ammunition and baggage trains in tow, Ali's army stretched for some eighty miles, head to tail. Moltke wanted to launch a spoiling attack at the vulnerable column, but Hafiz refused. Two days later, the Egyptians were in their attack positions and embarked on a reconnaissance in force against Biradschik. The Turks turned them back. Believing the battle won, Hafiz declared himself victor. Moltke, however, remained concerned. He noticed that the Egyptians had begun maneuvering into position to launch an attack against the flank and rear of Nezib. Once again, he advised the Turkish commander to conduct a spoiling attack, but Hafiz refused. Moltke then recommended that Hafiz mass his guns so as to protect his flanks. Yet, Hafiz, whose religious advisors warned him that the omens were not favorable for such a move, failed to act. Moltke then resigned his post as Hafiz's chief of staff and took charge of the Turkish artillery. The ensuing battle of Nezib, which occurred on 24 June, lasted a mere two hours, with the Turkish army essentially firing a few volleys, then running away. Purportedly, the Turkish artillery under Moltke gave a reasonable account of itself before fleeing.

With the collapse of the Turkish army, Moltke made his way back to Berlin over the course of several months. He arrived, broken in spirit and health, in December 1839. Much to his surprise, he was hailed as a hero and received the Pour le Mérite.[13] Several months later, Moltke was appointed to the staff of the IV Corps, stationed in Berlin. The following year, he met Marie Burt, the stepdaughter of his sister Auguste. Marie was sixteen at the time, and Moltke forty-one. The two married on 12 April 1842, the same day that Moltke was promoted to major.

While in Berlin he became intensely interested in the development of railways and served as one of the first directors of the Hamburg-Berlin Railway. The following year, he published a review article entitled "What Considerations Should Determine the Choice of the Course of Railways?" in which he maintained that military necessity should rank among the top considerations for railroad construction.[14]

Moltke then served as the personal adjutant to Prince Heinrich of Prussia, then in Rome, until the prince's death in 1846. He returned to Germany to serve on the staff of the VIII Corps at Coblenz. In 1848 he became chief of staff of the IV Corps at Magdeburg, where he remained for the next seven years. He was promoted to lieutenant colonel in 1850 and colonel in 1851. In 1855 he was appointed first adjutant to Prince Friedrich Wilhelm (later crown prince and kaiser), and was promoted to major general one year later. On 23 October 1857 Wilhelm became prince regent. Six days later, he selected Moltke for the post of chief of the General Staff of the Prussian army.

If it is true that tacticians solve military problems by considering the terrain while strategists turn to a map, then Moltke was both. He wrote several essays in the 1850s and 1860s that demonstrated his astuteness as a tactician. Within a year of his appointment as chief of the General Staff, Moltke observed that "improvements in infantry weapons necessitated a complete change in the tactics of all arms."[15] It was now "more advantageous to allow oneself to be attacked, than to attack."[16] The artillery still ruled the battlefield from 700 to 1,800 meters, but the infantry had become its undisputed master at ranges less than 700 meters. Accordingly, the Prussian army's existing method of attack—in which swarms of skirmishers "shattered" the defender through an intense and often prolonged firefight before a general assault with attack columns—had to change. Moltke advocated countering an opponent's rifle fire with a greater concentration of artillery fire and moving more swiftly across the enemy's fire zone with skirmishers or troops deployed in open order. Attack columns—once the decisive formation—would merely support the advance of the skirmishers and occupy ground that had already been won. He later stressed that shattering the enemy by fire-effect must always come before the bayonet assault. The army's junior leaders "should see in the bayonet attack not the first but the last act of battle." Moreover, an attack must use all available cover and avoid the front—the strength—of an enemy's position and strike against his flank.[17]

Moltke built on these observations in subsequent essays. Two years before the war with Denmark he had recommended a concept called the "offensive-defensive," in which the attacker assumed the offensive strategically, but shifted to the defensive to fight battles. The attacker could thus use the improved power of the defense to break up an adversary's attack, and then launch an annihilating counter-attack to finish the job. "The correct course of action," Moltke explained, "may be that we calmly await the attack until the very last moment to exploit the effects of infantry fire at close range and then reply to the attack directly thereafter with fresh energy and firm resolve."[18]

The offensive-defensive could never amount to more than a partial solution, however. To employ it properly, one had to find a position that the enemy could not ignore and thus would have to attack. There was also the risk that the enemy might opt to outflank the position and render it untenable, rather than assaulting it directly. Arguably, Moltke put this theory into practice only once—at the Battle of Sedan in which the French spent themselves in futile attempts to break out of a German defensive ring. Encircled and subjected to incessant pounding from highly accurate and effective German artillery, the French had little choice but to assume the tactical offensive or be smashed to pieces.

Tactical and strategic aspects of war remained closely linked for Moltke. He viewed the latter as the application of established principles for the purpose of bringing about conditions favorable for tactical success, which formed the cornerstone of Moltke's way of war. The strategy for a campaign remains "silent" until tactical success is achieved, but then becomes vocal again to build upon that success, taking advantage of the new circumstances.[19] Moltke equated grand strategy with policy—the province of statesmen—and insisted that while policy had the right to establish the goals for the conflict, even changing them when it sees fit, it had no right to interfere with the conduct of military operations. In Clausewitzian terms, Moltke acknowledged the initial importance of the logic of war, but insisted that its grammar took precedence during the actual fighting.

On 2 October 1862 Otto von Bismarck, the new minister-president of the kingdom of Prussia, sent a request to Moltke (through the war minister, Albrecht von Roon) asking for a military appraisal of a potential war against Denmark. Drawing from his own knowledge of Denmark, a General Staff study of the 1848–49 Schleswig-Holstein War, several terrain analyses, and some recent assessments of the fighting strength of the Danish armed forces, Moltke informed Bismarck that Prussia's options were limited since it did not have a navy capable of challenging the Danish fleet. The terrain of Denmark with its large islands and countless deep fjords would enable the Danish fleet to interfere with the Prussian army's operations—unless Prussia attacked in the dead of winter when the coastal waters would be frozen. Moltke noted that the Schleswig-Holstein War of 1848–49 had dragged on indecisively since the Danes were able to withdraw behind a series of island fortifications and earthworks and avoid destruction. To prevent such a stalemate from recurring, Moltke proposed attacking in January or February along the flanks of the famed Danewerk, a long line of stone fortifications and earthworks just north of the German border. The intent would be to cut off the fortresses at Düppel and Fredericia along with the Danish line of retreat and to seize Jütland as a basis for concluding a favorable peace.[20] Moltke and Bismarck both also agreed that the war had to be won quickly in order to avoid intervention by Britain and the other Great Powers.

Unfortunately, while Moltke's plan was sound, the commander in chief of the German forces, Field Marshal Friedrich von Wrangel, an old veteran of the Napoleonic wars and the 1848–49 campaign, failed to execute it properly. Wrangel proved too old and set in his ways for the task that lay before him. He was, however, the only Prussian officer with wartime experience, a condition demanded by the Austrians if they were going to allow their forces to be commanded by a Prussian. Thus, Moltke himself remained in Berlin, attempting to influence events from afar. Colonel Karl von Blumenthal, chief of staff of the I Corps then under the command of Prince Friedrich Karl, kept Moltke informed. Austrian and German troops invaded Denmark on 1 February 1864. But as a result of Wrangel's mishandling of the initial phases of the campaign, the Danish army managed to withdraw into the fortresses of Düppel and Fredericia, each of which commanded an important avenue of approach into Denmark. The Prussians and Austrians then laid siege to Düppel and Fredericia respectively.

Bismarck grew anxious over the lack of progress in the campaign and pressured the king into ordering an assault on Düppel. The Prussian army needed a clear-cut victory, he argued, one that would win the respect of Europe for Prussian arms and allow him to sit at the negotiating table with confidence.[21] Moltke delayed the assault long enough for heavy artillery to arrive from Berlin. An intense, twenty-five-day bombardment of Düppel ensued until 18 April, when Prussian troops took Düppel by storm. The barrage had caused such extensive damage to the defenses that the fortress fell within twenty minutes. The Prussians had killed or wounded 1,800 Danes and captured 3,600 prisoners while suffering negligible casualties. The Danes abandoned Fredericia shortly thereafter and fell back to the islands of Alsen and Fünen. An armistice ensued from 25 April to 25 June, while the British attempted to bring about a peace.

During the armistice, the king sent Moltke forward, finally, to serve as chief of staff to Prince Friedrich Karl, the new commander in chief of the German forces. Moltke persuaded the prince to cross the Sundewitt as soon as the armistice ended and to attack the Danes in the island of Alsen. The landing succeeded on 29 June, and the Danes evacuated Alsen. Moltke next proposed a landing on Fünen, but it proved unnecessary. On 1 August the Danes sued for peace. The Treaty of Vienna, signed on 30 October, officially ended the conflict.

In the months that followed the campaign in Denmark, relations with Austria worsened. Never one for the idealistic doctrines of eternal peace, Moltke believed war with Austria likely, if not inevitable. He began putting reforms into effect that accelerated the Prussian army's mobilization timetables and made better use of the north German rail network. During the spring and summer of 1865, he developed and wargamed a number of invasion scenarios that were then tested in the Prussian army's autumn maneuvers. Some two and one-half months before the conflict began, Moltke had essentially envisioned how it would play out—a Prussian main effort pushing from Silesia into Bohemia and oriented on Vienna with decisive battle likely in the area of Pardubitz-Königgrätz-Josefstadt. His foreknowledge proved correct, with one glaring exception. He assumed that the Austrians would attack, moving strong forces through Silesia toward Berlin, to split the patchwork of Prussian provinces in two. Instead, the Austrians prepared to remain on the defensive against an enemy they knew could mobilize faster than they. Thus, while Moltke's assumption about Austrian intentions proved wrong, his vision of the course of events basically came to pass.

On 2 June the king made Moltke the war commander of the Prussian army and, six days later, promoted him to general of infantry so that he would have rank and authority commensurate with his responsibilities. Essentially, this change meant that the king shared operational command with Moltke, who could now bypass the Military Cabinet and the War Ministry. It also resulted in a faster command cycle, which complemented Moltke's battle rhythm of issuing orders in four-hour cycles.[22] It also convinced Moltke that he had earned the confidence of the king to the degree that he now stood on par with Bismarck. This understanding would create a certain amount of friction—much discussed by historians—in the months to come.[23] In reality, however, Moltke's control over Prince Friedrich Karl and the king remained less than he might have desired.

Moltke concentrated the main Prussian force, some 270,000 men, against the combined Austro-Saxon armies, numbering about 240,000 troops. In a remarkable supporting campaign, a small Prussian force of 48,000 men overran the north and south German armies, capturing Hanover and preempting the mobilization of some 120,000 troops that could have aided the Austrian cause. Meanwhile the main Prussian force, divided into three armies—the Elbe Army near Torgau, the First Army under Prince Friedrich Karl in western Silesia, and the Second Army under the Crown Prince between Landshut and Waldenburg—marched south against the Austro-Saxon forces.[24]

Outmatched tactically, the Austrians under Field Marshal Ludwig Benedek could not mount a coherent defense along the Bohemian mountains and fell back toward Königgrätz. On 3 July Moltke planned to launch the Prussian First Army, under Prince Friedrich Karl and the king, in a pinning attack against the Austrian front, while the Second and Elbe Armies assaulted the Austrian right and left flanks respectively. The Second Army, however, did not receive its orders and the First and Elbe armies became intermixed and the advance stalled. The Second Army finally arrived on the right flank of the Austrians by mid-afternoon and turned a desperate situation into a victory. The Austrians were defeated, losing some 45,000 casualties while the Prussians lost 10,000 men. A sizable part of the Austrian army escaped, however, falling back toward Vienna.[25] Although Moltke was ostensibly the war commander, he had no real authority over the king or Prince Friedrich Karl, who tended to act independently at times. In the aftermath of the battle, Moltke, confident of victory even if the French should intervene, wanted to press on toward Vienna and annihilate the remainder of the Austrian army. Bismarck, on the other hand, desired to keep France out of the war, and objected to the pursuit.[26] In the end, Bismarck's view prevailed. A few days later, the French emperor stepped in to act as mediator, and the Austrians eventually signed the Treaty of Prague on 23 August, which ended the conflict.

Soon after the conflict with Austria, the Prussian Diet voted Moltke a large sum, which he used to purchase the estate of Kreisau in Silesia. Moltke, at last, became a member of the landed nobility. The happiness that came with this entitlement was short-lived, however, as his wife died soon thereafter, on Christmas Eve of 1868.

War with France formed a major planning concern for Moltke almost from the moment he assumed his responsibilities as chief of the General Staff in 1857. The General Staff updated its war plans as a matter of course whenever political conditions, force ratios, and the capacity of the combatants' railway systems changed. In the fall of 1867, however, planning efforts intensified as conflict with France moved from possibility to probability. Moltke, who had long believed that war with France was inevitable, worked and reworked several scenarios concerning timing, distance, and force allocation.[27] As before, he had to get more men in the field, and faster, than his foe. But now the distances with which he had to reckon were much greater, and he had to leave a sizable force along the Austrian border to deter any potential threat.

As in the war with Austria, Moltke essentially worked out in advance how the campaign would unfold. The General Staff's extensive wargaming revealed that by concentrating the German forces to the south of Mainz in three armies, Moltke would have the most operational flexibility, especially since the French would have to assemble the bulk of their forces near Metz and Strasbourg due to the limitations of their rail system. The German armies would advance in a rough semicircle. If the main French force appeared in strength in front of the center army, it would be attacked in the flanks by the German armies on the wings. If the main French army should turn up along the northern or southern axis, the German army on that axis would launch a pinning attack to fix it while the other two armies attacked it in the flank and rear. Essentially, Moltke envisioned fixing the principal French army and attacking it so as to drive it away from Paris and sever its lines of communication. The events of the campaign basically unfolded according to Moltke's vision.

On 15 July 1870 the French declared war on Prussia. Five days later, the Prussian king appointed Moltke "Chief of the General Staff of the Army at the Headquarters of his Majesty the King" for the duration of the war. This appointment gave Moltke the right to issue orders in the king's name, making them tantamount to royal commands. Now a matter of routine, Moltke took what amounted to a "mobile General Staff" with him on campaign. In addition to the customary adjutants and curriers, this mobile staff consisted of a deputy chief and the department heads from operations, intelligence and communications, and supply and railroads. Each department also brought along its own complement of staff officers, for a total of some sixty to eighty personnel, to include security and support troops.[28]

Prussian mobilization for the campaign against France occurred with remarkable speed. By 30 July Moltke had 468,000 German troops deployed along the French border, and another 95,000 men in arms (excluding Landwehr), serving as reserves and as a safeguard against the possibility of an Austrian intervention. The German armies crossed the French border in early August. The First Army, consisting of two corps under the command of Gen. Carl von Steinmetz, moved along the Prussian right flank with the object of securing the Moselle region just below Metz. In the center, the Second Army under Friedrich Karl formed the main effort, its six corps advanced to seize the area between Metz and Nancy. The Third Army, consisting of approximately five corps under the Prussian crown prince, made up the left flank, and advanced to capture Strassburg and occupy the Alsace region.[29]

The early frontier battles of Wörth, Froeschwiller, and Spicheren resulted in German successes, but were brought on prematurely, enabling the French to retreat and avoid being enveloped as Moltke desired. The two battles of Mars-la-Tour (16 August) and Gravelotte-St. Privat (18 August) drove French Marshal François Achille Bazaine's army away from Paris and into the fortress of Metz, where he was encircled and later captured. French Marshal Patrice MacMahon's army marched to Bazaine's aid along with the French emperor, Napoleon III, only to be encircled at Sedan and defeated on 2 September.

The French, now under a provisional government, refused to admit defeat. They barricaded Paris and waged a controversial guerilla war against the Germans from October 1870 through January 1871. In an equally controversial move, Bismarck ordered the bombardment of Paris, which began in late December. Moltke opposed the bombardment on the grounds that it was unnecessary, as the city's population would be starved into submission within a few months.[30] Bismarck had his way, but Moltke's reasoning proved correct. With Parisians on the verge of starvation, the French finally capitulated on 28 January and signed the Treaty of Frankfurt on 10 May 1871, ending the conflict.

On 29 October, two days after the fall of the fortress of Metz, Moltke was made a *Graf* (count). On 16 June 1871, six weeks after the Treaty of Frankfurt, he was promoted to field marshal. He was later elected to the Reichstag where he gave a number of addresses on military matters. In 1888 he resigned his post as chief of staff and was succeeded by Count Alfred von Waldersee. Moltke died suddenly, though not unexpectedly, on 24 April 1891, during a visit to Berlin.

Although clearly a legend, few historians today describe Moltke as a military genius. One can certainly refer to him as the first modern war-planner, however, and therefore the most important chief of staff of the nineteenth century. Moltke made brilliant use of, and helped develop, one of the first "deep future" military planning organizations, the Prussian General Staff.[31] The high standards he set for thorough planning and wargaming, and simplicity in concept and execution remain hallmarks of the German military tradition. Indeed, one could well argue that Moltke established the German way of war.

Ironically, while Moltke was a "Renaissance man" of exceptional literature and letters, it was during his tenure as chief of staff that the curriculum of the War Academy shifted away from a general education toward greater emphasis on developing technically proficient officers. Some historians have maintained that this shift produced officers with very narrow—purely military—perspectives, unable or unwilling to incorporate political perspectives into military planning. However, given the changing character of warfare toward the end of the nineteenth century, which was rapidly increasing in technological complexity, and the fact that the German public education system was at the same time providing one of the best and broadest educations in Europe, the shift was justified. As Clausewitz's masterwork reveals, the friction between the logicians and grammarians of war predated Moltke. German strategic planning shunned political influence in the World War I, but was permeated with it in World War II. In both cases, victory proved elusive, suggesting that neither view is inherently better than the other.

Notes

1. Selected biographical references: Arden Bucholz, *Moltke and the German Wars, 1864–1871* (New York: Palgrave, 2001); Eberhard Kessel, *Moltke* (Stuttgart: K. F. Koehler, 1957); Rudolf Stadelmann, *Moltke und der Staat* (Krefeld: Scherpe, 1950); William O'Connor Morris, *Moltke: A Biographical and Critical Study* (reprint, New York: Haskell, 1971); Roland G. Förster, ed., *Generalfeldmarschall von Moltke: Bedeutung und Wirkung* (Munich: R. Oldenburg, 1991); Hajo Holborn, "The Prusso-German School: Moltke and the Rise of the General Staff," and Gunther E. Rothenberg, "Moltke, Schlieffen and the Doctrine of Envelopment," in *Makers of Modern Strategy*, ed. Peter Paret (Princeton,

N.J.: Princeton University Press, 1986), 281–95 and 296–325 respectively; and Roland G. Foerster, "The Operational Thinking of the Elder Moltke and Its Consequences," in Foerster et al., *Operational Thinking in Clausewitz, Moltke, Schlieffen, and Manstein* (Bonn: E. S. Mittler, 1988), 21–40.

2. Although not the focus of this essay, Moltke also helped to shape, or at least to reinforce, the principal cultural and political attitudes within the Prusso-German officer corps. Antulio J. Echevarria II, "Moltke and the German Military Tradition: His Theories and Legacies," *Parameters* 26 (Spring 1996): 91–99.

3. Bucholz, *Moltke and the German Wars*, 18ff. By way of comparison, Moltke's General Staff served a different function than its contemporary equivalent in the Pentagon. War-planning staffs in the Pentagon merely conduct cross-coordination and prioritize the flow of forces for the regional combatant commanders who do the actual scenario and contingency planning.

4. "Über Strategie," in *Moltkes Militärisches Werke*, ed. Großer Generalstab, 14 vols. (Berlin: E. S. Mittler, 1892–1912), here vol. 4, pt. 2, pp. 287–93; see also Helmuth Graf von Moltke, *Moltke on the Art of War: Selected Writings*, ed. and trans. Daniel Hughes (Novato, Calif.: Presidio, 1993).

5. The maps were published in 1852.

6. Actually, service on the General Staff required the purchase of two mounts, though Moltke could not afford even one.

7. Peter Paret, *Clausewitz and the State* (Princeton, N.J.: Princeton University Press, 1976).

8. "Holland und Belgien in gegenseitiger Beziehung seit ihrer Trennung unter Philipp II. bis zu ihrer Wiedervereinigung unter Wilhelm I." and "Darstellung der inneren Verhältnisse und des gesellschaftlichen Zustandes in Polen," in *Gesammelte Schriften und Denkwürdigkeiten des General-Feldmarschalls Grafen Helmuth von Moltke*, 8 vols. (Berlin: E. S. Mittler, 1892), here 2:1–60 and 2:61–170, respectively.

9. "Die beide Freunde," in *Gesammelte Schriften*, 1:40–102. The story was primarily an effort to raise money. He also contracted to translate Gibbon's *Decline and Fall of the Roman Empire* into German during this time in the hope of earning enough money to buy a horse. He finished translating nine volumes out of twelve, but the publisher reneged on the project and so Moltke received only a third of the amount he was promised—not enough to buy a mount.

10. Letter to Dr. Johann Caspar Bluntschli, dated 11 November 1880. Moltke wrote his famous statement that "eternal peace is a dream and not even a good one." Helmuth von Moltke, *Leben und Werk in Selbstzeugnissen, Briefe, Schriften, Reden* (Birsfelden bei Basel, Switzerland: Verlag Schibli-Doppler, 1966), 351.

11. Eberhard Kessel, *Moltkes erster Feldzug: Anlage und Durchführung des türkisch-ägyptischen Feldzuges 1839* (Berlin: Mittler, 1939), 21.

12. Ibid., 22.

13. While away, he had written a stream of letters to his mother and sisters, which he later revised and published as *Letters on Conditions and Events in Turkey in the Years 1835 to 1839*. Moltke's *Letters from Turkey* are still considered a classic; *Briefe über Zustände und Begebenheiten in der Türkei aus den Jahren 1835 bis 1839* (Berlin: Mittler and Sohn, 1876).

14. "Welche Rücksichten kommen bei der Wahl der Richtung von Eisenbahnen in Betracht?" *Gesammelte Schriften*, 2:229–74.

15. "Bemerkungen vom 12. Juli 1858 über Veränderungen in der Taktik infolge des verbesserten Infanteriegewehrs," in *Militärische Werke* (Berlin: Mittler and Sohn, 1896), vol. 2, pt. 2, p. 7.

16. "Bemerkungen vom 1858," in ibid., 7–10.

17. "Bemerkungen vom Jahre 1865 über den Einfluß der verbesserten Feuerwaffen auf die Taktik," in ibid., 47–58, 65.

18. Großen Generalstabe, ed., "Der Angriff über die freie Ebene (1861/62)," in ibid., vol. 4, pt. 3, p. 136; and "Bemerkungen vom April 1861 über den Einfluß der verbesserten Feuerwaffen auf die Taktik," in ibid., vol. 2, pt. 2, pp. 27–41.

19. "Über Strategie (1871)," in ibid., vol. 2, pt. 2, pp. 187ff.

20. "Denkschrift vom 6. Dezember 1862 über Operationen gegen Dänemark," in ibid., vol. 1, pt. 1, pp. 1–6.

21. Gordon A. Craig, *The Politics of the Prussian Army, 1640–1945* (Oxford: Oxford University Press, 1955), 188–89.

22. Bucholz, *Moltke and the German Wars*, 119ff.

23. Craig, *Politics of the Prussian Army*, 180ff.

24. Geoffrey Wawro, *The Austro-Prussian War: Austria's War with Prussia and Italy in 1866* (Cambridge: Cambridge University Press, 1995).

25. Gordon A. Craig, *The Battle of Königgrätz: Prussia's Victory over Austria* (Philadelphia: Lippincott, 1964). See also Theodor Fontane, *Der deutsche Krieg von 1866*, 2 vols. (Berlin: R.v. Decker, 1871–72).

26. Craig, *Politics of the Prussian Army*, 200ff.

27. Eberhard Kolb, "Helmuth von Moltke in seiner Zeit: Aspekete und Probleme," in *Generalfeldmarschall von Moltke*, 11.

28. Bucholz, *Moltke and the German Wars*, 119.

29. Michael Howard, *The Franco-Prussian War: The German Invasion of France, 1870–1871* (London: Routledge, 1989).

30. Craig, *Politics of the Prussian Army*, 209ff.

31. The term is from Bucholz, *Moltke and the German Wars*, 50–64. For a discussion of the influence that Moltke's successes had on the rise of the General Staff, see Lothar Burchardt, "Helmuth von Moltke, Wilhelm I und der Aufstieg des preußischen Generalstabes," in *Generalfeldmarschall von Moltke*, 19–38.

Part Two
World War I

CHRONOLOGY OF ERICH LUDENDORFF

9 Apr 1865	Born in Kruszczewina, Posen.
1877	Attended Ploen Cadet School.
1879	Attended Lichterfelde Senior Cadet School.
15 Apr 1882	Appointed second lieutenant, 57th Infantry Regiment.
1 Apr 1889	Assigned to the Marine Infantry, 2nd Sea Battalion.
24 Mar 1890	Promoted to first lieutenant.
12 Aug 1890	Assigned to the 8th Grenadier Regiment.
1 Oct 1890	Student, Kriegsakademie.
17 Mar 1894	Appointed candidate member of the Great General Staff.
22 Mar 1895	Promoted to captain and appointed full member of the General Staff.
19 Mar 1896	Assigned to the General Staff of IV Corps.
22 Mar 1898	Assigned as company commander, 61st Infantry Regiment.
22 July 1900	Assigned to the General Staff of the 9th Division.
19 Sep 1901	Promoted to major.
18 Oct 1902	Assigned to the General Staff of V Corps.
10 Mar 1904	Assigned to the Great General Staff, Berlin.
13 Sept 1906	Assigned as instructor, Kriegsakademie.
10 Apr 1908	Assigned as assistant department chief, Great General Staff.
18 May 1908	Promoted to lieutenant colonel and assigned as department chief, Great General Staff.
21 April 1911	Promoted to colonel.
27 Jan 1913	Assigned as commander of the 39th Fusilier Regiment.
22 Mar 1914	Promoted to major general and assigned as commander of the 85th Infantry Brigade.
1 Aug 1914	Assigned as Oberquartiermeister, Second Army.
6–7 Aug 1914	Assigned as acting commander, 14th Infantry Brigade.
8 Aug 1914	Awarded the Pour le Mérite.
22 Aug 1914	Assigned as chief of General Staff, Eighth Army.
15 Sep 1914	Assigned as chief of General Staff, Ninth Army.
11 Nov 1914	Assigned as chief of the General Staff, Supreme Command East.

27 Nov 1914	Promoted to lieutenant general.
23 Feb 1915	Awarded the Oak Leaves to the Pour le Mérite.
29 Aug 1916	Promoted to general of infantry and assigned as first quartermaster-general of the German army.
1 Nov 1917	Appointed colonel-in-chief, 39th Fusilier Regiment.
24 Mar 1918	Awarded the Grand Cross of the Iron Cross.
26 Oct 1918	Retired from the German army.
1919	Published *My War Memoirs*.
13–17 Mar 1920	Supported the Kapp-Lüttwiz Putsch.
1921	Published *The General Staff and Its Problems*.
1922	Published *War Leadership and Politics*.
8 Nov 1923	Participated in the Beer Hall Putsch.
1 Apr 1924	Acquitted for his role in the Beer Hall Putsch.
1924–28	Served as a Nazi delegate to the Reichstag.
1925	Unsuccessfully challenged Hindenburg in the German presidential elections.
20 Dec 1937	Died, Munich, Germany.

Erich Ludendorff

Paul J. Rose

W orld War I, or the Great War as it was called before there was the necessity of numbering such events consecutively, started in 1914 when Europe stood on the verge of a golden age. It was one of the greatest catastrophes in European history. In the opening phase of that war, Russia's massive thrust into East Prussia brought to the aid of Imperial Germany the brilliant and successful team of Paul von Hindenburg and Erich Ludendorff, who steered the German armies to victory at Tannenberg (now known as Stebark, Poland) and other battles on the eastern front. They then guided Germany's destiny on the western front from 1916 until the end of the war.

This chapter is about Ludendorff's role as chief of staff to Hindenburg in the critical battle of Tannenberg, where a relationship was established that lasted throughout the war and came very close to bringing a German victory over a much stronger coalition of allied nations. But it is inevitably about more than Ludendorff at Tannenberg in order to make clear his place in such an enormous and complex struggle and in history. The operation of the Schlieffen Plan, which Ludendorff helped develop and was instrumental in implementing, brought about the situation in East Prussia, which then led to his being chosen as chief of staff of the Eighth Army under Hindenburg.

Ludendorff's role as chief of staff can best be understood if we examine his immediate activities before his assignment, how he acted under the pressures of battle, and explore something of his life after Tannenberg. The Battle of Tannenberg (27–30 August 1914) was a major victory over Russia which led to the defeat of Tsarist Russia and then to the victory of Communism in Russia and ultimately to World War II and to the Cold War. As it turned out,

Tannenberg would be one of the very few clear-cut battlefield victories for Germany in the Great War.

Ludendorff was born on 9 April 1865 in Kruszczewina, near Posen, Prussia (now called Poznan, Poland). He went to cadet school before joining the Prussian army in 1882. He was a commoner from a middle-class, landowning family, which lacked the aristocratic "von" usually seen before the name of other officers of Ludendorff's rank and prestige. Because of the important role Ludendorff played during the war, Kaiser Wilhelm II offered to award him a "von" to place before his name, but Ludendorff refused it, saying he wanted no title that his father had not possessed. In the two volumes of his memoirs he wrote only two paragraphs about his youth, and these stressed the financial hardships he experienced as a young officer. Because of his outstanding military potential he was selected for general staff duties. He studied operations and tactics under Count Alfred von Schlieffen, chief of the Great General Staff and author of the Schlieffen Plan.

Ludendorff was a complex and enigmatic figure, but a soldier of great intellect, stamina, and competence. He has been called a genius of war. He became the most dominant figure in Germany between 1916 and 1918. In addition to making national policy, he initiated changes in tactical doctrine that brought the German army to its highest ever level of excellence. But he was a tormented warrior, a victim of his own unrelenting drive for perfection in everything he did. He was prone to panic under pressure. Consequently he needed a strong figure around him to steady his nerves and prevent his unstable nature from distorting his judgment. This role was played ably by Paul von Beneckendorff und von Hindenburg, whom Ludendorff would serve so brilliantly as his chief of staff.[1] In many important aspects, however, Ludendorff came to eclipse Hindenburg.

Each member of the Hindenburg-Ludendorff team was a person of considerable individual ability, yet each displayed substantial individual limitations. By working together, the soldierly abilities of each served to offset the manifest weaknesses of the other. It is perhaps fair to say that neither general acting alone would have been considered a great captain of war. Together, however, their great individual abilities melded together to produce an outstanding military team.

It is worth noting that these two great partners in war also represented the basic flaws so evident in German militarism, which ultimately contributed more to German defeat than did allied superiority in manpower and resources. They made up a leadership that epitomized the values, strengths, capabilities, and limitations of the German General Staff. They were the men who, above all others, were most responsible for what was both good and bad in the process, whereby the German army gradually and somewhat reluctantly came to dominate all aspects of the war effort of the Central Powers.

The early relationship between Hindenburg and Ludendorff was and remains difficult to determine with any degree of exactness. Later personal, professional, and political developments show them working together as a perfectly harmonized team. Winston Churchill saw them as such a perfect pair, or a symbiosis of two men, that he often referred to them by their joint initials, "HL." Ludendorff later wrote that "Hindenburg and I worked together like one man in the most perfect harmony." Hindenburg saw the team as a "happy marriage" which was "one in thought and action."

There were very practical reasons for them to cooperate. They had been put into a chaotic and dangerous situation together and they would either succeed or fail together. Being products of the German military system, they both realized that the degree of cooperation to be achieved by a commander and his chief of staff was largely a matter of personalities. Each man knew his own strong and weak points. Each man was willing to provide support for the other, who in many special ways was superior to himself. Each knew that he could drive ahead and take risks, knowing that if he slipped or failed the other would provide any needed assistance and support.

The Schlieffen Plan, as modified by Helmuth von Moltke (the Younger), had little chance of success even under the best of circumstances, and practically none unless the German army could move swiftly through the Low Countries into western France without delay. To accomplish this, Fortress Liège had to be taken very quickly. Through his personal battlefield intervention, Colonel Ludendorff contributed greatly to the German army's first major success in the war, leading the capture of the formidable Belgian fortress on 7 August 1914.

Before the outbreak of war, Ludendorff had spent six years planning the capture of Liège, the linchpin of the entire Belgian defensive system. During the attack he successfully guided 8,000 troops up from the Meuse Valley, between two defensive rings to attack Fortress Liège. He was in Belgium as a staff officer and an observer and was not supposed to take part in the combat. But when the 14th Brigade stalled after its commander, Maj. Gen. Friedrich von Wussow, was killed, Ludendorff took personal command and led the troops through some very difficult house-to-house fighting, while bypassing the perimeter forts. Ludendorff's men fell in great numbers under heavy fire when three attempts to rush the Belgian line failed. "I shall never forget hearing the thud of bullets striking human bodies," Ludendorff later wrote in his memoirs.[2]

Schlieffen had been wrong about the Belgians in one respect. Terror, horror, and even mass murder did not force them to give way and allow the Germans to pass without a fight. Ludendorff blamed German brutality on the Belgians, who had the audacity to fire on German troops. It was true, he wrote, that innocent people might have to suffer, but "the Belgian Government can alone be held responsible. For my part, I had taken the field with chivalrous and human conception of warfare. This *franc-tireur* warfare was bound to disgust any soldier. My soldierly spirit suffered bitter disillusion."[3]

Ludendorff's brigade was quickly cut off from the rest of the German army during the attack. After bombarding Liège with his limited artillery, his troops occupied the city, but the fortress was still in Belgian hands. Believing incorrectly that Colonel von Oven, in command of an advance guard, had already captured the citadel, Ludendorff walked up and started pounding on the gate with the hilt of his sword.[4] Several hundred Belgian soldiers, seeing this imposing German officer at the door and assuming their fortifications had been overrun, surrendered. With Ludendorff holding the citadel, the Belgians were unable to coordinate their defensive efforts. One by one the twelve individual forts of the outer defensive ring were destroyed, and the German army streamed through Belgium on its way to France. By his bold and courageous leadership, Ludendorff made possible the success of the early phase of the Schlieffen Plan. This heroic effort won him the prestigious Pour le Mérite. It also identified him as a senior officer who could get things done without waiting for orders to act.

Ludendorff was at Namur, Belgium, preparing for the attack on that fort when he received word of his new assignment in the east. It was exactly at 0900 hours on 22 August when a staff officer delivered the message. Together with his orders were two letters from Moltke and General Hermann von Stein, the deputy chief of staff. Moltke's letter informed him:

> A new and difficult task is entrusted to you. . . . I know of no other man in whom I have such absolute trust. You may yet be able to save the situation in the East. . . . Of course you will not be responsible for what has already happened, but with your energy you can prevent the worst from happening.[5]

Stein's letter spoke similarly. It ended by saying, "Your task is a difficult one, but you are equal to it."[6]

Ludendorff questioned the messenger but was able to learn only that a retired general of infantry named Hindenburg was being considered as the new Eighth Army commander, and Ludendorff would become his chief of staff. He was well aware that this was an opportunity that would come only once in a lifetime. Within twenty minutes he had packed his bag and was in a staff car on his way to General Karl von Bülow's Army Supreme Headquarters (OHL—Oberste Heeresleitung) in Koblenz. On his arrival Moltke briefed him immediately on the situation in the east.

There was little in Ludendorff's appearance to suggest the victorious commander. In many ways he resembled the typical Prussian officer, little different from hundreds of other officers who came from the same windy East Elbian plains. He was heavy-set and bullet-headed, with a visible roll of fat on the nape of his neck. He had a large mustache and close-cropped hair, which resembled a brush. His stare was cold and his eyes reflected intelligence. He projected an air of brutal vigor that often had a chilling effect on those around him. On this particular day he looked tired, with a haunted expression and deeply etched lines on his face. But as he studied the map with Moltke he thought about East Prussia, which he knew well. This land of clay and sand, many small lakes, small streams, and stunted forest of birch and pine was, after all, his home. He had often surveyed this land together with Schlieffen as they contemplated the two-front war they felt was sure to come.[7]

While the Schlieffen Plan had assumed the Russians could not attack before six weeks of mobilization, they were crossing the border into East Prussia within two weeks of the start of the war. The Russians planned a two-pronged attack into East Prussia, which jutted into Russian territory north of Poland. They well understood that the Masurian Lakes, which lay just inside the Prussian border, was a difficult obstacle, but an obstacle that could be turned to their advantage. Their plan called for Gen. Pavel K. Rennenkampf, commander of the Russian First Army, to attack just north of the lakes in an area known as the Insterburg Gap. The intent was to draw the German Eighth Army as far from East Prussia as possible. Then Gen. Aleksandr Samsonov would enter East Prussia from the south with the Second Army and strike the German rear. At that point the two Russian armies would come together to crush the German Eighth Army. At least that is the way the Russians hoped it would happen. Rennenkampf crossed the German border on 17 August.

At mid-day on 23 August the new partners in command, Hindenburg and Ludendorff, arrived at Marienburg on the Vistula and were greeted by Maj. Gen. Paul Grünert, the quartermaster general of the Eighth Army and

Lt. Col. Max Hoffmann, the chief of operations. These two officers had persuaded Gen. Maximilian von Prittwitz, the recently sacked Eighth Army commander, that the correct course of action was a plan devised by Hoffmann. Hoffmann's plan called for concentrating almost all of the German forces in an attack against Samsonov to the south, leaving only one division to guard against Rennenkampf, who would be dealt with later. This plan was both bold and dangerous, leaving as it did one division to guard against an entire army. This was risky but nevertheless correct strategy under the extreme circumstances they faced. If Rennenkampf moved faster than expected, the Germans would find themselves trapped between two armies. Following the cardinal principle of war known as mass, the German plan called for the greatest concentration of force at the decisive point. Such action was necessary if the badly outnumbered Germans were to have any chance of success. Due to the folly of the Russian commanders in sending radio messages in the clear, the Eighth Army commander was able to anticipate every move of the Russian forces.

The Hoffmann plan was almost identical to orders that had been telephoned from Koblenz by Ludendorff, who did not know at that time what Hoffmann was considering. These two able officers, both thoroughly trained in German military methods and doctrine, had arrived at similar solutions to the same problem. This says much about the high level of German staff training and the cohesiveness of their doctrine.

Hindenburg and Ludendorff anxiously plotted the movement of Rennenkampf, who was on the move without resting his troops as long as the Germans had expected. When Rennenkampf failed to put any intensive pressure on the thin screen of forces left to watch him and, instead of moving toward Samsonov, headed due west, Hindenburg and Ludendorff set about executing their plan.

On the evening of 24 August Hindenburg and Ludendorff had not yet decided to risk an all-out attack against Samsonov because all of their forces were not yet in place. The I Corps of Gen. Hermann von François was just moving up by train to the right of the XX Corps, commanded by Gen. Friedrich von Scholtz. Gen. August von Mackensen's XVII Corps and Gen. Otto von Below's I Reserve Corps were resting and refitting south of Friedland. Hindenburg and Ludendorff debated whether to send them south to attack Samsonov or move them back to checkmate Rennenkampf. They hesitated because they were unsure of Rennenkampf's intentions. Ludendorff later noted; "Rennenkampf's formidable host hung like a threatening cloud to the north east" throughout the entire operation.[8]

The Eighth Army commander was reluctant to throw all of his available force against Samsonov when another large army was threatening his left flank and rear. While he was weighing the options, the first of many valuable intercepted messages informed him that Samsonov had been ordered to pursue Scholtz's XX Corps, which Yakov Zhilinsky assumed was in retreat. While still worrying over Rennenkampf's plans, Hindenburg and Ludendorff decided to take advantage of the knowledge of Samsonov's orders and to exploit his ignorance of what forces he was facing. Accordingly, Mackensen and von Below were ordered south to take their place on Scholtz's left, while François' forces would be on his right.

The move against Samsonov was to take place on 26 August, with a strong attack on each of his flanks. By turning Samsonov's flanks, Ludendorff hoped to trap his center and crush it. The Germans needed to destroy the Russian Second Army quickly, so they could throw all of their forces against Rennenkampf's First Army, which threatened from the north.

Although François had the reputation of being a very aggressive officer, he refused Ludendorff's order to attack until all of his troops, including his heavy artillery, had arrived. Ludendorff, fearful of any delay, repeated the orders to François while ordering Scholtz's XX Corps to attack toward Tannenberg against Samsonov's VI Corps commanded by General Blagovchensky. Concurrently with Scholtz's attack, Ludendorff sent the German center forward.

The battle started in earnest in the area of the Masurian Lakes, near the villages of Frogenau and Tannenberg on 27 August. At a decisive moment in the battle Ludendorff lost his nerve, as he was prone to do. He was so upset that he proposed recalling General François and canceling the encirclement of Samsonov's Second Army, as required by his own instructions and Hoffman's plan. Ludendorff was both furious and somewhat confused. Did not others realize how disastrously everything might turn out? What would the irresponsible François do next, and could old Mackensen be relied upon, since he had not handled himself brilliantly at Gumbinnen?

Ludendorff's anxieties are easier to understand in the context of the German army's lack of official doctrine for fighting a delaying action against superior numbers. Their doctrine emphasized the attack, with any defense being a temporary situation. The illogical assumption that the German army would always retain the offensive was very strong. Their limited techniques for defensive warfare provided that a commander would remove his forces as quickly as possible from the enemy's reach. This provided little help in the situation in which Ludendorff now found himself. Hoffmann recorded that

Hindenburg, noticing Ludendorff's concerns being expressed openly before everyone in the mess, told him he would like to see him privately after dinner.

Hindenburg later wrote, "We overcame the inner crisis, held by the decision we had taken, and tried to find a solution by an attack with all of our forces." Cool and unshaken, Hindenburg demanded that everyone support the original plan and the fight continued. Here one sees the new team working at its best. Both generals were playing their assigned roles. Ludendorff acted the part of the abrasive genius and Hindenburg that of the calm, father figure.[9]

Having regained his equilibrium, Ludendorff took control of the battle once again. Early on 28 August he urged General François to turn his advancing forces in support of the weaker sector of the front. But François disobeyed and pressed his attack against the center, driving the Russian forces forward without even attempting to inform Ludendorff that he had disobeyed a direct order. A British historian of the battle, Gen. Sir William Ironsides, later wrote, "To the disobedience of von François, Ludendorff undoubtedly owed the magnitude of his victory on succeeding days."[10]

By the end of August Samsonov's army was defeated and the Russians were in retreat. East Prussia was restored to German control. Much hard fighting still lay ahead, but the Battle of Tannenberg was essentially over. The victory had indeed been great. The Germans captured 30,000 wounded and 100,000 healthy troops, 500 guns, and thousands of horses. It required sixty trains to haul the captured equipment back to Germany.

Having recovered from his case of bad nerves, Ludendorff prepared the triumphal report for his superiors at OHL. When he started to date the dispatch from Frogenau, Hoffmann suggest changing the name to Tannenberg, which had been the scene of a lost battle five hundred years earlier in which the Teutonic Knights, among whom there was a Hindenburg, were defeated by an army of Lithuanians and Poles. Other towns played a more important role in the battle, but the name Tannenberg was chosen to help erase the humiliation of an earlier defeat. The defeat of Russia at Tannenberg is considered by many experts to have been the greatest battlefield defeat suffered by any of the warring powers during World War I.

Generals Martos and Kliouev were taken prisoner during the battle. Martos' account of his treatment at the hands of Hindenburg and Ludendorff tells much about the character of the two generals. Ludendorff taunted Martos constantly about the great defeat the Russians had suffered. Noting the anguish on Martos' face resulting from his treatment by Ludendorff, Hindenburg took the old general's face in his hands to comfort him and told him that his troops had fought well. He promised that his sword would be returned to him. Before departing he bowed and said, "I wish you happier days."[11] Samsonov, feeling that he could not face the czar after having failed his trust, walked off into the woods and shot himself.

Both Hindenburg and Ludendorff were grateful that the gods of war had once again favored Germany's forces in battle. On the evening of 31 August, the two attended a thanksgiving service in a Protestant Church in Allenstein, situated near an old castle of the Teutonic Knights. The church was filled with worshipers in Feldgrau uniforms. Hindenburg appeared overcome with emotions and he swelled with pride and satisfaction as strong, young German voices were raised, triumphally singing Martin Luther's famous hymn, "Eine feste Burg ist unser Gott" (A Mighty Fortress Is Our God). Respectfully, Ludendorff knelt beside Hindenburg, but to those who knew him well, he was understood to be giving his thanks and gratitude to Schlieffen rather than to the Almighty. In any event, he had little time to show emotions because the Eighth Army had to be regrouped for a strike at Rennenkampf, who still lurked nearby.[12]

The news of the great victory electrified Germans everywhere. Hindenburg became an instant hero. The victory was a great morale booster on every front and at home. But to whom should credit for the victory go? Hoffmann was at the time happy to receive the Iron Cross for his "humble role of sitting behind a desk." But in 1919 he called himself the sole initiator of the battle and the savior of East Prussia. In the public mind, however, the only heroes produced at Tannenberg were Hindenburg and Ludendorff.

The receipt of the Iron Cross to wear with his Blue Max reinforced Ludendorff's image as a genius of war. Most people had regarded him from the beginning as the real brains and driving élan behind the more stolid Hindenburg. Some historians believe that the Battle of Tannenberg could have been won had Hindenburg not been there. But one should not discount his steadying influence on Ludendorff during times of crisis. Because of his position as the senior member of the duo, however, Hindenburg received the lion's share of the glory. He felt that he deserved the credit for the victory because in his words, "if it had been lost, I would have lost it alone."[13] The German high command and the German people apparently agreed, since Hindenburg was subsequently promoted to field marshal and awarded the Pour le Mérite.

Who really deserved the credit for winning the Battle of Tannenberg? Ludendorff had conceived the tactics to be followed and had made the important decision on 24 August to attempt a double envelopment using all

available forces. But Hoffmann had independently arrived at the same decision and had smoothed the way by his initial troop disposition before receiving any orders from Ludendorff to do so. Hoffmann, however, was not crucial
to the victory, which could have been won without him. François made
important contributions by insisting on not moving until he had gathered all
of his forces together. He was also true to the teaching of Schlieffen's principle
of attacking not against the flank but "against the line of retreat . . . for a battle
. . . of annihilation, a battle with an obstacle in the rear of the enemy."[14]

   After due credit is given to all others, Ludendorff must surely be considered
the victor of Tannenberg. It was his plan that produced the victory. It was at
the time a crucial victory for Germany, which cast a warm glow over the
many failures to come. It was the most important German victory of the long,
bloody, and indecisive struggle that was World War I.

   During the war Tannenberg retained some relevancy to diplomatic and
military realities. Afterwards many myths and legends grew up that have
resonated through German history. They continued to fuel the sentiments
of German nationalist ideology as well as their military policy long after
the battle was over. Changes in European balance of power that came with
the collapse of the Soviet Union in the early 1990s remind us that history
continues to instruct us and that Tannenberg as a history lesson has still not
lost its relevance.

   When Hindenburg became commander in chief of all of Germany's forces
in the field in August 1916, Ludendorff went with him as his closest adviser
and eventually became the director of the entire German war effort. Promoted
to first quartermaster general, he used this new authority to supervise and
control military supply production and gain control of the entire German
economy. By 1917 his influence was so great that he was able to bring about
the removal of Chancellor Theobald von Bethmann Hollweg, with whom he
had policy disagreements. By this action he gained at least de facto control
over the entire German government and economy.[15]

   Germany's subsequent failures on the battlefield brought a decline in
Ludendorff's prestige and power. He was blamed for supporting the policy of
unrestricted submarine warfare, which served to bring the United States into
the war against Germany. His darkest moment came with the Allied assault
that shattered the German lines on 8 August 1918 at Amiens, ending any
remaining hopes Germany might have had of winning the war. Ludendorff
referred to this event as "the Black Day of the German Army." After that
event he experienced one of his most intense nervous crises, which were

occurring more frequently. His concerned staff arranged for him to consult with the famed psychiatrist, Dr. Hochheimer. After one visit Hochheimer told Ludendorff he was "overworked" and that his "drive and creative power" were impaired. Medical treatment and a period of rest were recommended. Ludendorff continued to work, but he lacked his old resilience and showed little evidence of recovery.

Ludendorff's final break with Hindenburg was a bitter one. After being dismissed by the kaiser for having countersigned a proclamation calling for continued resistance by the troops, Ludendorff saluted and departed. Because of Hindenburg's value as a symbol to the German people, the kaiser refused to accept his offer to resign also. Hindenburg then took his leave. Outside the palace, he approached Ludendorff and suggested that they continue their voyage together by car. Turning and giving Hindenburg a cold, glassy, hostile stare, Ludendorff replied, "I refuse to drive with you." Astonished, Hindenburg inquired why, and Ludendorff answered: "I refuse to have any more dealings with you because you treat me so shabbily."[16]

Ludendorff then turned his back on his old friend and climbed into another staff car and went home. Falling into an overstuffed chair looking pale as death, he told Frau Ludendorff, "The Kaiser has sacked me. I have been dismissed." After sitting slumped over for a few minutes he muttered, "In a fortnight we shall have no Empire and no Emperor left, you will see."[17] It was a moment of great despair for the tired, old warrior.

Ludendorff's loss of influence caused him to take an extended leave of absence until he finally resigned from the army on 26 October 1919. In 1926 he divorced the charming Margarethe Ludendorff, his last and most faithful friend, and married Frau Mathilde von Kemnitz. In 1927 at a ceremony to dedicate the Tannenberg Memorial, he created an unsightly scene by refusing to stand at the side of then President Hindenburg. Offended, Hindenburg departed before Ludendorff spoke, after which the latter, being shunned by his former comrades, went to his car alone. General Max Hoffmann had not been present at this nostalgic ceremony, having earlier passed away at Berchtesgaden at the age of fifty-eight. It was perhaps just as well, because Hoffmann, who was first and foremost a gentleman, would have no doubt been saddened by the sorry spectacle between the two old partners in war.[18]

By some clever maneuvering Ludendorff managed to avoid personal responsibility for Germany's surrender and he also helped to establish the "stab-in-the-back myth" of how Germany lost the war. And like many other Germans who were embittered by the loss of the war, Ludendorff became an active supporter of Adolf Hitler's Nazi Party. In 1923 he participated, without great enthusiasm, in the Beer Hall Putsch. After the Putsch a certain coolness developed between Ludendorff and Hitler. From 1924 to 1928, however, Ludendorff did serve as a Nazi delegate in the Reichstag. In 1925 he unsuccessfully challenged Hindenburg for the presidency of Germany.

After gaining power in Germany, Hitler tried to improve relations with Ludendorff, who was once again hailed as a great national hero. Hitler offered him a promotion to field marshal, which he declined. After refusing Hitler's peace offer, Ludendorff spent the rest of his life advocating a return to the worship of the pagan Nordic gods. In particular he espoused the semireligious worship of the Teutonic tribal gods Odin, Hertha, Wotan, and Siegfried; accepted the Nazi theory of German racial superiority; and advocated that the German people should worship their racial heritage, their blood, and their soil. Among other things, he renounced Free Masonry and wrote his theories of total war. Ludendorff died in Munich on 20 December 1937, less than two years before the outbreak of World War II.[19]

Hindenburg, the other member of the great military partnership, served as president of the Weimar Republic from 1925 until his death in 1934. Today his fame greatly exceeds that of his old chief of staff. Hindenburg's name can be found in almost any standard collegiate dictionary, while that of Ludendorff cannot.

Notes

1. D. J. Goodspeed, *Ludendorff: Genius of World War I* (Boston: Houghton Mifflin, 1966), throughout.
2. Erich Ludendorff, *My War Memories, 1914–1918*, 2 vols. (London: Hutchinson, 1919), 1:32.
3. Ibid.
4. Goodspeed, *Ludendorff*, 49.
5. Ibid., 63.
6. Ibid.
7. Dennis E. Showalter, *Tannenberg: Clash of Empires* (New York: Archon Books, 1991), 65.
8. Trevor N. Dupuy, *The Military Lives of Hindenburg and Ludendorff of Imperial Germany* (New York: Watts, 1970), 35.
9. Max Hoffmann, *War Diaries and Other Papers*, trans. Eric Sutton, 2 vols. (London: Martin Secker, 1929), 2:49.
10. Martin Gilbert, *The First World War: A Complete History* (Toronto: Stoddart Press, 1996), 49.

11. Martos, as quoted in Gen. Nicholas N. Golovine, *The Russian Campaign of 1914*, trans. Capt. A. G. S. Muntz (Fort Leavenworth, Kan.: Command and General Staff School Press, 1933), 327.

12. Paul von Hindenburg, *Out of My Life*, trans. F. A. Holt (New York: Harper and Bros., 1921), 99.

13. Ibid., 78.

14. Dupuy, *Hindenburg and Ludendorff*, 45.

15. Georg von Muller, *The Kaiser and His Court: The Diaries, Note Books and Letters of Admiral Georg Alexander von Muller, Chief of the Naval Cabinet, 1914–1918* (London: Macdonald, 1961), 280.

16. Ludendorff, *My War Memories*, 2:684.

17. Margarethe Ludendorff, *My Married Life with Ludendorff*, trans. Raglan Somerset (London: Hutchinson, 1929), 173.

18. Goodspeed, *Ludendorff*, 307.

19. David Zabecki, ed., *World War II in Europe: An Encyclopedia*, 2 vols. (New York: Garland, 1999), has some excellent material related to Ludendorff and the Nazi theories that he espoused. See Justin Murphy, "Ludendorff," 394; and "Beer Hall Putsch," "Munich Crisis and Agreement," and "National Socialism," all by Paul J. Rose (22–23, 116–20, and 121–24, respectively).

CHRONOLOGY OF CARL ADOLF MAXIMILIAN HOFFMANN

25 Jan 1869	Born at Bad Homberg, near Kassel.
1879–87	Attended Gymnasium in Nordhausen.
1887–93	Assigned to 72nd Infantry Regiment.
19 Sep 1888	Promoted to lieutenant.
15 Jul 1893	Married Cornelia (Nelly) Stern. One daughter.
1893–1903	Assigned as battalion adjutant, 45th Infantry Regiment.
14 Jul 1895	Promoted to first lieutenant.
1895–98	Attended the War Academy.
1898–99	Language study in Russia (Kharkov).
1 Apr 1899	Posted to the Great General Staff. First Department (Russia and the Nordic States).
23 Mar 1901	Promoted to captain.
1 Apr 1901	Assigned as Ib, V Army Corps (Posen).
17 Feb 1903	Assigned as company commander, 33rd Fusilier Regiment.
11 Feb 1904	Posted to the Great General Staff (attached to the Japanese Army 23 Feb 1904 to 2 Oct 1905).
27 Jan 1907	Assigned as Ia, 1st Division (Königsberg).
11 Sep 1907	Promoted to major.
1 Oct 1909	Posted to the Great General Staff, First Department.
1 Oct 1911	Assigned as instructor, War Academy.
1 Oct 1913	Assigned as battalion commander, then staff officer, 112th Infantry Regiment.
27 Jan 1914	Promoted to lieutenant colonel.
2 Aug 1914	Assigned as Ia, Eighth Army.
18 Sep 1914	Assigned as Ia, Ninth Army.
2 Nov 1914	Assigned as Ia, Oberost.
16 Aug 1916	Promoted to colonel.
30 Aug 1916	Assigned as chief of staff, Oberost.
7 Oct 1916	Awarded Pour le Mérite.
25 Jul 1917	Awarded Oak Leaves, Pour le Mérite.
29 Oct 1917	Promoted to major general.
16 Jan 1919	Assigned as commander, 10th Infantry Brigade.
31 Mar 1920	Retired.
8 Jul 1927	Died, Bad Reichenhall, Bavaria.

Carl Adolf Maximilian Hoffmann

Ulrich Trumpener

Except for Erich Ludendorff and Hans von Seeckt, Col. Max Hoffmann (major general from 29 October 1917) is probably the best-known German staff officer of the Great War. Widely credited with playing a major role in the German victory at Tannenberg in August 1914 and seen as a key figure in the eastern theater of war during the following years, Hoffmann was rated by some historians as "perhaps the most brilliant German staff officer of his generation" and used as a model at the U.S. Army's Command and General Staff College.[1] Other authors have asserted that from 1916 on Hoffmann was in effect Germany's supreme commander on the eastern front.[2] By contrast, Field Marshal Paul von Hindenburg, at whose headquarters Hoffmann had labored for over two years, did not even mention him in his postwar memoirs.[3]

After serving as first general staff officer (Ia hereafter) at Germany's High Command East (Oberost hereafter) since November 1914, Hoffmann became the chief of staff at that headquarters on 30 August 1916. On the same day, Field Marshal Prince Leopold of Bavaria succeeded Hindenburg as the commander of Oberost, with permanent quarters in and around Brest-Litovsk. Leopold—a brother of the reigning king of Bavaria and a son-in-law of Emperor Franz Joseph of Austria—had been a professional soldier for over forty years and previously had commanded both an army and an army group on the eastern front. It would therefore be quite wrong to assume that the elderly prince was merely a figurehead in his new post and that Hoffmann could henceforth do whatever he wished. It is clear, on the other hand, that on some occasions, and particularly during the armistice and peace negotiations with the Bolsheviks at Brest-Litovsk, the field marshal did indeed give his chief of staff a free hand.[4]

When Colonel Hoffmann took over as chief of staff, he could count on several seasoned veterans of the previous regime to help him with his new responsibilities. Among these were the deputy chief of staff for logistics (Oberquartiermeister), Maj. Gen. Ernst von Eisenhart-Rothe, and the highly talented senior intelligence officer, Maj. Fritz Gempp (who later created the Abwehr service of the Reichswehr).[5] Of the staff officers newly recruited by Hoffmann, three were particularly noteworthy. To fill the Ia slot he himself had just vacated, Hoffmann chose Maj. Viktor Keller, a very capable man who previously had served in a similar capacity at corps and army headquarters on the Russian front.[6] After Keller was promoted to a more senior position, Hoffmann recruited Maj. Friedrich Brinckmann to take his place. Brinckmann not only was a seasoned staff officer with extensive experience on the eastern front, but also was quite versatile. Before the war he had served as a military attaché in Belgium and the Netherlands, and in 1918–19 he would once again be used in politically sensitive posts.[7] It seems clear that during his posting to Oberost (from November 1916 to June 1918) Brinckmann was Hoffmann's closest advisor, while Maj. Karl Hofmann, the second general staff officer (Ib), became an equally trusted executor of Hoffmann's wishes. Admired for his "incredible stamina and zest for work," Hoffmann had begun his career in the corps of engineers, and was thus particularly suited to deal with the technological aspects of modern war.[8] In 1918 General Hoffmann also relied heavily on Maj. Edmund Wachenfeld, who acted as a roving observer of frontline units for his deskbound chief.[9]

After Gempp was transferred to other duties in November 1916, the senior intelligence post at Oberost was filled in succession by two brothers, Emil and Robert von Winterfeld. The latter, another engineer by background, had joined Oberost as a junior intelligence officer in 1914 and would spend the entire war period and much of the 1920s in that field.[10] When he was reassigned to the central office of the secret military intelligence branch (Abteilung IIIb), Capt. Siegfried Hey succeeded him at Oberost. A reserve officer with long experience both in military intelligence work and civilian journalism, Hey was of great use to Hoffmann on a broad range of issues, and he was officially included in the German peace delegation at Brest-Litovsk.[11] In May 1918 Field Marshal Prince Leopold secured the appointment of his elder son, Prince Georg, as the new senior intelligence officer at Oberost. Although Georg had previously served in a similar capacity at various headquarters on the Russian front and in Turkey, it is doubtful that Hoffmann was pleased with this nepotistic arrangement.[12]

Hoffmann's work as chief of staff at Oberost divides itself roughly into two periods. During the first period, from August 1916 to December 1917, developments at the front were of primary concern. Despite growing war weariness in Russia, the tsar's armies continued to be formidable opponents of the Central Powers. Even after the overthrow of the tsarist regime, in March 1917, Oberost repeatedly had to deal with local crises at the front. Though it ultimately was unsuccessful, the Kerenski Offensive in July 1917 inflicted some serious losses on both Austro-Hungarian and German troops, and forced Oberost into several hasty redeployments of forces. As often before, Hoffmann resented the "incompetence" and "lack of staying power" among Austro-Hungarian troops. He confided to his wife how unpleasant it was to have to work with those people.[13]

When Prince Leopold and Hoffmann took charge at Oberost, they assumed responsibility for three army groups. The northernmost group, headed by Col. Gen. Hermann von Eichhorn, held a line stretching from the Gulf of Riga to the Smorgon region in Byelorussia. On Eichhorn's right was Col. Gen. Remus von Woyrsch's army group, which included an Austro-Hungarian corps and stretched down to the southwestern reaches of the Pripyat Marshes. The third army group, commanded by General of Infantry Alexander von Linsingen, included an entire Austro-Hungarian army, and held a precarious line in Volhynia. All three of these army group commanders were seasoned veterans of combat against the Russians, and Eichhorn was widely regarded as a man of outstanding personal qualities and military talent. From October 1916 until early 1918 Oberost's authority was extended to an Austro-Hungarian army group in eastern Galicia, which was headed by Col. Gen. Eduard von Böhm-Ermolli. It was in this sphere of command that some of the heaviest fighting took place in 1916 and 1917, thus requiring special attention from Hoffmann and his staff.[14]

As it was customary in the Prussian army, Hoffmann's daily contacts with the subordinate army groups were handled primarily through the staffs at those commands. Until the eastern front more or less closed down—that is, until December 1917—Hoffmann was well served by most of the senior staff officers in the field. Col. Wilhelm Heye, the chief of staff at Army Group Woyrsch until September 1917, was a highly competent officer. Like Hoffmann, Heye had an excellent knowledge of Russian and extensive experience in intelligence work.[15] Col. (later major general) Walter Baron Schmidt von Schmidtseck, who served consecutively as chief of staff under Eichhorn and Woyrsch, was likewise an accomplished officer in his field. Although he had experienced considerable difficulties with his headstrong corps commander, Hermann von François, in August 1914, the baron survived that ordeal unscathed and thereafter repeatedly distinguished himself in senior staff positions on the Russian front.[16] Somewhat less outstanding was Maj. Gen. Traugott von Sauberzweig, who followed Schmidt von Schmidtseck as Eichhorn's chief of staff. A pastor's son who had been ennobled shortly before the outbreak of the Great War, Sauberzweig was a very capable staff officer, but he was plagued by a heart condition that often interfered with his work. Moreover, while serving as governor of Brussels in 1915, he had shown very poor judgment by his refusal to spare the life of nurse Edith Cavell, as senior civilian officials in the Belgian capital had advised him.[17] As for Army Group Linsingen, Hoffmann had one of his favorites, Lieutenant Colonel Keller, in charge of its staff until March 1918.[18]

Ever since the Russian armies had been pushed out of Poland, Lithuania, and most of Courland in 1915, the administration and economic exploitation of some of these areas had become part of Oberost's responsibilities. Most of the captured Polish lands had been placed under the control of a German governor-general headquartered in Warsaw, and an Austro-Hungarian military governor with offices in Lublin. Oberost was in charge of all the other captured territories, including the Baltic provinces, parts of Byelorussia, and a small strip of land in eastern Poland. By the time Prince Leopold and Hoffmann took over from Hindenburg and Ludendorff, an elaborate system for the maintenance of public order and the utilization of the region's resources already had been put in place.[19] As time went by, however, Oberost's role in this sphere became more complex, for both in Lithuania and in Courland certain political or ethnic groups began to demand better treatment and greater political rights from the German administration. Hoffmann's time, therefore, was increasingly taken up having to deal with these issues. In 1918, both during the peace negotiations at Brest-Litovsk and afterwards, he often found himself in an awkward position between the harsh and imperialistic demands of his superiors at OHL and the more moderate policies advocated by the German foreign ministry.[20]

Hoffmann's encounters with Leon Trotsky and other prominent Bolsheviks at Brest-Litovsk, and his sometimes acerbic comments to various Austro-Hungarian dignitaries during the negotiations with the Soviet government in Russia and the Rada regime of the Ukraine, have been the subject of many studies. While some historians depict him as a typical representative of German militarism and imperialism, others have acknowledged that

Hoffmann was much more open to progressive ideas than many of his fellow officers.[21] Indeed, on several occasions both Hindenburg and Ludendorff were quite upset by his views and proposals, and right-wing circles in Germany even criticized him in the press. The fact that Hoffmann's wife came from a family of Jewish converts and was fairly liberal in her outlook undoubtedly contributed to the animus against him.[22]

Fortunately for Hoffmann, for about seven months (from December 1917 until July 1918) the purely administrative side of maintaining order in the ever-enlarging occupation zones of Oberost was handled quite deftly by Lt. Gen. Georg Count von Waldersee. (In August 1914 Waldersee had been Hoffmann's immediate superior at the headquarters of the Eighth Army in East Prussia.)[23] Waldersee's last postings eventually took him to Sevastopol, where he served briefly as the military governor.[24]

Hoffmann's remarkable skills in operational planning, his resourcefulness, and his coolness under pressure had become evident during the very first weeks of the war and manifested themselves again and again in the ensuing two years. By the time he succeeded Ludendorff at Oberost in late August 1916, the military challenges facing the Central Powers on the Russian front were no longer quite as daunting as they had been so often in the past. As a result, Hoffmann's military accomplishments during his tenure as Oberost's chief of staff perhaps do not look quite as impressive as his earlier feats.

Among the operations that added further luster to his name, the German offensive in Galicia beginning on 18 July 1917 is probably the best known. Long before the Russians launched their own Kerensky Offensive there and in several other sectors of the eastern front, Hoffmann had worked out an effective scheme for dislodging the enemy from both Galicia and the Bukovina. While both Prince Leopold and OHL actively participated in the final preparations, the German advance along the Siret River certainly owed much of its success to Hoffmann's input and determination. Within a few weeks, the Russians were driven back to the prewar borders of the Habsburg empire. Both Hoffmann and Prince Leopold were duly rewarded by the kaiser, receiving the Oak Leaves to the Pour le Mérite. To Hoffmann's annoyance, Emperor Charles of Austria "did not even say thanks" for the recovery of his crown lands.[25]

At the beginning of August 1917, Hoffmann complained to his wife that he was tired and in need of a break; but since everyone held him—rather than Prince Leopold—responsible for everything that happened on the Ostfront, he simply could not get away.[26] The Bavarian field marshal obviously appreciated Hoffmann's hard work, for a few weeks later he proposed to the kaiser that his chief of staff receive an accelerated promotion to major general. Although the head of the kaiser's military cabinet, Gen. Moritz Baron von Lyncker, initially blocked the proposal, Leopold, backed by Hindenburg and Ludendorff, finally got his way at the end of October. The fact that in the meantime further glories had been added to Oberost's record, including the capture of Riga by the German Eighth Army on 3 September and the seizure of the large islands at the northern end of the Gulf of Riga between 12 and 21 October, undoubtedly strengthened Hoffmann's cause.[27]

Even before a formal armistice had been concluded on the eastern front (the relevant negotiations at Brest-Litovsk dragged on until 15 December 1917), OHL and its Austro-Hungarian counterpart, the AOK, had begun a significant transfer of divisions from the eastern front to the western and Italian theaters of war. At the same time, the command structure in Oberost's realm was simplified somewhat through the dissolution of Army Group Woyrsch, with a corresponding enlargement of General von Linsingen's responsibilities.[28]

Trotsky and his delegation walked out of the peace conference at Brest-Litovsk on 10 February 1918 with the bold announcement that Russia was "leaving the war," but would not accept the terms drawn up by the Central Powers. OHL promptly authorized Oberost to resume hostilities as soon as the armistice grace period had elapsed. Accordingly, on 18 February, Prince Leopold and Hoffmann launched their famous "railroad offensive" to the east. Within the next two weeks, the divisions of Army Group Eichhorn advanced rapidly to a line running from Narva, near the Gulf of Finland, via Pskov to the eastern fringes of Byelorussia. Farther south, at the invitation of the Ukrainian Rada, German divisions of General von Linsingen's army group quickly moved into southern Russia. After hesitating for over a week, the Austro-Hungarian government sent its own divisions into the Ukraine and eventually secured the right to occupy the western half of Volhynia, as well as the provinces of Podolia, Kherson, and Yekaterinoslav.[29] This eastward drive continued in April. On 1 May German units reached Taganrog on the Sea of Azov, as well as Sevastopol, in the Crimea. The following day Bavarian cavalry closed up to the Strait of Kerch, while a number of other units, including an Austro-Hungarian battalion, occupied Rostov-on-Don a week later.[30]

While the advance into the Ukraine and other southern portions of the old Russian empire was coordinated initially by Oberost, its influence in those regions steadily declined during the spring season. On 21 March 1918

Field Marshal von Böhm-Ermolli's Austro-Hungarian troops returned to the direct control of AOK. Moreover, the German army group in the Ukraine, headed by Field Marshal von Eichhorn since 31 March, removed itself more and more from Hoffmann's supervision. Perhaps the most important factor in that development was the appointment of Lt. Gen. Wilhelm Groener as Eichhorn's chief of staff. Senior in rank to Hoffmann and certainly his equal in political savvy and administrative talent, Groener soon became the key figure in Kiev and gained even more clout after Eichhorn was assassinated on 30 July. Eichhorn's place was taken by Col. Gen. Günter Count von Kirchbach. He was an amiable and fatherly figure well liked by his troops, who would hold out in the strife-torn Ukrainian capital until mid-January 1919.[31]

It appears that in the months following the conclusion of peace at Brest-Litovsk Hoffmann sided with those in the German government who believed that the survival of Lenin's regime in Russia was in Germany's best interest. He gradually changed his stance, however. As he explained to Berlin in August 1918, the Bolsheviks increasingly were becoming a threat to the Central Powers, especially by their revolutionary propaganda among German and Austro-Hungarian troops. Their removal from power in Moscow was, therefore, highly desirable.[32] This recommendation brought Hoffmann closer to the views held by the kaiser, Ludendorff, and former vice-chancellor Karl Helfferich, but the new head of the German foreign ministry, retired admiral Paul von Hintze, successfully resisted all attempts to pursue a militant line against the Bolshevik regime. Indeed, after months of bickering, the Soviet government signed a series of treaties on 27 August, agreeing to cooperate with the Germans on a number of political and economic issues.[33]

When the German revolution broke out in November 1918, followed on the eleventh of that month with the Armistice of Compiègne, the German Ostheer had close to 300,000 soldiers stationed in Ukraine and other parts of southern Russia. Another 200,000 mostly middle-aged militia troops were scattered over the Baltic region and Byelorussia.[34] Prince Leopold and Hoffmann, who had moved their headquarters to Kovno (Kaunas) in May, were well aware of the growing disaffection and homesickness in most of Oberost's garrisons. An orderly withdrawal from all the occupied territories was, therefore, not likely to succeed. Their problems were compounded by the insistence of the Western Allies (embedded in the Armistice text) that the evacuation of the eastern territories should be timed in consonance with their wishes. Within a few days after the armistice, Oberost warned OHL and the new government in Berlin that it needed volunteers to help maintain some semblance of order in its sphere of responsibility. At the same time it tried to coordinate the phased withdrawal of Kirchbach's army group in the south and the retreat of the Eighth and Tenth armies in the northern region. But various transportation bottlenecks, as well as active intervention by Red Guards, Ukrainian republicans, local brigands, and a host of others, soon produced well-nigh chaotic conditions in many areas. While most of the German troops eventually reached East Prussia by train, some cavalry brigades marched home in harsh winter conditions over distances exceeding one thousand miles.[35]

At the end of December, long before the evacuation program had been completed, Oberost moved its headquarters to Königsberg. Two weeks later, on 14 January 1919, both Prince Leopold and Hoffmann went on leave and Oberost's functions were transferred to other institutions. Although Hoffmann eventually received a brigade command near the Polish border, neither General Groener (Ludendorff's successor at OHL), nor Maj. Gen. Hans von Seeckt (the new head of the Reichswehr's Truppenamt), appears to have shown much interest in keeping their colleague in the service.[36] Officially retired in March 1920, Hoffmann settled in Berlin and kept himself busy with writing about his experiences and various other topics. In 1921 his close friend, Maj. Gen. Hans Kundt, whom he had known since their common service as subalterns in the 72nd Infantry Regiment, left Germany for Bolivia, where he would preside over the General Staff until the 1930s.[37]

After years of working under great stress and often with little or no regular sleep, Hoffmann was in rather poor health during the remaining years of his life. He died in 1927 at the age of fifty-eight at Bad Reichenhall, a spa in the Bavarian Alps.[38]

Notes

1. Cf. B. H. Liddell-Hart, *History of the First World War* (London: Pan Books, 1972), 68, 100ff., 305ff.; Holger H. Herwig and Neil M. Heyman, *Biographical Dictionary of World War I* (Westport, Conn.: Greenwood, 1982), 188–89; and the well-balanced assessment in Dennis F. Showalter, *Tannenberg* (North Haven, Conn.: Archon Books, 1991), 140, 330, 349, and passim. John W. Wheeler-Bennett, *Brest-Litovsk: The Forgotten Peace* (London: Macmillan, 1963), 78; John Keegan and Andrew Wheatcroft, *Who's Who in Military History from 1493 to the Present Day* (New York: William Morrow, 1976), 162; and D. K. R. Crosswell, *The Chief of Staff: The Military Career of General Walter Bedell Smith*, Contributions in Military Studies (New York: Greenwood, 1991), 60–61. Crosswell notes

that Eisenhower's future chief of staff, Walter Bedell Smith, was among those who "played the role" of Hoffmann in a dramatized re-creation of the Battle of Tannenberg.

2. See, e.g., Isaac Deutscher, *The Prophet Armed: Trotsky 1879–1921* (Oxford: Oxford University Press, 1965), 354; John G. Williamson, *Karl Helfferich, 1872–1924. Economist, Financier, Politician* (Princeton, N.J.: Princeton University Press, 1971), 279; and Spencer C. Tucker, *The Great War* (Bloomington: Indiana University Press, 1998), 149, 156, 160.

3. Field Marshal Paul von Hindenburg, *Aus meinem Leben* (Leipzig, 1934), published in English as *Out of My Life* (New York: Harper and Bros., 1921).

4. Hoffmann himself rated Leopold as a smart soldier with a clear vision and strong nerves. He also thought that Leopold was "much more intelligent than Hindenburg," though both men left too much work on his shoulders. See Bundesarchiv-Militärarchiv Freiburg, *Nachlass* Hoffmann N/37 (hereafter *Hoffmann Papers*), passim.

5. Since he was senior in rank to Hoffmann, the latter arranged Eisenhart-Rothe's reassignment to OHL at the end of 1916, where he became the "intendant-general of the German field army." As a result of his long involvement with German military intelligence (1913–27 and again 1939–43), Major General Gempp was arrested by the Soviets in 1946 (at age seventy-three) and never seen again.

6. Keller concluded his war service as chief of staff of Army Group von Gallwitz on the Western Front. For his accomplishments against the Russians, he received the Pour le Mérite in March 1918.

7. After retiring from the army in1920, Brinckmann became a successful businessman and eventually a senior executive of the Arado Aircraft Company in Berlin.

8. See Karl Friedrich Nowak, ed., *Die Aufzeichnungen des Generalmajors Max Hoffmann*, 2 vols. (Berlin: Verlag für Kulturpolitik, 1929), 2:156.

9. See ibid., 2:159. After retiring from the army in 1932, Wachenfeld joined Göring's new Luftwaffe in 1934 and was promoted to three-star rank the following year.

10. Robert von Winterfeld retired in 1933, but was recalled to active duty as a two-star general in World War II.

11. Hey joined the German foreign service in 1920. Before his retirement in 1935, he spent seven years in the Soviet Union and served as Deputy Director for East European Affairs at the Wilhelmstrasse from 1932 on.

12. Like some other royals, Prince Georg had advanced more rapidly through the ranks than ordinary mortals, holding the rank of colonel at age thirty-eight.

13. See Kriegsgeschichtliche Forschungsanstalt des Heeres, *Der Weltkrieg 1914 bis 1918* (Berlin: Kriegsgeschichtliche Forschungsanstalt des Heeres, 1942), 13:148–58; Bundesministerium für Landesverteidigung/Kriegsarchiv, *Oesterreich-Ungarns letzter Krieg 1914–1918* (Vienna: Bundesministerium für Landesverteidigung/Kriegsarchiv, 1936), 6:236ff.; and *Hoffmann Papers*, Hoffmann to his wife, 10 July and 17 July 1917. Norman Stone, *The Eastern Front, 1914–1917* (New York: Macmillan, 1975), for reasons unknown, dismisses the Russian war effort in 1917 in four lines (p. 282).

14. Böhm-Ermolli's Army Group in 1917 was composed of the Austro-Hungarian Second and Third Armies, and the German Southern Army (Südarmee). The latter included some Austro-Hungarian and Turkish divisions.

15. Heye later rose to four-star rank and headed the German army from 1926 to 1930.

16. He ended his war service as a divisional commander on the western front. His baronial title was quite new (1907).

17. On the Cavell case, see Oscar Freiherr von der Lancken-Wakenitz, *Meine dreissig Dienstjahre* (Berlin: Kulturpolitik, 1931), 238ff.; and the article on Edith Cavell by Meredith L. Bragg in *The European Powers in the First World War: An Encyclopedia*, ed. Spencer C. Tucker (New York: Garland, 1996), 177–78.

18. See Lancken-Wakenitz, *Meine dreissig Dienstjahre*.

19. See Gen. Erich Ludendorff, *My War Memoirs, 1914–1918* (London: Hutchinson, 1919), 1:180–207, for his proud recital of Oberost's "work for civilization" in the occupied lands during his tenure there.

20. Cf. Fritz Fischer, *Griff nach der Weltmacht: Die Kriegszielpolitik des kaiserlichen Deutschland, 1914–1918* (Düsseldorf: Droste Verlag, 1967), passim; Gerhard Ritter, *Staatskunst und Kriegshandwerk*, vols. 3–4 (Munich: Oldenbourg Verlag, 1964–68), passim; Winfried Baumgart, *Deutsche Ostpolitik 1918* (Munich: Oldenbourg Verlag, 1966); and Nowak, *Die Aufzeichnungen des . . . Hoffmann*, passim.

21. See Wheeler-Bennett, *Brest-Litovsk*, passim; Wolfdieter Bihl, *Oesterreich-Ungarn und die Friedensschlüsse von Brest-Litovsk* (Vienna: Broschiert, 1970), 33–34, 57–58, and passim; and Werner Hahlweg, ed., *Der Friede von Brest-Litowsk* (Düsseldorf: Droste Verlag, 1971), passim.

22. Cf. Martin Kitchen, *The Silent Dictatorship: The Politics of the German High Command Under Hindenburg and Ludendorff, 1916–1918* (London: Croon Helm, 1976), 168 and passim; Ritter, *Staatskunst und Kriegshandwerk*, vol. 4, chaps. 2 and 4; and the readable but often unreliable account in Robert B. Asprey, *The German High Command at War: Hindenburg and Ludendorff Conduct World War I* (New York: Morrow, 1991), chap. 31. Quite a few senior officers of Wilhelmian Germany had married women from converted Jewish families, including the future creator of the Reichswehr, General Hans von Seeckt.

23. Along with the army commander, Waldersee had been fired by Moltke on 22 August 1914 for contemplating a general retreat to the Vistula River.

24. After the war, Waldersee became deeply involved in conservative politics and served as president of the National Association of German Officers until 1925.

25. See *Der Weltkrieg 1914 bis 1918*, 13:159–79; *Österreich-Ungarns letzter Krieg*, 6:289ff.; and *Hoffmann Papers*, Hoffmann to his wife, 25 and 26 July 1917.

26. Ibid., letter of 2 August 1917.

27. Ibid., letters of 10 September and 30 October 1917. On the Riga Offensive, see *Der Weltkrieg 1914 bis 1918*, 13:189–98; and David T. Zabecki's article, "Riga, Battle of," in *The European Powers*, ed. Tucker, 597ff. On the amphibious operations in the Gulf of Riga, see Erich von Tschischwitz, *Armee und Marine bei der Eroberung der Baltischen Inseln* (Wolfenbüttel: Melchior Verlag, 2007); and *Der Weltkrieg 1914 bis 1918*, 13:200–205.

28. See Tschischwitz, *Armee und Marine*, 207, 331, 342–45, and Beilage 28a.

29. See Tschischwitz, *Armee und Marine*, 353–56, 362–70, 374–80; *Oesterreich-Ungarns letzter Krieg*, vol. 7 (1938), 114–39 and passim; and Deutscher, *The Prophet Armed*,

380ff. Cf. Oleh S. Fedyshyn, *Germany's Drive to the East and the Ukrainian Revolution, 1917–1918* (New Brunswick, N.J.: Rutgers University Press, 1971), chaps. 4–5.

30. See *Der Weltkrieg 1914 bis 1918*, 13:380–87; *Österreich-Ungarns letzter Krieg*, 7:140–45.

31. Cf. Baumgart, *Deutsche Ostpolitik*, 117–55; Fedyshyn, *Germany's Drive to the East*, chaps. 6–10; and Wilhelm Groener, *Lebenserinnerungen: Jugend, Generalstab, Weltkrieg*, ed. Friedrich Freiherr Hiller von Gaertringen (Göttingen: Vandenhoeck and Ruprecht, 1957), 383–418, 566–73.

32. See Baumgart, *Deutsche Ostpolitik*, 306ff., 322ff., and passim; Ritter, *Staatskunst und Kriegshandwerk*, 4:316ff.; and Williamson, *Karl Helfferich*, 270ff.

33. See Baumgart, *Deutsche Ostpolitik*, and E. H. Carr, *The Bolshevik Revolution, 1917–1923*, vol. 3 (London: Macmillan, 1953), 80–95.

34. Forschungsanstalt für Kriegs- und Heeresgeschichte, *Die Rückführung des Ostheeres* (Berlin, 1936), 2ff.; Günter Frantz, "Die Rückführung des deutschen Besatzungsheeres aus der Ukraine 1918–1919," *Wissen und Wehr* 15 (1934): 445ff.

35. See Frantz, "Die Rückführung"; also Fedyshyn, *Germany's Drive to the East*, chap. 11.

36. Forschungsanstalt, *Die Rückführung*, 154; and Hoffmann to his wife, 3 May 1919, Hoffmann Papers. See also his letters of 3, 6, and 7 September 1916, 4 October 1916, and 29 September 1917, on his frequent clashes with Generalmajor von Seeckt while the latter had served as chief of staff of an independent Austro-Hungarian army group (Heeresfront).

37. For a sampling of Hoffmann's postwar writings about the dangers of Bolshevism, see Nowak, *Die Aufzeichnungen*, 2:317ff.; on Hoffmann's admiration for Kundt, see 2:22. Cf. Kurt von Borcke, *Deutsche unter fremden Fahnen* (Berlin: Schlieffen Verlag, 1938), 298–307.

38. According to Nowak and others, Hoffmann had a tendency to overindulge in food, and during the war years he often drank cognac and large doses of Turkish coffee to stay awake and alert.

CHRONOLOGY OF HANS VON SEECKT

22 Apr 1866	Born in Schleswig.
4 Aug 1885	Appointed Fahnenjunker, 1st Battalion Emperor Alexander Guard Grenadier Regiment.
11 Mar 1886	Promoted to Fähnrich.
15 Jan 1887	Promoted to second lieutenant.
18 Feb 1892	Appointed adjutant, 1st Battalion, Emperor Alexander Guard Grenadier Regiment.
1 Oct 1893	Student, War Academy.
27 Jan 1894	Promoted to first lieutenant.
1 Apr 1897	Assigned to the 5th Guard Grenadier Regiment as General Staff candidate.
25 Mar 1899	Assigned to the Great General Staff, Berlin.
3 Jul 1899	Assigned XVII Corps, as General Staff candidate.
13 Sep 1899	Promoted to captain.
27 Jan 1900	Appointed as General Staff officer.
22 Mar 1902	Assigned to the 39th Fusilier Regiment.
22 Apr 1902	Assigned as a company commander, 39th Fusilier Regiment.
25 Jul 1904	Assigned as a General Staff officer, 4th Infantry Division.
17 Nov 1906	Promoted to major.
20 Dec 1906	Assigned to the Great General Staff, Berlin.
6 Apr 1909	Assigned as a General Staff officer, II Corps.
20 Feb 1912	Assigned as a battalion commander, 109th Grenadier Regiment.
4 Apr 1913	Promoted to lieutenant colonel and assigned as chief of the General Staff, III Corps.
27 Jan 1915	Promoted to colonel.
9 Mar 1915	Assigned as chief of the General Staff, Eleventh Army.
14 May 1915	Awarded the Pour le Mérite.
22 Jun 1915	Promoted to major general.
14 Sep 1915	Assigned as chief of the General Staff, Army Group von Mackensen.
27 Nov 1915	Awarded the Oak Leaves to the Pour le Mérite.

14 Jun 1916	Assigned as chief of the General Staff, Austro-Hungarian Seventh Army.
1 Jul 1916	Assigned as chief of the General Staff, Austro-Hungarian Army Group Archduke Karl, then Archduke Joseph Austro-Hungarian Army Group.
2 Dec 1917	Assigned as chief of the Army General Staff, Turkish army.
20 Dec 1917	Assigned as chief of staff, Turkish Field Army.
6 Aug 1918	Assigned as chief of staff, Turkish Great General Headquarters.
10 Jan 1919	Assigned as chief of staff, Army High Command North, East Prussia (border defense and evacuation of German units from East Europe).
26 Apr 1919	Assigned as military advisor to the German delegation to Versailles Peace Conference.
3 Jul 1919	Assigned as chief, Defense Staff, Great General Staff.
1 Oct 1919	Appointed chief of the Truppenamt (the Great General Staff by another name).
17 Mar 1920	Appointed commander, General Command I.
20 Apr 1920	Appointed chief, Heeresleitung.
19 Jun 1920	Promoted to lieutenant general.
18 Dec 1920	Promoted to general of infantry.
1 Jan 1925	Promoted to colonel general.
9 Oct 1926	Retired from the army.
1930–32	Served as a member of the Reichstag, German People's Party.
1934–35	Served as senior military advisor to Chiang Kai-shek, China.
22 Apr 1936	Appointed colonel in chief, 67th Infantry Regiment.
27 Dec 1936	Died, Berlin.

Hans von Seeckt

N. H. Gaworek

J ames S. Corum, in his important book, *The Roots of Blitzkrieg: General Hans von Seeckt and German Military Reform*, could have contributed to the introductory chapter of this volume. He wrote:

Even though a great commander might provide the vision and set the army's grand strategy, all of his efforts would be for naught unless the framework of his grand vision were fleshed out by the detailed work of capable staff officers and military specialists. Great commanders and military theorists are useful only to a point. A brilliant theory is useless if the officers who have to make it a reality are mediocre.[1]

General Hans von Seeckt was the quintessential staff officer and chief of staff par excellence.

The purpose of this brief essay is to highlight and summarize von Seeckt's career and achievements in World War I. The reader should keep in mind, however, that von Seeckt's career did not end abruptly in November 1918, because it extended into the postwar period in which he continued to leave his mark as leader in the transition of the imperial army to the Reichswehr and then to the Wehrmacht. He was placed in charge of the orderly withdrawal of German forces from Eastern Europe and the defense of Germany's eastern borders by Field Marshal Paul von Hindenburg, chief of the Great General Staff. He spent a few weeks as military advisor to the German peace delegation to Versailles, where he sought a mitigation of the severe military clauses of the Treaty of Versailles. Then he was charged with implementing these restrictive military provisions, first as chief of the Defense Staff of the Great General Staff, which the Allies ordered abolished, then as chief of the Truppenamt in October 1919, and finally as commander of General Command I. On 20 April 1920 he was appointed chief of the Heeresleitung, commander in chief of the new army, the Reichswehr, until his forced resignation in October 1926. During this period, several promotions followed until he achieved the rank of colonel-general on 1 January 1925.

Rebuilding Germany's armed forces within the severely restrictive framework of the Treaty of Versailles was a formidable task. Part V of that treaty stipulated the military, naval, and air clauses: reduction of the army to ten divisions for a total of 100,000 men, including 4,000 officers; dissolution of the Great General Staff; severe limits on guns, machine guns, mortars, rifles, ammunition, and the calibers of guns and their manufacture and importation; prohibitions of the production and storage of all gases; and the abolition of compulsory military service and the institution of long-term service (twelve years for enlisted men and NCOs, twenty-five years for officers). Likewise, Germany's navy was reduced in the type and size of ships and their armaments; naval personnel were shrunk to 15,000 officers, warrant officers, and men (their length of service was the same as for army personnel). Submarines were forbidden. Germany was prohibited from having an air force.[2] But, taking advantage of several opportunities—including clandestine rearmament, dummy corporations, and secret funds; emphasizing several of the virtues of the old army (such as training and selection of high-quality personnel; collaboration with Soviet Russia; Allied laxness; and the absorption of the lessons of the war—von Seeckt was able to rebuild a coherent force. Circumventing and violating the treaty was endorsed by practically all governments and all parties and their civilian leaders.

Von Seeckt is credited with creating a cadre army (Führerheer) of officers and NCOs, an army that was expandable with the introduction of obligatory military service. The Reichswehr's new doctrine was based on principles of movement and technology; in other words, it became the nucleus of the army that fought the Blitzkrieg of 1939. Von Seeckt had written ten years earlier that not mass armies, but small, professional, motorized units, supported by combined arms and air forces, would bring about military decisions in a future war. A fully trained reserve would augment this force in case of war.[3]

Although he remained a monarchist all his life, von Seeckt served the republic well, making virtue out of necessity under the post-Versailles conditions. He was relieved of command of the Reichswehr in October 1926. His last military task before his death in December 1936 was as senior military advisor to Gen. Chiang Kai-shek, leader of the Kuomintang government and armed forces in China.

Johannes Friedrich Leopold von Seeckt was born on 22 April 1866 in Schleswig, where his father was stationed. Both his father and his grandfather were general officers. Von Seeckt attended school wherever his father was on duty until he graduated from Strasbourg's gymnasium in 1885. Most other staff officers attended cadet schools.

According to his biographer, Hans Meier-Welcker, von Seeckt appears to have had in mind following in his father's footsteps by becoming an officer.[4] His basic training took place in Berlin in the Emperor Alexander Guard Grenadier Regiment. In 1886 he spent nine months in Hannover's military school, from which he emerged as an officer candidate. After returning to his regiment, he was promoted to second lieutenant. Service in that Berlin regiment had many social advantages as well. In 1893 he married into a prominent family. In the fall of that year he attended the War Academy for three years, advancing to first lieutenant during this preparatory training, which he completed with excellent grades. This practically guaranteed him a position in General Staff duties.[5]

The remainder of von Seeckt's training included service as General Staff candidate in a troop unit, duty in the Great General Staff in Berlin, and staff duties in the VIII Corps, during which he was promoted to captain. His appointment to the Great General Staff came in early 1900. Between that appointment and staff service in the 4th Infantry Division, the II and the III Corps, he returned a couple of times to the Great General Staff. He completed two tours of duty as line officer with an infantry company and an infantry battalion. He advanced to major and then to lieutenant colonel in 1913.[6]

The beginning of the world war found von Seeckt as chief of staff of the III Corps of the First Army, which, following the Schlieffen Plan, advanced into Belgium and northern France on the right wing of the German offensive. Von Seeckt's corps was heavily involved in the Battle of the Marne. In 1927 von Seeckt explained that there were several reasons for Germany's defeat in that battle. The troops needed rest; personnel, especially junior officers and seasoned NCOs, needed to be replaced; and trust had to be restored in the higher military leadership.[7]

War on the western front became increasingly static after the "race for the sea." Trench warfare set in from the Swiss border to the North Sea. Costly and bloody offensives and counteroffensives and the use of innovative tactics and new weapons, from poison gas to the tank, were attempts to bring back a war of movement.

Von Seeckt came to the attention of his superiors after his unit was attacked in early January 1915 by French forces in the area of Soissons. He devised a successful counterattack that yielded thousands of prisoners and dozens of guns. This success was achieved, according to Meier-Welcker, "because of skillful leadership and the excellent use of combined arms, and thus became the model for limited attacks in trench warfare."[8]

Von Seeckt was promoted to colonel in March 1915 and soon received a new assignment as chief of staff of the newly formed Eleventh Army. It was initially formed to conduct offensive operations on the western front, and von Seeckt was charged with examining a suitable attack location. Things turned out differently, however. That army, now commanded by Gen. August von Mackensen, deployed to the east to relieve the hard-pressed Austro-Hungarian armies on the Carpathian front.[9] The Russian army spilling into the Hungarian plain was a dreadful prospect that might encourage Italy and Romania to enter the war on the Allied side. This change in mission exemplified several fundamental dilemmas that haunted German military leaders. To what extent was Germany able to support its weaker allies? Where should a decision be sought? In the West or in the East? Where should increasingly scarce resources be sent, not only to sustain Germany's own war effort but also to bolster resource-deficient allies who were always clamoring for assistance of all kinds? Last but not least was the question of who should be in overall command on the eastern front and in the Balkans. Even among the armies of one front, there was often an intense competition for replacements and materiel.[10]

The Germans chose the Gorlice-Tarnow area for unhinging the Russian front. The attack began on 2 May 1915. Chief of the Great General Staff Erich von Falkenhayn chose the site, assumed general command, and issued the initial operations orders, which von Seeckt fine-tuned. He wrote to his wife on the morning of the attack: "I look forward with confidence to the outcome. First prepare everything, then give the commanders on the front freedom of action, then draw the consequences of their actions and initiate something new. In a few words, that is my task."[11]

Years later von Seeckt would amplify his thoughts regarding the role and function of the chief of staff, especially the relationship between the commander in chief and his chief of staff. He opined that despite his many experiences in the war, he found it difficult to delineate clearly that position. "The chief is, according to our present view, the adviser and assistant to the commander in chief, who fully and responsibly participates in all matters."[12]

Von Seeckt saw the crucial element in the answer to the questions: Who commands? Who can command? Who may command? He then proceeded to answer his questions: Only one person can give orders. And that is the commander in chief. It followed that the relations between the two authorities are of utmost importance. In the "union" between the two lies the sureness of command. The commander in chief gives orders through the chief of staff. Even more senior officers must bow without resisting. Both officers must have complete trust in one another's capabilities, judgment, military knowledge, and thinking. Differences must be resolved.[13]

The success at Gorlice-Tarnow and continuing successes prompted intense debates during and after the war whether or not the opportunity to defeat Russia decisively and knock it out of the war in 1915 had perhaps been lost.[14] Nonetheless, the attack by the Eleventh Army, supported on both flanks by Austro-Hungarian armies, was successful. "In the first twelve days we reconquered West Galicia and forced the Russians to vacate the best and largest part of Poland; we drove him [the Russians] away from the Upper Silesian border, secured Krakow as well as Hungary; destroyed one of his armies and forced two others to retreat," wrote Seeckt, who was awarded Germany's highest decoration, the Pour le Mérite.[15] Five weeks later, Seeckt was promoted to major general.

In early June the Eleventh Army was reinforced by units from the western front, and the Second and Fourth Austro-Hungarian armies were placed under Mackensen's command. "Eighteen army corps are obedient to my will," von Seeckt declared to his wife. The campaign resumed and von Seeckt proposed to defeat the Russian armies.[16] In late August, the Russians abandoned Brest-Litovsk. However, sizable elements of the Russian Army managed to slip away.

At the end of September, the fighting died down. Russia had abandoned Poland and much of the Baltic, and German troops stood on Russian soil. Tsar Nicholas assumed personal command, which would have fateful consequences. In September 1915 von Seeckt became chief of staff of Mackensen's army group command, which included Austro-Hungarian and Bulgarian units. The group's mission was to bring the Balkans under the control of the Central Powers by defeating Serbia, against which Austria-Hungary had been unsuccessful so far, and open the railroad connection to Istanbul via Belgrade and Sofia. The military situation had become more complicated when the Allies landed at Gallipoli on 25 April 1915 in an attempt to force Turkey out of the war and secure shorter supply routes to Russia. After that fiasco, the Allies sent an expeditionary force into Salonika in early October 1915.

Army Group Mackensen crossed the Danube in early October 1915 and Bulgaria declared war on Serbia on 12 October. Faced with attacks from the north and the east, the Serbian Army ascaped westward. Appalling conditions prevailed everywhere. Von Seeckt commented that he was more "diplomat and commercial agent" than soldier in daily attempts to steer between local rival factions and securing supplies.[17] The pursuit of the Serbs continued to the Adriatic Sea. The remnants of the Serb army were taken to Corfu and eventually joined the Allies at Salonika. Von Seeckt was awarded the Oak Leaves to the Pour le Mérite. He considered the campaign against Serbia strenuous but a success.

What was to be done next? Von Seeckt favored attacking to expel the Allies from Salonika. That in turn was supposed to preserve the neutrality of Greece and Romania in the face of the Allies' designs to liberate Serbia and entice Greece and Romania into the war on their side. But the Battle of Verdun consumed most manpower reserves in the West. The Eleventh Army and its Bulgarian allies, therefore, assumed a defensive position on the Greek border.[18]

The collapse of the Austro-Hungarian Fourth Army at the beginning of Russia's Brusilov Offensive in early June 1916 brought a change in von Seeckt's post as well. While German and other reinforcements arrived, von Seeckt was made chief of staff of the Austro-Hungarian Seventh Army, commanded by Gen. Karl Baron von Pflanzer-Baltin. He and von Seeckt did not get along.[19]

Field Marshal von Mackensen, who remained in the Balkans to keep an eye on Romania and Greece, reflected very positively on von Seeckt's tenure as his chief of staff: "highly skilled militarily," "penetrating intellect," "clear, concise and determined in judgment," "fully knowledgeable in all aspects of general staff duties and army command." Mackensen regretted that von Seeckt was not given his own command and that he later was sent to Turkey, instead of becoming the successor to Gen. Franz Conrad von Hötzendorf, who was dismissed as Austro-Hungarian chief of General Staff. Mackensen believed that von Seeckt reflected perfectly Count Schlieffen's dictum regarding general staff officers: "accomplish much without standing out."[20]

Having left behind familiar surroundings and fellow officers, von Seeckt found his position tenuous from the start. There were conflicts of personality, differences in military styles and methods, and the obvious difficulties of having as chief of staff of Austro-Hungarian units a Prussian officer who also reported directly to the German High Command. When the military situation did not improve, Pflanzer-Baltin was relieved of his command. Von Seeckt was transferred to the newly formed Austro-Hungarian Army Group under the command of Archduke Karl, whose chief of staff he became on 1 July 1916. He remained in that post until December 1917, first under Archduke Karl and later under his brother, Archduke Joseph, when Karl succeeded to the thrones of the Dual Monarchy. The Russians continued to attack on that front, but the tide finally turned after substantial German and Austro-Hungarian reinforcements arrived.

In the meantime, Romania entered the war against the Central Powers. Army Group Mackensen, joined by the Ninth Army under General Falken-hayn and Army Group Archduke Karl, began the campaign against Romania, while keeping the Russian army at bay. Similar tensions that characterized von Seeckt's relationship with Pflanzer-Baltin also emerged between him and Austro-Hungarian officers and political camps. Although he was ready for reassignment after Karl became emperor, von Seeckt remained at his post.

Reflecting on the year 1916, von Seeckt wrote that it was a year of events without "stars, crosses, and dispatches."[21] The campaign against Romania was a success. Its army was driven out of Romania, whose resources were now available to the Central Powers. However, half the Romanian army survived and would fight again.

The Russian Revolution of March 1917 changed the nature of warfare and politics in the East. Von Seeckt spent much of 1917 recuperating from a broken leg, dealing with political questions, training troops, and studying supply and armaments issues. The calm was interrupted by a Russian offensive in July 1917. Achieving some initial successes against the Austro-Hungarian armies, German reinforcements and Russian weaknesses soon led to a stabilization of the southeastern front. Indeed, the Russian army began to dissolve. The Bolshevik coup d'état in November created yet again a period of new opportunities for the Central Powers, but also created political and economic differences among them in regard to who was going to get what in East Europe.

On 18 November 1917 Gen. Erich Ludendorff, first quartermaster general of the German High Command, inquired whether or not von Seeckt would consider accepting the position of chief of staff of the Turkish army. Von Seeckt accepted.[22] What did these Austrian commanders think of von Seeckt? Like his brother Karl before him, Archduke Joseph thought very highly of von Seeckt, with whom he developed a cordial and consensual team relationship: "I cannot imagine having a better chief of general staff," he noted. Archduke Joseph also believed that von Seeckt was superior to Ludendorff in military talent.[23]

Von Seeckt's first task upon arriving in Turkey was to acquaint himself personally with the conditions of the various fronts and armies. Other German officers were much in evidence. General Otto Liman von Sanders, who had conducted the defense at Gallipoli, headed the German military mission and now commanded the Fifth Army in Anatolia. Falkenhayn commanded in Palestine and Mesopotamia. Colonel Friedrich Kress von Kressenstein commanded the Seventh Army between Jaffa and the Dead Sea. Von Seeckt did not get along with them. Von Seeckt's first major recommendation was that defensive operations were preferable to offensive ones and that supplies of all kinds had to be delivered to the armies.[24]

Much of von Seeckt's time was absorbed by inter-Turkish political squabbles, and the issues raised in the negotiations that led to the Treaty of Brest-Litovsk with Bolshevik Russia. German annexationist ambitions also began to clash with those of the Ottoman empire, and von Seeckt was called upon to keep the Turks away from German interests.[25] Von Seeckt characterized his ambiguous position: "and [I] mediate, telegraph, speak, write and calculate in Turkish service and in Germany's interest." He was busier with politics than with war, he wrote, deploring his fate of having to attend meetings of the Turkish council of ministers and having to negotiate with representatives of the various Caucasus peoples over conditions of peace.[26]

The end came swifter than expected. The Central Powers no longer were able to cope with the demands of war after the Allied and Associated Powers resumed the offensive on practically all fronts, now reinforced by the U.S. Army. Bulgaria collapsed in September 1918 and concluded an armistice on 30 September. British and Arab forces assumed the offensive in September and decimated the opposing Turkish forces. A new sultan, Mohammed VI, dismissed the Germanophile Enver Pasha and Talaat Pasha and concluded an armistice with the Allies on Mudros on 30 October. A few days later, on 3 November, Austria-Hungary signed the armistice.

Von Seeckt's main task now consisted in extracting many troops and officers and returning them to Germany. Von Seeckt arrived in Berlin on 13 November 1918, after the armistice of 11 November and the abdication of Kaiser Wilhelm II. Meier-Welcker wrote that while von Seeckt was traveling back to Germany he had hoped to get a command on the western front.[27]

Reflecting on Germany's defeat in the Great War, von Seeckt remarked that Germany overestimated its own strengths; these strengths were insufficient to force a military decision while simultaneously supporting the other fronts and conducting expansionary politics. He also mentioned the failure of the military leadership in 1914 to adhere to the Schlieffen Plan. The failure of that modified plan led to the efforts to knock Russia out of the war. Despite a string of victories in the East, however, German power was insufficient to succeed. Increasingly, Germany lacked the means to bring about a strategy of deciding the war. Von Seeckt also was critical of the Army High Command under Hindenburg and Ludendorff, whose leadership he labeled "mindless" and lacking strategic thought.[28]

From the military point of view, von Seeckt concluded that the war was more a war by general staffs rather than a war by generals. Superiority in men and materiel, not the conduct of battles, had been decisive.[29]

Notes

1. James S. Corum, *The Roots of Blitzkrieg: Hans von Seeckt and German Military Reform* (Lawrence: University Press of Kansas, 1992), xiii. A very useful introduction to practically all major subjects relating to World War I, with cross-references and bibliographies, can be found in Spencer T. Tucker, ed., *The European Powers in the First World War: An Encyclopedia* (New York: Garland, 1996). The Von Seeckt Papers are available in the U.S. National Archives; the *Nachlass Seeckt* and other pertinent documents are also in the German military archives in Freiburg and Potsdam.
2. Great Britain, Foreign Office, *The Treaty of Peace between the Allied and Associated Powers and Germany* (London: HMSO, 1925).
3. Hans von Seeckt, *Gedanken eines Soldaten* (Berlin: Verlag fur Kulturpolitik, 1929). See especially the chapter "Modern Armies." Yet, in a sensationalized article in *Die Zeit* (7 March 1997), which was based on a recently discovered secret *Reichswehr* document, it was announced that Seeckt had commissioned in 1925 a table of organization and equipment study by *Truppenamt* officers, which examined the feasibility of establishing an army of 102 divisions with 2.8–3 million men. We know, of course, that these early efforts to circumvent the Treaty of Versailles and re-create a powerful armed force had not come to fruition. Until the beginnings of the 1930s "the scope and military importance of the various illegal measures remained relatively small in terms of the personnel and equipment involved." Research Institute for Military History, Freiburg im Breisgau, *Germany and the Second World War: The Buildup of German Aggression* (vol. 1 of a projected ten-volume study), ed. W. Deist, M. Messerschmidt, H.-E. Volkmann, W. Wette, trans. P. Pella, D. McMurray, and E. Osers (Oxford: Clarendon Press, 1990), 376. An excellent and still current account of Germany's military development during the Weimar Republic is F. L. Carsten, *The Reichswehr and Politics, 1918–1933* (Berkeley: University of California Press, 1973). Carsten has many illuminating observations of Seeckt's *Reichswehr* leadership. See especially 103ff., "Seeckt's Personality."
4. Hans Meier-Welcker, *Seeckt* (Frankfurt: Bernard und Graefe Verlag, 1967), 20.
5. Ibid., 24.

6. See chronology above.

7. Meier-Welcker, *Seeckt*, 41.

8. Ibid., 44. General Wilhelm Groener remarked that the success at Soissons was possible largely through Seeckt's "deft dispositions." He added: "From here started Seeckt's reputation." Wilhelm Groener, *Lebenserinnerungen: Jugend, Generalstab, Weltkrieg*, ed. Friedrich Freiherr Hiller von Gaertringen (Göttingen: Vandenhoeck and Ruprecht, 1957), 216.

9. The divisions of this army were formed by downsizing western front divisions.

10. Major-General Max Hoffmann, Chief of Staff at Headquarters, High Command East, wrote in his diaries several times that the Austro-Hungarian armies' needs cut into his own meager reserves. "Seeckt sent up a wail for help" in August 1916 while chief of staff under Archduke Karl. In September Hoffmann "had a pathetic appeal from him [Seeckt] early in the morning." See also Hoffmann's entry for 11 August 1917. Max Hoffmann, *Die Aufzeichnungen des Generalmajors Max Hoffmann*, 2 vols. (Berlin: Karl Friedrich Nowak, 1929), 1:141, 151, 193.

11. Meier-Welcker, *Seeckt*, 52–53. The plan originated from Austro-Hungarian Chief of General Staff Conrad von Hotzendorf.

12. Seeckt, *Gedanken eines Soldaten*, 156.

13. Ibid., passim. Seeckt may have had in mind his senior generals Liman von Sanders and Erich von Falkenhayn during his tour of duty in Turkey.

14. Hoffmann, *Die Aufzeichnungen*, 2:107ff. He stated that Falkenhayn, concerned with events on the western front, actually wanted to break off operations at several stages. Hoffmann and Ludendorff advocated the envelopment of the Russian front from the north in the direction of Kovno. Both Ludendorff and Falkenhayn fought for their own strategic plans, but the emperor decided in favor of Falkenhayn's. Groener, *Lebenserinnerungen*, 222–53. The military historian Gerhard Ritter, who described Colonel von Seeckt as an ambitious staff officer, called the breakthrough at Gorlice-Tarnow the only great military success achieved by Germany in the war, and largely because of Seeckt's meticulous planning and execution. Gerhard Ritter, *Staatskunst und Kriegshandwerk: Das Problem des Militarismus in Deutschland*, 4 vols. (Munich: R. Oldenbourg, 1954–64), 3:85.

15. Meier-Welcker, *Seeckt*, 53.

16. Ibid., 55, 56–57. General Erich von Falkenhayn, chief of the Great General Staff, commented: "Again and again there were local commanders who maintained that they had discovered a sure way of striking a more or less serious, indeed decisive blow—if only the necessary means were placed at their disposal. Now it was four, now twenty or more divisions, of course with the corresponding heavy artillery and ammunition, which were to suffice. But unfortunately the advisers usually forgot two very important facts. These escaped them because they were only perceptible from the centre and not from the periphery." Erich von Falkenhayn, *General Headquarters 1914–1916 and Its Critical Decisions* (London: Hutchinson, 1919), 99.

17. Meier-Welcker, *Seeckt*, 68. General Groener commented that everyone had been looking forward to participating in a war of movement in the Balkans and that "Seeckt would be the guarantor of victory." If success came, "Seeckt will be the man

of the future." Groener, *Lebenserinnerungen*, 253. Falkenhayn gave a lot of credit for success to Lieutenant Colonel Hentsch, Seeckt's quartermaster. Falkenhayn, *General Headquarters*, 186–87.

18. General Max von Gallwitz, who commanded the Eleventh Army, which was part of Army Group Mackensen in the Balkans, mentioned a "visit" by Seeckt's quartermaster, Lieutenant Colonel Hentsch, who complained that "Seeckt loved to make operational decisions without consulting his quartermaster in advance." Max von Gallwitz, *Meine Führertätigkeit im Weltkriege 1914/1916: Belgien, Osten, Balkan* (Berlin: Verlag E. G. Mittler, 1929), 493. This account also contains a few of Seeckt's operational orders to units (496, 504, and 506).

19. This appointment came at the insistence of Falkenhayn. Martin Kitchen, *The Silent Dictatorship: The Politics of the German High Command under Hindenburg and Ludendorff, 1916–1918* (New York: Holmes and Meier, 1976), 29. Seeckt's appointment was controversial because of the ongoing issue of overall command of the Eastern and Balkan fronts.

20. August von Mackensen, *Briefe und Aufzeichnungen des Generalfeldmarschalls aus Krieg und Frieden*, ed. Wolfgang Foerster (Leipzig: Bibliographisches Institut, 1938), 138.

21. Meier-Welcker, *Seeckt*, 110.

22. Ibid., 127. Ludendorff's judgment of Seeckt is contained in his memoirs: "Thanks to his keen intellect and clear judgment this officer became one of the most prominent in the war." Erich Ludendorff, *My War Memories*, 2 vols. (London: Hutchinson, 1919), 1:140–41. Ludendorff also mentioned that the breakthrough of May 1915 was "brilliantly carried out by the troops." Ibid., 145.

23. Ibid., 133. Seeckt's opinion of Ludendorff was that he had no personal relations with him, but he recognized his unflagging energy and his organizational talent. "Without him we would not have been able to carry on the war so long." Ibid., 165. After Ludendorff was dismissed from his post, his suggested replacements included Seeckt, who, however, was not acceptable to Ludendorff, despite several people who suggested his name.

24. Meier-Welcker, *Seeckt*, 140.

25. Kitchen, *Silent Dictatorship*, 239. See also Fritz Fischer, *Griff nach der Weltmacht: die Kriegszielpolitik des kaiserlichen Deutschland, 1914–1918* (Düsseldorf: Droste Verlag, 1964), 742, 744; for a map delineating German war aims, the "New Order" in the East, see 716. According to Fischer, Seeckt had proposed in 1915 the establishment of German satellite states from the Atlantic to Persia (862).

26. Meier-Welcker, *Seeckt*, 140, 146, 148.

27. Ibid., 175.

28. Ibid., 190, 192–93.

29. Ibid., 194–95.

CHRONOLOGY OF HERMANN VON KUHL

2 Nov 1856	Born in Koblenz.
Aug 1878	Received doctorate from the University of Tübingen.
1 Oct 1878	Appointed Fahnenjunker in the 33rd Infantry Regiment.
13 May 1879	Promoted to Fähnrich.
12 Aug 1879	Promoted to second lieutenant.
1 Apr 1886	Assigned as adjutant of the Wesel Area Command.
16 Feb 1889	Promoted to first lieutenant.
1 Oct 1889– 21 Jul 1892	Attended the Kriegsakademie.
25 Mar 1893	Seconded to Great General Staff, Berlin.
14 Sep 1893	Promoted to captain and assigned as company commander, 3rd Grenadier Regiment.
10 Sep 1897	Assigned to the Third Department, Great General Staff.
1 Oct 1898	Assigned as military history instructor, Kriegsakademie.
13 Sep 1899	Promoted to major.
24 Sep 1899	Married Helene Richter.
1 Oct 1905	Assigned as military history instructor, Kriegsakademie.
10 Apr 1906	Promoted to lieutenant colonel and assigned as Department Chief, Third Department, Great General Staff.
24 Mar 1909	Promoted to colonel.
4 Jun 1912	Promoted to major general.
3 Jun 1913	Assigned as commander, 5th Infantry Brigade (Münster).
16 Jun 1913	Ennobled by Kaiser Wilhelm II.
1 Jan 1914	Assigned as Oberquartiermeister in the Great General Staff.
1 Aug 1914	Assigned as chief of the General Staff, First Army.
18 Jun 1915	Promoted to lieutenant general.
22 Sep 1915	Assigned as chief of the General Staff, Twelfth Army.
24 Nov 1915	Assigned as chief of the General Staff, Sixth Army.
28 Aug 1916	Awarded the Pour le Mérite and assigned as chief of the General Staff of Army Group Crown Prince Rupprecht.
20 Dec 1916	Awarded the Oak Leaves to the Pour le Mérite.
12 Apr 1917	Given the position of Kommandierender General.

12 Jan 1919	Retired from the German army.
10 Sep 1919	Promoted to general of infantry on the retired list.
6 Dec 1924	Awarded Pour le Mérite für Wissenschaft und Künst.
4 Nov 1958	Died (102 years old).

Hermann von Kuhl

Robert T. Foley

During the height of the first stage of the Battle of the Somme in July 1916, the intelligence section of the staff of the British Second Army compiled profiles of the commanders of the German formations that they faced. One of the most important of these during this bloody but inconclusive battle was the German Sixth Army, commanded by Col. Gen. Rupprecht von Bayern, the crown prince of Bavaria. The Second Army's intelligence report duly provides information about Rupprecht, whom they assumed to be the guiding force behind the army's actions. Among other things, it noted that the crown prince was "a keen sportsman, being very fond of chamois shooting." However, when it came time to profile the chief of the General Staff of this army, the true brains behind the command, the report notes only: "Not known."[1] In fact, Rupprecht's chief of staff in 1916 was one of the keenest students of Alfred von Schlieffen and one of the most experienced General Staff officers in the German army, then Lt. Gen. Hermann von Kuhl.

Unlike many of his contemporaries, von Kuhl did not come from a military background and only decided late to make the military his career. He was born in Koblenz on 2 November 1856. His father, Dr. Mattias Kuhl, was a professor of philosophy at, and later rector of, the Jülich Progymnasium, and it seemed initially as if the younger Kuhl would follow in his footsteps. He studied philosophy, Latin, Greek, and German at the universities of Leipzig, Tübingen, Berlin, and Marburg, finally gaining his doctorate, magna cum laude, from the University of Tübingen at the age of twenty-two in 1878. Having fulfilled his father's wishes regarding education, von Kuhl now fulfilled his own "inner wish" to become a soldier by entering Infantry Regiment Nr. 53 in Jülich as a "one-year volunteer."[2]

As a highly educated and motivated volunteer, von Kuhl was undoubtedly a prime recruit for his regiment. Initially, however, the young academic was not to find promotion and advancement easy in the Prussian army. After completing his training as a one-year volunteer, he was promoted by his regiment to second lieutenant in August 1879.[3] Despite being made use of as adjutant of the regional command above his regiment, von Kuhl was not given the opportunity to take the entrance examination to the Kriegsakademie until 1889, which he duly passed. Upon completion of this important school, von Kuhl gained a glowing recommendation from his instructors. He was judged to be "clear and sensible in decision making, firm and determined in implementation, with a good eye for terrain. Hard-working and reliable, he is recommended for assignment to the General Staff."[4]

Once again, von Kuhl would find the going more difficult than he thought after passing out of Kriegsakademie. After the normal six-month secondment to the Great General Staff in Berlin, the now thirty-seven-year-old captain was transferred to the command of a company in the Grenadier Regiment Nr. 3 in Königsberg. There, his career languished for three and a half long years. Finally, in the autumn of 1897, von Kuhl got the call for which he had long been waiting—he was assigned to the Third Department of the Great General Staff. His hard work had paid off. From that point, his career took off, and he would, with the exception of a single six-month period, spend the next twenty-two years serving at the heart of the Imperial German military establishment as a General Staff officer.

Von Kuhl entered an institution dominated by the presence of its head— Alfred Graf von Schlieffen. Having become chief of the Great General Staff just before the signing of the Franco-Russian Military Convention in 1892, Schlieffen was driven by the need to find a way out of Germany's strategic dilemma—a two-front war against numerically superior enemies. He made it his mission to prepare his staff, the future leaders of the German army, for a war in which their forces would be outnumbered and to construct a plan that would give Germany the best chance of success in such a war. Ultimately, this process resulted in what has become known as the "Schlieffen Plan." This plan called for the bulk of the German army to be deployed in the west against France during any future war. The heavily fortified Franco-German border would be bypassed by a powerful German right wing advancing through Holland, Belgium, and Luxemburg. This powerful wing was to annihilate the French army and deliver a decisive victory against France before Russia could mobilize fully. The victorious German forces could then be transported to the east to finish off the Russian army. Schlieffen hoped that this plan would provide Germany with the rapid victory he believed she needed in any future war.[5]

As a member and later chief of the Third Department, the section responsible for monitoring France, Great Britain, and the Low Countries, von Kuhl played a key role in the formation of Schlieffen's war plans. Around the time von Kuhl entered the General Staff, Schlieffen began developing his plan, and the intelligence supplied by the Third Department was crucial to the plan's success. This section provided crucial information on the order of battle of the western armies, their armaments, their fortress construction, and important for Schlieffen, information about their wartime deployments. Based upon this information, Schlieffen took his first tentative steps toward violating the neutrality of the Low Countries in 1899 and brought his plan to completion on the eve of his retirement in 1905.[6]

Another key area of Schlieffen's process, both for developing the German war plans and for training his staff for the difficult war to come, was wargaming. Throughout the year, the chief of the General Staff would set his subordinates tactical and strategic problems. Additionally, several times a year he would take a number into the field to conduct staff rides, and once a year a great two-front war game would be played out in the General Staff building in Berlin. These war games helped Schlieffen work out different ideas that he would then incorporate into his war plans. These war games also were an important means of transmitting Schlieffen's ideas about the conduct of war. Central to Schlieffen's plan was the necessity for a rapid and decisive victory. He therefore used his war games as a means of inculcating his subordinates with the imperative to annihilate whatever enemy they were facing.[7]

Unsurprisingly, Schlieffen took these games very seriously, but his zeal was not always appreciated by his subordinates. Von Kuhl later wrote of his experience:

> Many long years ago, the bell to my flat rang on Christmas Eve. A special messenger brought me [Schlieffen's] Christmas gift—a scenario, drawn up by him, of a large-scale war along with the task of drawing up a plan of operations. It would have been absolutely astounding if the final solution had not been in his hands by the evening on Christmas Day. On Boxing Day, there arrived the continuation of the problem, again composed by Schlieffen, with additional tasks. In [Schlieffen's] opinion, Sundays and

holidays were ideal for bigger tasks, as one required quiet, continuous work, undisturbed by the routine of everyday life.[8]

Despite not always appreciating Schlieffen's zeal, the young von Kuhl was nonetheless heavily influenced by his superior, and after Schlieffen's retirement in 1906 von Kuhl continued to visit Schlieffen and seek his advice. Schlieffen reciprocated von Kuhl's attention, believing him to be a "great captain of the future."[9]

Working well with the often-difficult Schlieffen, von Kuhl's career flourished in the General Staff. In 1899 he was promoted to major. In addition to his duties in the Third Department, in 1899 and again in 1905, he served as a military history instructor in the Kriegsakademie.[10] After Schlieffen's retirement, von Kuhl was named as chief of the Third Department and steadily made his way through the ranks. At major general, however, von Kuhl stalled briefly. In order to be promoted to lieutenant general von Kuhl needed command experience, to serve "at the front," as it was called at the time. Having commanded nothing since his company in 1897, he was stuck. Schlieffen's successor, Helmuth von Moltke the Younger, stepped in to aid his subordinate. Moltke appealed to the chief of the kaiser's Military Cabinet to have von Kuhl transferred to command the 5th Infantry Brigade in Münster, while its commander was on leave. Thus, from June to September 1913, von Kuhl spent his only period out of the General Staff since 1897 and gained the experience necessary for further promotion.[11]

Since von Kuhl had spent most of his career in the General Staff in the Third Department and worked closely with Schlieffen on his plan, Moltke maintained that von Kuhl was the "best man to serve as Chief of the General Staff of an army that he could recommend."[12] Therefore, it was only fitting that on the outbreak of World War I von Kuhl should be named chief of the General Staff of Colonel General Alexander von Kluck's First Army. To this five-corps-strong army fell the important role of being the outermost formation of the powerful right wing demanded by the Schlieffen Plan. Together with the Second Army, it was to bring about the decisive battle with the French army. Von Kuhl was to be, then, at the heart of the action against the Entente, and from this position he would play a key role in the initial stages of the war.

Von Kuhl and Kluck first met shortly after mobilization was declared in early August 1914. The contrast between the two men is reminiscent of that between Gneisenau and Blücher. While von Kuhl had spend most of his career in the General Staff, Kluck had spent his entire forty-nine-year career with the troops, progressing steadily from command to command until being named army inspector in January 1914.[13] With a great deal of command experience, including combat experience in the Wars of Unification, Kluck brought a steadiness and a command presence to this important army. His chief of staff, on the other hand, brought a deep knowledge of the French army and long experience of planning complex operations. In this team, then, Kluck was to provide the instinct and von Kuhl the intellect for the First Army.[14]

The campaign got off to a good start for the First Army. The army's staff successfully managed to squeeze their 320,000 men through a six-mile strip of land between Liège and the Dutch border.[15] Once they deployed, the First Army immediately began its advance against France on 18 August. On 23 August they met the British Expeditionary Force (BEF) at Mons and forced their retreat. At Le Cateau two days later, the First Army again engaged the British, who once again were forced to retreat after suffering high casualties. Reports from the western armies were so good that Moltke believed the end was in sight in the west and he began ordering the transfer of troops to the east.[16]

While the First Army was meeting with success, however, its neighboring Second Army was beginning to run into difficulties. On 29 August it had been dealt a tactical blow by the French Fifth Army at the battle of Guise and had called upon the First Army for assistance. After successfully fending off this counterattack, the Second Army began to pursue the beaten French forces to the south. Short of intelligence, it appeared to the First Army as if the main French forces were being pursued by the Second Army, and Kluck and von Kuhl made the difficult decision to abandon their current march direction, which would have taken them around Paris to the north, in favor of a southern march. They hoped thereby to fall upon the French and force the decisive battle demanded by Schlieffen's plan.[17] However, this change of direction would expose their right flank to Paris during their southward march, and there, unknown to the First Army, the French were assembling a new army. The stage was set for what von Kuhl and many other observers would later term the "turning point of the war"—the Battle of the Marne.[18]

After the failure of the French offensive into Alsace and Lorraine, the French commander, Joseph Joffre, belatedly recognized the danger posed by the powerful German right wing. He ordered the creation of a new army in Paris and another behind the French Fifth Army composed of units stripped from his right wing. On 5 September, the French launched a general counterattack along their entire line. The new French Sixth Army advanced from Paris into the right flank of the German First Army, which had by this point crossed the Marne River and advanced far south of the slower-moving Second Army.[19] Convinced, however, that this attack was being carried out by weak forces, Kluck and von Kuhl initially did nothing, focused as they were on what they believed would be the decisive battle to the south.

The First Army had been advancing under the assumption that the German armies along the entire western front had been victorious and that they were engaged in a flanking movement that would seal the fate of the French army. Although their cavalry reported enemy forces on their right flank, Kluck and von Kuhl assumed them to be weak. They were totally unaware of the build-up of French forces in Paris or of the setbacks of the other German armies. Thus, when Lt. Col. Richard Hentsch arrived from the Oberste Heeresleitung (OHL) on the evening of 5 September to report that across the rest of the front the German armies were facing setbacks, Kluck and von Kuhl were shocked. The aggressive Kluck immediately ordered the other corps of his army to turn to the east to join the IV Reserve Corps and the III Army Corps in their battle against the French Sixth Army.[20] While this stopped the French Sixth Army's advance in its tracks, the movement had the unfortunate effect of widening the gap between the First Army and the slower Second Army.

While the First Army wheeled to fight with the French Sixth Army, the BEF and the French Fifth Army drove into the twenty-mile gap that had grown between the First and Second Armies. On the night of 8 September OHL again sent Hentsch to the embattled armies of the German right wing. Hentsch first visited Bülow's Second Army. There, he found a command badly shaken by the Entente flanking attacks.[21] Bülow and his chief of staff, Lauenstein, concluded that a retreat was necessary in order to avoid a disaster, and Hentsch, infected by the Second Army's pessimism, could only agree.[22]

On 9 September Hentsch proceeded to the First Army headquarters to confer with Kluck and von Kuhl. There, he found a very different atmosphere. The First Army had been successful in repulsing the attacks of the French Sixth Army and was in the process of beginning a counterattack. Von Kuhl met with Hentsch without Kluck being present, a fact that shows how plans were made within the First Army. The meeting was a stormy one. Hentsch outlined the poor situation facing the Second Army and insisted that a retreat was necessary to avoid the defeat of the First Army. Von Kuhl objected strenuously, arguing that the enemy on the First Army's right flank was all but beaten and that a decisive victory was within their grasp. Hentsch, however, would not be moved. Von Kuhl recorded the moment of decision in a memorandum written the following day: "He [Hentsch] explained . . . there was nothing left but to retreat. . . . He stressed that this directive was official . . . he had full *Vollmacht*."[23] Faced with such a situation, von Kuhl could do nothing but report to Kluck with Hentsch's directive, and Kluck in turn ordered the First Army to retreat.[24]

The Battle of the Marne did indeed turn out to be a pivotal battle, but not in the way von Kuhl had hoped. It marked the abandonment of Schlieffen's ideas and of Germany's prewar plan of outflanking the French army and defeating them rapidly in a great, decisive battle. As such, it went against von Kuhl's every grain to agree to Hentsch's directive. A student of Schlieffen and a coauthor of the prewar plan, von Kuhl was convinced of the need to maintain focus on the goal of annihilating the French army in the field by means of a flanking maneuver. On 9 September 1914 von Kuhl was convinced that the prewar plan could still be carried out. He wrote after the war:

> In difficult, back-and-forth fighting during the days between 6 and 8 September, the situation of the First Army became all the better. Only on the morning of the 9th had all the elements of the army arrived on the battlefield. On the decisive northern wing, General von Kluck possessed considerable superiority. The enemy there, completely outflanked, was beaten and withdrew in the direction of Paris. Around mid-day *a complete victory* beckoned, and in the distance, our troops saw the Eiffel Tower rising above Paris. Then, the order to break off the battle and retreat arrived in the afternoon. . . . The hour of Germany's fate had rung.[25]

On a certain level, von Kuhl would never recover from the defeat at the Battle of the Marne. His prewar career had been intertwined with the plan to defeat France rapidly in mobile warfare, and the position warfare that developed after the Marne brought other, younger officers to the fore. Yet, the German army could not do without his experience, and von Kuhl, unlike his superior in the General Staff, Helmuth von Moltke, found other employment after the defeat at the Marne. After a brief stint on the eastern front, he was again called back to France in November 1915, this time to serve as the chief of staff to the Bavarian Crown Prince Rupprecht, who commanded the Sixth Army and later the Army Group Crown Prince Rupprecht.[26]

In contrast to Kluck, Rupprecht received his command at the outbreak of war for political reasons rather than military ability. Rupprecht was not a career soldier, but, as Bavaria was the second-largest kingdom in the German empire, politics and tradition demanded he be placed as an army commander, just as the German Crown Prince Wilhelm received the Fifth Army. Erich Ludendorff described him as "a soldier from a sense of duty" and believed that "his inclinations were not the least bit military."[27] Erich von Falkenhayn believed he was a difficult commander with whom to deal and informed von Kuhl on the eve of his taking up his position as chief of staff: "The Crown Prince of Bavaria is somewhat difficult, particular. One minute he is extraordinarily optimistic, the next terribly down."[28] All this meant that von Kuhl would be the backbone of the Sixth Army, providing guidance and planning operations for his royal commander.

The western front was now very different from that of late 1914. After the Battle of the Marne, the field positions on both sides of the front had extended to the English Channel and trench warfare had set in. With this, the command relationship had also changed. Locked into near-permanent positions, armies no longer had the independence of action that they possessed in the open warfare of 1914. Their actions were dictated by the OHL, and most undertakings were carried out at a much lower level. For a General Staff officer like von Kuhl, imbued with the ideas of Bewegungskrieg (mobile warfare) and Auftragstaktik (mission orders), this was not an easy position.

Indeed, lack of resources meant that the Germans were largely on the defensive on the western front. Falkenhayn's offensive at Verdun was limited to a relatively small area of the front around the fortress. Although Falkenhayn had intended the Sixth Army to play a role in administering a coup de grâce to what he hoped would be exhausted Entente forces, the Verdun offensive did not go as Falkenhayn planned, and the support of the Sixth Army was not needed.[29] Later in 1916, von Kuhl's army suffered the Battle of the Somme, but this was a battle fought largely by subordinate units. All that von Kuhl and the Sixth Army command could do to influence the battle was provide reserves—likewise the Battle of the Third Ypres in 1917. The chance for von Kuhl to once again play an active role in Germany's bid for victory would only come after Falkenhayn's replacement as chief of the General Staff by Paul von Hindenburg and his deputy and the brains behind the team, Erich Ludendorff.

Ludendorff was a contemporary of von Kuhl's and had served in the Second Department of the Great General Staff while von Kuhl served in the Third Department. Like von Kuhl, Ludendorff had absorbed Schlieffen's lessons about the need for a decisive battlefield victory to win a war and came to command in August 1916 intending to bring the war to an end in just such a manner.[30] By late 1917, having re-equipped and retrained the German army in addition to forcing Russia out of the war, he was ready to make an attempt against the western allies. In November Ludendorff hosted a conference of the army commanders from the western front and their chiefs of staff in which various offensive options were discussed. Von Kuhl and Rupprecht, now the command team of Army Group Crown Prince Rupprecht, were skeptical of the offensive abilities of the rapidly tiring German troops on the western front.[31] Therefore, von Kuhl put forward a plan for a relatively limited attack. He wanted to attempt to break through the British line in Flanders and push toward Hazebrouck. This, he hoped, would split the British forces and place the large number of units north of the breakthrough in an untenable position and lead, perhaps, to some political end to the war.[32]

Ludendorff, however, had grander ambitions. While he agreed that the British were to be the target of the 1918 offensive, he felt that von Kuhl's plan was too limited. Instead, he wanted a bigger attack aimed at breaking through at St. Quentin, which would split the British forces from the French. He then intended to advance north and roll up the whole British line, causing the defeat of the British and the rupture of the alliance.[33] This was to be the largest German offensive since 1914—Ludendorff scraped together 192 German divisions, or around 1.3 million troops, to take part in what was supposed to be the decisive battle of the war.[34]

Once again, von Kuhl was fated to play a leading role in a pivotal battle of World War I. Although Ludendorff had thought von Kuhl's planned offensive too limited, he incorporated it into the larger attack. Von Kuhl's plan became Operation Georg, which was to be launched shortly after the main offensive further south along the junction between the British and French armies, Operation Michael. To Army Group Crown Prince Rupprecht was allotted responsibility for Operation Georg and for two-thirds of Operation Michael. Rupprecht's Seventeenth and Second Armies would launch Operations Michael I and II, while Army Group German Crown Prince's Eighteenth Army would launch Michael III.[35] This strange division of command was instituted to allow the German Crown Prince Wilhelm to take part in the final destruction of the Entente and, importantly, to divide command of the offensive amongst two headquarters, thereby giving the OHL greater control.[36] Thus, although as chief of staff to one of the two army groups carrying out the offensive von Kuhl would play an important role in the upcoming battle, he would not be the prime decisionmaker. This was left to Ludendorff.

Indeed, most of the subordinate commanders were unhappy with Ludendorff's proposed operations. As noted earlier, von Kuhl and Rupprecht had their doubts about the capabilities of the troops to conduct such a large-scale operation. Now, the two expressed their fears about the operation's objectives. Von Kuhl believed that Ludendorff's offensive lacked a clear operational level goal, that it focused too much on achieving the tactical breakthrough and not enough on where operations would proceed once this breakthrough had been achieved.[37] When Army Group Crown Prince Rupprecht questioned Ludendorff on this, he replied angrily, "I object to the word 'operation.' We will punch a hole in their line. For the rest, we will see. We did it like this in Russia!"[38] Nothing could show more clearly the role in the offensive that had been assigned to Rupprecht and von Kuhl by Ludendorff.

Despite the offensive getting off to a spectacular start, events quickly proved von Kuhl's doubts correct. Rupprecht's Seventeenth and Second Armies smashed through the British front lines on 21 March 1918, while to the south Wilhelm's Eighteenth Army did the same. Within two days, the three armies had ripped a hole fifty miles wide in the British lines and had advanced forty miles. Moreover, they had killed or wounded some 200,000 British soldiers, taking another 90,000 prisoner and capturing 1,300 guns.[39] However, here is where things began to go wrong for the Germans. While the Entente commanders were badly shaken by the German success, they did not lose their nerves. Reserves were rushed in to fill the gaps in the Entente lines and new defensive positions were hurriedly constructed. Moreover, just as von Kuhl had feared, the German armies did not have the energy to maintain the pace of combat demanded by a war of movement.[40] Although a great tactical victory had been achieved, little more than the destruction of enemy forces had been achieved.

While Ludendorff continued to launch offensives across the western front until July, the failure of Operation Michael to cause the Entente to collapse within the offensive's first few days meant that it had been a waste of Germany's precious resources. With the Americans arriving in ever-greater numbers, the Entente could make good its losses, while the already weary German army could not. Ludendorff's offensive was indeed Germany's last card, but it was trumped by the Entente. Within several months, an exhausted Germany would be forced to sue for peace and the once mighty German army would return to its garrisons in Germany and disband itself.[41]

Once more, von Kuhl had been part of a pivotal battle, but one that resulted in victory for the other side. After seeing his troops home, von Kuhl submitted his resignation from an army he could no longer recognize. However, a new career beckoned for this experienced General Staff officer. In retirement, von Kuhl continued to play an active role in the military affairs of his country.

In 1920 he published his first history of the war, *The German General Staff in Preparation and Conduct of the World War*, and its success occasioned a second edition later in the year. Building upon his experience in the General Staff, this book established von Kuhl's reputation as a commentator on the war. He was called to give evidence at the commission established by the Reichstag to examine the causes for Germany's defeat, and he later became a member of the commission that oversaw the publication of the German official history of the war. These were followed by the editorship of the *Deutsches Offizierblatt* in 1924. Perhaps the highlight of his postmilitary career, however, was receiving the Pour le Mérite für Wissenschaft und Künst, making von Kuhl the only general aside from Helmuth von Moltke the Elder to be awarded both the military and civilian classes of Prussia's highest award.[42]

Yet, despite the central role von Kuhl played in writing the history of the war in its immediate aftermath, his work, much like his work as chief of staff to Crown Prince Rupprecht, remains largely unknown to the outside world. While the works of many of his contemporaries were translated into other languages, his were not and have been largely forgotten by historians. Moreover, the central role he played in two of Germany's three attempts to find victory in the west has also been all but forgotten. Perhaps, though, von Kuhl would have seen this as proof that he was living up to Schlieffen's instructions to his General Staff officers: "[d]o much, but stand out little—be more than you appear," and perhaps he would have been proud.[43]

Notes

1. Second Army Daily Intelligence Summary, 26 July 1916, Public Record Office, War Office Files, Series 157, Nr. 103, Kew, England. My thanks to James Beach for bringing this document to my attention.
2. Hanns Möller-Witten, *Festschrift zum 100.Geburtstag des Generals der Infanterie a.D. Dr. Phil. Hermann von Kuhl* (Frankfurt: E. S. Mittler, 1956), 3–6.
3. It wasn't until 1899 that the Prussian army abolished all foreign words from its vocabulary. Thus, in 1879 Kuhl was given the French-sounding rank of "Seconde-Lieutenant" rather than the Germanic "Leutnant."
4. Möller-Witten, *Festschrift*, 7.
5. On this process and Schlieffen's ideas, see Robert T. Foley, *Alfred von Schlieffen's Military Writings* (London: Frank Cass, 2002).
6. Despite gaining some notable intelligence successes, the Third Department often got things wrong. See Robert T. Foley, "The Origins of the Schlieffen Plan," *War in History* (April 2003): 222–32.

7. Arden Bucholz, *Moltke, Schlieffen, and Prussian War Planning* (Oxford: Berg, 1991), 140ff. For the most current scholarship on the Schleiffen Plan see Hans Ehlert, Michael Epkenhans, and Gerhard P. Gross, *Der Schleiffen-Plan: Analysen und Dokumente* (Munich: Ferdinand Schöningh, 2006).

8. Hermann von Kuhl, *Der deutsche Generalstab in Vorbereitung und Durchführung des Weltkrieges*, 2nd ed. (Berlin: E. S. Mittler, 1920), 126.

9. Hugo Rochs, *Schlieffen* (Berlin: Vossische Buchhandlung Verlag, 1926), 114–15.

10. Bernhard Schwertfeger, *Die großen Erzieher des deutschen Heeres: Aus der Geschichte der Kriegsakademie* (Potsdam: Akademische Verlagsgesellschaft Athenaion, 1936), 138.

11. Möller-Witten, *Festschrift*, 17–18. Interestingly, Kuhl joined the same army corps (VII) as Erich Ludendorff had done when he was reassigned out of the General Staff in January 1913 as "punishment" for advocating the expansion of the German army. See Erich Ludendorff, *Mein militärischer Werdegang* (Munich: Ludendorffs Verlag, 1933), 162ff.

12. Quoted in Hanns Möller-Witten, "General der Infanterie v.Kuhl zum 95.Geburtstag," *Wehr-Wissenschaftliche Rundschau* (June–July 1951): 78.

13. On Kluck's career, see "Note on von Kluck's Military Career," in Alexander von Kluck, *The March on Paris and the Battle of the Marne 1914* (London: Edward Arnold, 1920), xi–xii.

14. See von Kuhl, *Der deutsche Generalstab*, 193ff.

15. Holger Herwig, *The First World War: Germany and Austria-Hungary 1914–1916* (London: Arnold, 1997), 60.

16. Hermann von Kuhl, *Der Weltkrieg 1914–1918*, 2 vols. (Berlin: Verlag Tradition Wilhelm Kolk, 1929), 1:35ff.

17. Hermann von Kuhl, *Der Marnefeldzug 1914* (Berlin: E. S. Mittler, 1921), 100ff; Kluck, *March on Paris*, 80ff.

18. Kuhl, *Der Weltkrieg*, 1:45.

19. Sewell Tyng, *The Campaign of the Marne 1914* (London: Humphrey Milford, 1935), 187ff.

20. Von Kuhl, *Marnefeldzug*, 127ff.; Kluck, *March on Paris*, 107ff.

21. Karl von Bülow, *Mein Bericht zur Marneschacht* (Berlin: August Scherl, 1919), 59ff.

22. Tyng, *Campaign of the Marne*, 274f.

23. Von Kuhl, *Marnefeldzug*, 219. *Vollmacht* was the authority to act and issue orders on the spot in the name of the High Command.

24. Given its significance, the "Hentsch Mission" has received a great deal of attention from contemporaries and historians alike. For a recent analysis, see Annika Mombauer, *Helmuth von Moltke and the Origins of the First World War* (Cambridge: Cambridge University Press, 2001), 250ff.

25. Kuhl, *Der Weltkrieg*, 1:43.

26. Möller-Witten, *Festschrift*, 29.

27. Erich Ludendorff, *Meine Kriegserinnerungen 1914–1918* (Berlin: E. S. Mittler, 1919), 16–17.

28. Hermann von Kuhl, "Kriegstagebuch," entry for 28 November 1915, Bundesarchiv/ Militärarchiv, Freiburg, W10/50652.

29. Robert T. Foley, "Attrition: Its Theory and Application in German Strategy, 1880–1916," Ph.D. diss., University of London, 1999, 181ff.

30. Franz Uhle-Wettler, *Erich Ludendorff in seiner Zeit* (Berg: Kurt Vowinckel-Verlag, 1995), 38ff.

31. Kronprinz Rupprecht von Bayern, *Mein Kriegstagebuch*, 3 vols. (Munich: Deutscher National Verlag, 1932), 2:326.

32. Von Kuhl, *Der Weltkrieg*, 2:303–4.

33. Ludendorff, *Kriegserinnerungen*, 473ff.

34. Herwig, *First World War*, 400–401; Kuhl, *Der Weltkrieg*, 2:325ff.

35. Kuhl, *Der Weltkrieg*, 2:307–8.

36. Ludendorff, *Kriegserinnerungen*, 475.

37. Kuhl, *Der Weltkrieg*, 2:309.

38. Quoted in Rupprecht, *Kriegstagebuch*, 2:372.

39. Herwig, *First World War*, 406.

40. Kuhl, *Der Weltkrieg*, 2:328ff. See also von Kuhl's evidence to the Reichstag committee on the causes of the German defeat, "Durchführung und Zusammenbruch der deutschen Offensive im Jahre 1918," in Albrecht Philipp et al., *Die Ursachen des Deutschen Zusammenbruchs im Jahre 1918*, Bd. III (Berlin: Deutsche Verlagsgesellschaft für Politik und Geschichte, 1925), 90–238.

41. Von Kuhl, *Der deutsche Generalstab*, 199ff.

42. Möller-Witten, *Festschrift*, 45ff.

43. Foley, *Alfred von Schlieffen*, xvi.

CHRONOLOGY OF KONSTANTIN SCHMIDT VON KNOBELSDORF

13 Dec 1860	Born in Frankfurt/Oder.
1870–78	Educated in the Prussian Cadet Corps.
15 Apr 1878	Assigned as lieutenant, 67th Infantry Regiment.
1881–90	Assigned as battalion adjutant, 98th Infantry Regiment.
1884–87	Attended the War Academy.
1885	Married Helene Hoppe. One son, Günter.
16 Aug 1887	Promoted to first lieutenant.
1890–1893	Posted to the Great General Staff.
29 Mar 1892	Promoted to captain.
1893–1897	Assigned as company commander, 4th Foot Guards Regiment.
20 May 1897	Assigned as Ia, 2nd Division.
1 Apr 1898	Promoted to major.
3 Jul 1899	Assigned as Ia, IX Army Corps.
18 Apr 1901	Assigned as battalion commander, 74th Infantry Regiment.
31 May 1904	Assigned as chief of staff, X Army Corps.
15 Nov 1904	Promoted to lieutenant colonel.
14 Apr 1907	Promoted to colonel.
1 Aug 1908	Assigned as commander, 4th Foot Guards Regiment.
27 Jan 1911	Assigned as chief of staff, Guards Corps.
20 Mar 1911	Promoted to major general.
16 Nov 1912	Assigned as Oberquartiermeister III, Great General Staff (deputy chief of staff, in charge of staff training, operational studies, and so on).
27 Jan 1914	Promoted to lieutenant general.
2 Aug 1914	Assigned as chief of staff, Fifth Army.
1 Aug 1915	Simultaneously assigned as chief of staff, Army Group German Crown Prince and Fifth Army.
17 Oct 1915	Awarded Pour le Mérite.
21 Aug 1916	Assigned as commanding general, X Army Corps; awarded Oak Leaves, Pour le Mérite.
18 Oct 1918	Promoted to general of infantry.
30 Sep 1919	Retired.
1 Sep 1936	Died, Gluecksburg, Schleswig-Holstein.

Konstantin Schmidt von Knobelsdorf

Ulrich Trumpener

When Germany mobilized in August 1914, nearly seven-eighths of its ground forces, distributed among seven field armies, were deployed along its western border. While two armies (the Sixth and the Seventh) were slated to conduct a flexible defense in the southern half of Lorraine and the adjacent Alsatian region, the other five armies (the First through the Fifth) would wheel into France through Belgium and Luxembourg in accordance with the Schlieffen Plan as modified by Col. Gen. Helmuth von Moltke, Schlieffen's successor as chief of the Great General Staff.[1]

In this offensive scheme, the Fifth Army was expected to form the pivot for the wheeling movement in the heavily fortified Metz-Thionville region; eventually, it would participate in the advance into France in alignment with the other four armies on its right.[2]

According to the mobilization schedule for 1914, command of the Fifth Army would be assumed by Col. Gen. Hermann von Eichhorn, one of Germany's most capable and respected senior generals. The chief of staff position would be filled by the highly talented Bavarian staff officer, Maj. Gen. Konrad Krafft von Dellmensingen.[3] Unfortunately, Eichhorn, age sixty-six, was injured in a riding accident a few months before the outbreak of the war. Even though by late July he felt well enough to lead the Fifth Army into battle, his offer was rejected and his post given instead to the German crown prince, Wilhelm of Prussia. This was a silly decision (for which both Moltke and the kaiser must take the blame), for the Kronprinz was only thirty-two years old, never had commanded more than a regiment of hussars, and barely had reached the rank of major general.[4] To guide him through the intricacies of leading an army of several hundred thousand men, Moltke, after consultation with the kaiser, chose Lt. Gen. Konstantin Schmidt von Knobelsdorf to serve as Wilhelm's chief of staff.

Von Knobelsdorf, as he is usually called, had over thirty years of experience in various staff and command positions and was considered by some of his colleagues suitable for replacing Moltke someday.[5] Moreover, during the spring and summer of 1914, he personally had supervised the Kronprinz's training at the Great General Staff in the finer points of tactics and strategy. As the kaiser reminded his son on 1 August, he must follow the advice of his chief of staff in the months ahead.[6]

Having made this awkward arrangement, Moltke at least made sure that von Knobelsdorf would have capable staff officers to assist in his thankless task. The Ia post was given to Lt. Col. Gerhard von Heymann, aged forty-eight, who previously had proved himself in various staff positions, including a stint at the Sixth Army Inspectorate under the elderly field marshal Colmar Baron von der Goltz.[7] The post of deputy chief of staff for logistics (Oberquartiermeister) was filled by Maj. Gen. Johannes Rogalla von Bieberstein, scion of an old Polish family, who likewise had distinguished himself in previous postings.[8] Both these men would remain at von Knobelsdorf's side until the spring of 1916. A third officer, Maj. Robert Matthiass, stayed even longer at Fifth Army headquarters, serving as Ib until August 1916, and then as Ia for another three months.[9]

Von Knobelsdorf also was well served by the intelligence officers assigned to the Fifth Army. The first one, Capt. Wolfgang Richter, was a seasoned spymaster from prewar years. His successor, Captain Roepell, had less experience in intelligence matters but proved his aptitude in that field very quickly.[10] The third man to take charge of the intelligence desk—from May 1915 on—was a very bright Bavarian cavalry officer, Senior Lt. Franz Baron von Gebsattel. In January 1916 he in turn recruited Heinz Guderian (of World War II fame) as his assistant. Guderian liked and respected Gebsattel (who was his junior in both age and rank), but he also found his own workload too light and his assignments quite boring.[11] Parenthetically, it should be mentioned that the Ic of the Fifth Army, Capt. Walter Witting, had a multitude of duties unrelated to intelligence—unlike the Ic officers of Hitler's Wehrmacht.[12]

During the first three weeks of August 1914, the various units assigned to the Kronprinz's army assembled in the Saar region, northern Lorraine, and Luxembourg. On the right wing was the V Army Corps from Poznania. Next to it stood the XIII Army Corps from Württemberg and the VI Reserve Corps from Silesia. Behind them, ready to be inserted into the central sector of the upcoming offensive, stood the V Reserve Corps from Prussia's Polish-speaking areas. The left wing was formed by the XVI Army Corps, whose peacetime headquarters always had been at Metz, near the French border. In addition, several Landwehr (militia) brigades, a cavalry division, and the "main reserve" of the Metz fortified region—the 33rd Reserve Division—were placed under Fifth Army control.[13] Most of these units began their advance into southern Belgium and French Lorraine on 22 August. Within the next four days, they gained ground almost everywhere, but also suffered several local setbacks.[14] On 26 August the kaiser expressed great satisfaction with the progress made by his son's army, whereupon the head of his military cabinet, Gen. Moritz Baron von Lyncker, rather tactlessly reminded his royal master that the Fifth Army's operations were directed by von Knobelsdorf and not by the Kronprinz.[15]

On that same day, the German Supreme Army Command (OHL) ordered V Army Corps to march back to Thionville, so it could entrain for redeployment to the Russian front. Shorn of one corps, Fifth Army nevertheless was expected to continue its advance toward the line Châlons sur Marne-Vitry le François and simultaneously seal off the fortified region around Verdun.[16] After fighting its way across the Meuse River north of Verdun in the last days of August, the Fifth Army resumed its advance in a generally southwestern direction. In the area north and west of Verdun, it now had an additional corps at its disposal, the VI Army Corps, which previously had belonged to the adjacent Fourth Army. Moreover, the V Army Corps, after useless marches in the rear, had meanwhile been returned to von Knobelsdorf, so that he could now operate with four corps on the west bank of the Meuse and with another two on the eastern side of the river.[17]

By 9 September the right wing of the Fifth Army had moved through the Argonne Forest, while the corps in the middle had pushed south toward the Rhine-Marne Canal. The result was an enormous bulge around the Verdun fortified region, with some of the Kronprinz's divisions on the western side of that bulge facing east toward Verdun, and others sealing it off in the north and on the right bank of the Meuse.[18]

This rather promising situation ended abruptly on 11 September. As the fiasco of the German right wing armies on the Marne became increasingly evident, Moltke and his advisers at OHL decided that the Third, Fourth, and a large part of the Fifth Army should be pulled back to more defensible positions as well. Disagreements among the top men of those three armies as to where exactly the new defense lines should be established eventually led to the abandonment of more territory than was necessary, and it appears that von Knobelsdorf was at least partly responsible for this.[19]

With the retreat to shorter lines largely completed by the middle of the month, the central and southern portions of the western front gradually froze in place. The Fifth Army, with permanent headquarters in Stenay, henceforth held a line running from an area west of the Argonne across the Meuse to the Woevre Plain, with its front marked at a right angle northeast of Verdun. For this defensive mission, the Kronprinz was left with four corps, V Army Corps holding the eastern sector and the other three deployed on the western side of the Meuse. On 25 November 1914, OHL, by now under the control of Gen. Erich von Falkenhayn, divided the German armies on the western front into three groups. Each group would be headed by a senior general, who simultaneously would retain command of his own army. (This was a German practice in the Great War that was designed to keep "costs" down, but hardly a recipe for smooth sailing.) Under this arrangement, the Kronprinz and von Knobelsdorf found themselves in charge of both their own army and three adjacent Armee-Abteilungen (in effect mini-armies), which held the somewhat "quieter" sectors between the Woevre Plain and the Swiss border.[20] Since each of the three Armee-Abteilungen was headed by a man with vastly superior experience and seniority, it must have been difficult for the Kronprinz to gain their respect.[21] Von Knobelsdorf, on the other hand, had no such difficulty, for all the chiefs of staff serving in the Armee-Abteilungen were clearly his juniors in both rank and age.[22]

In March 1915 von Knobelsdorf's workload was significantly reduced, inasmuch as the two Armee-Abteilungen not immediately adjacent to the Fifth Army were withdrawn from his operational control. Four and a half months later, on 1 August 1915, the previous arrangement was put back into effect and an official label placed on it. Henceforth, the Kronprinz and von Knobelsdorf would preside over the Fifth Army and the three Armee-Abteilungen as a veritable army group, to be known as Heeresgruppe Deutscher Kronprinz.[23]

Seven weeks later, on 25 September, OHL added the Third Army in the Champagne to the Kronprinz's army group, in order to ensure better coordination of the German defensive efforts against the French onslaught in that region. Once that crisis had been mastered, on 7 December, the Third Army was withdrawn from Stenay's operational control.[24]

While von Knobelsdorf and his princely commander had been restricted to a basically defensive stance since mid-September 1914, General von Falkenhayn and his advisers at OHL decided in late 1915 that an attack on Verdun should be launched in February 1916. Falkenhayn's motives and objectives are still a matter of controversy today. Did he want to capture this important French fortress? Did he merely intend to draw the French into a costly defensive battle "to bleed them White"? Did he expect to provoke the British into launching a premature offensive somewhere else to relieve the pressure on their ally at Verdun? These and a number of other questions cannot be answered here.[25] What is clear is that the Kronprinz and his chief of staff were consulted extensively by Falkenhayn during the relevant deliberations at OHL, and that both of them agreed with the concept of hitting the French in the Verdun region. What they and many other German officers did not like was Falkenhayn's insistence that the initial attack must be limited to the right bank of the Meuse, and that not enough German divisions were available to launch a simultaneous assault on the left bank of the river.[26]

To deliver a massive punch against the French lines on the right bank, OHL moved hundreds of heavy guns and half a dozen new divisions into the staging areas. Bad weather forced the Fifth Army to postpone the start of the offensive from 12 February to 21 February, thereby further decreasing the surprise effect everyone had hoped for.[27] When the attacks finally got under way, with Gen. Hans von Zwehl's VII Reserve Corps on the right, the Hessian divisions of Dedo von Schenck's XVIII Army Corps in the middle, and the Brandenburg III Army Corps under Ewald von Lochow on the left, good progress was made almost everywhere during the first four days. The legendary Fort Douaumont was taken on 25–26 February. But from then on, the German advance (now joined by some other divisions) became more difficult, and Zwehl's divisions in particular were hampered increasingly by flanking artillery fire from the left bank.[28] By early March it had become clear that a supporting attack would have to be staged on the western side of the Meuse as well.

Initially, the burden of that offensive would fall on the shoulders of General Konrad von Gossler's VI Reserve Corps. His own 11th and 12th Reserve Divisions began their attacks on 6 March, ably supported by the 22nd Reserve Division in the Raven Woods, and the 11th Bavarian Infantry Division in the Avocourt Forest. But here too, the German progress soon slowed down, especially around Côte 304 and the adjacent Le Mort Homme ridge.[29]

With fierce fighting now raging on both sides of the Meuse, Fifth Army headquarters on 19 March delegated the day-to-day supervision of the right bank operations to Gen. Bruno von Mudra, with Maj. Erich Kewisch serving as his chief of staff.[30] Ten days later, Gen. Max von Gallwitz (who had distinguished himself as an army commander both on the Russian front and against the Serbs) took over as head of Assault Group West on the left bank.[31]

While these arrangements certainly made sense, giving the Kronprinz and von Knobelsdorf more time to look after the needs of their army group down to the Swiss border, the situation on the battlefields around Verdun improved only marginally under the new management. With French resistance stiffening on both sides of the Meuse, and German losses mounting, additional divisions were brought in by OHL.[32]

On the left bank, the older brother of OHL's chief, General of Cavalry Eugen von Falkenhayn, took over some of the divisions in that area.[33] Simultaneously, General von Gallwitz, ably assisted by Col. Bernhard Bronsart von Schellendorff and Maj. Max Stapff, tried valiantly to keep his assault group's casualties down by more systematic preparations. Little good, however, came of these efforts.[34] On the eastern side of the Meuse, things did not look any better, and by mid-April the coordinator of that assault group, von Mudra, was replaced by General Ewald von Lochow of the Brandenburg Corps, who brought along his trusted chief of staff, Maj. Georg Wetzell.[35]

In the meantime, soul-searching had begun both at OHL and in other places about the whole Verdun operation. There is conflicting evidence on what General von Falkenhayn and his chief of operations, Maj. Gen. Gerhard Tappen, thought about the rising cost and limited progress of the offensive, nor is it entirely clear where the Kronprinz and von Knobelsdorf stood on the matter.[36] What is apparent is that von Knobelsdorf was not simply pushing for more of the same (as some critics would later claim), and that he also recognized that if the offensive were to be halted now, many German units would have to abandon their present advanced positions and return to their start lines. Could Germany afford such a demoralizing spectacle after so many lives had been lost already?

Perhaps the best picture of von Knobelsdorf's attitude in April and May is provided in General von Gallwitz's notes of that period. On 8 April von Knobelsdorf agreed with the assault group commander that further advances must be prepared carefully, and that Falkenhayn was pushing too much. Two weeks later, both von Knobelsdorf and his new Ia, Col. Friedrich Count von der Schulenburg, "showed full understanding" for Gallwitz's decision to suspend further attacks. Setbacks by Eugen von Falkenhayn's troops early in May once again led to a meeting of minds between Gallwitz and von Knobelsdorf, with the latter explaining "the difficulty of his position vis-à-vis the Kronprinz." On 11 May the two generals had another discussion on the Verdun stalemate. Gallwitz proposed that priority should be given to his side of the Meuse, but "of course Knobelsdorf" could not be swayed "that easily." On 19 May, while German troops were once again trying to seize Le Mort Homme, von Knobelsdorf personally watched the advance through a telescope and repeatedly showed his concern. At the end of the month he once again visited Gallwitz and advised him that no fresh troops could be sent to the left bank in the foreseeable future.[37]

While developments in the Verdun region during the month of May were quite unsatisfactory from the German point of view, the Prussian war minister, Adolf Wild von Hohenborn, did his best to keep Falkenhayn's spirit up. A fairly firm supporter of the Verdun offensive since its inception in December 1915, General Wild von Hohenborn repeatedly reminded the head of OHL that a complete abandonment of the operation would do more harm than good, though the scope and tempo of the offensive could certainly be reduced. If that was done, offensive thrusts in other sectors of the Westfront should be attempted, for "we must retain the initiative."[38]

After receiving some reinforcements, General von Lochow's assault group scored several successes in June, highlighted by the capture of Fort Vaux on the seventh and of Thiaumont and Fleury the twenty-third of that month. But the onset of the Brusilov Offensive on the eastern front, which tore big holes into the lines held by Austro-Hungarian troops, forced OHL to husband its resources ever more carefully. To make matters worse, the Anglo-French offensive on the Somme, which began on 1 July, put additional strain on Falkenhayn. He nevertheless agreed to one last push at Verdun on the right bank. Carried out by some newly arrived units, especially the justly renowned Alpenkorps, the assault brought the Germans as close to the town of Verdun as they ever came, but then all major operations were suspended in the entire region.[39]

Having invested so many lives and material resources in the Verdun operation, both Falkenhayn and von Knobelsdorf found it very difficult to extract themselves from the mess. Many of the positions gained during the previous five months were completely unsuitable for defensive purposes, yet to withdraw to better positions or shorter lines after so much sacrifice seemed to be inadvisable too. The debates on this topic heated up in August and eventually the Kronprinz persuaded the kaiser and Falkenhayn that his army group should get a new chief of staff. On 21 August von Knobelsdorf was decorated with the Oak Leaves to the Pour le Mérite, and simultaneously reassigned to a corps command on the eastern front.[40] His place in the Kronprinz's headquarters was filled by Lt. Gen. Walther Baron von Lüttwitz, but he lasted in the position only about three months.[41] Only seven days after von Knobelsdorf's departure, Erich von Falkenhayn himself was removed from

OHL and replaced by the team of Hindenburg and Ludendorff.[42] The French in October, using new tactics, threw the dispirited German units on the right bank out of their positions, retaking Fleury, the Ouvrage de Thiaumont, and even the ruins of Fort Douaumont. Nine days later, the Germans abandoned Fort Vaux. On 15 December, the Fifth Army, now under the command of General von Lochow, lost another mile of ground north of Fort Douaumont. Lochow was sacked two days later.[43]

Many historians, especially those who focused on the tragic events at Verdun, have tended to depict General von Knobelsdorf as a man of limited talents and flawed character. In his widely read book on the Battle of Verdun, Alistair Horne contends that the general looked like a typical Prussian sergeant, with "all its connotations of brutal, unimaginative single-mindedness," and that he was probably "swept along by ambition, seeing himself as the organizer of victory at Verdun, exalted to become the Ludendorff of the Western Front."[44] As the foregoing pages suggest, that judgment is probably too harsh; it also ignores von Knobelsdorf's accomplishments as chief of staff in 1914 and 1915. Suffice it to add that most of von Knobelsdorf's colleagues and subordinates in the General Staff corps gave him fairly high marks, both at the time of his service and after the war in their memoirs.[45] Even the Kronprinz acknowledged in his reminiscences that he owed great thanks to von Knobelsdorf "in the military sphere," and that "despite frequent personal disagreements" between them, he always had been aware of the general's great achievements.[46]

Notes

1. See Reichsarchiv, *Der Weltkrieg 1914 bis 1918*, vol. 1, *Die Operationen des Jahres 1916 bis zum Wechsel in der Obersten Heeresleitung* (Berlin: Mittler and Sohn, 1925), 3–76, and passim; Gerhard Ritter, *Staatskunst und Kriegshandwerk*, 4 vols. (Munich: 1954–68), vol. 2, chaps. 9–10; and Jehuda L. Wallach, *Das Dogma der Vernichtungsschlacht* (Frankfurt/Main: 1967), 129–50 and passim (in English as *The Dogma of the Battle of Annihilation: The Theories of Clausewitz and Schlieffen and Their Impact upon the German Conduct of Two World Wars* [Westport, Conn.: Praeger, 1986]).

2. See Reichsarchiv, *Weltkrieg*, 1:69ff.

3. See Ulrich Trumpener's entries on Eichhorn and Krafft in *The European Powers in the First World War: An Encyclopedia*, ed. Spencer C. Tucker, History of the United States (New York: Garland, 1996), 238–39, 409–10. See also BA/MA *Krafft Papers*, diary 31 July and 1 August 1914; Kronprinz Rupprecht von Bayern, *Mein Kriegstagebuch*, 3 vols. (Munich: Deutscher National Verlag, 1929), 3:32; and Wilhelm Groener,

Lebenserinnerungen: Jugend, Generalstab, Weltkrieg, ed. Friedrich Freiherr Hiller von Gaertringen (Göttingen: Vandenhoeck and Ruprecht, 1957), 140, 544.

4. Made a lieutenant at age ten, the Kronprinz was slated to command a guards division in case of war. However, in late July 1914 he and Moltke decided that he was qualified to do "more." It also appears that the German chancellor, Theobald von Bethmann Hollweg, objected to exposing the heir to the throne to the hazards of a divisional command at the front. See Kronprinz Wilhelm, *Meine Erinnerungen aus Deutschlands Heldenkampf* (Berlin: E. S. Mittler, 1923), 3–4 (in English as Wilhelm, Crown Prince of Germany, *My War Experiences* [New York: Robert M. McBride and Co., 1923]), and Klaus W. Jonas, *The Life of Crown Prince Wilhelm* (London: 1961), 92.

5. See von Knobelsdorf's chronology, and Groener, *Lebenserinnerungen,* 161. Von Knobelsdorf's father, Karl Schmidt, had been ennobled in 1852 and on that occasion added his mother's maiden name, von Knobelsdorff, to his own surname, but dropped one "*f*" in the process.

6. See Kronprinz Wilhelm, *Meine Erinnerungen,* 4. On 2 August, an experienced general staff officer, Maj. Otto von Müller, was assigned to the crown prince as a personal adjutant. Müller remained at his side throughout the war.

7. It appears that the Kronprinz thought very highly of Heymann, but von Knobelsdorf got rid of him in April 1916 after they repeatedly had disagreed on the conduct of the Verdun offensive.

8. Since ethnic Poles made up a rather large proportion of the Fifth Army's manpower, his appointment was perhaps not entirely by accident. He later commanded the 9th (Silesian) Division at Verdun.

9. Matthiass ended his wartime service as chief of staff of a corps command on the western front.

10. Richter had run agents from Saarbruecken since 1912. Roeppel had begun his intelligence service in November 1914. He later ran the covert operations of the army's intelligence service, served as senior intelligence officer of the Fourteenth Army during the Caporetto campaign, and then moved to The Hague for further covert work.

11. See Dermot Bradley, *Generaloberst Heinz Guderian und die Entstehungsgeschichte des modernen Blitzkrieges* (Osnabruck: Biblio Verlag, 1978), 92–95.

12. Witting retired from the army in 1922. In the Third Reich he became a Luftwaffe general and died in a Soviet internment camp (Buchenwald) in 1948.

13. See *Weltkrieg,* 1:133–34, 227ff.

14. See ibid., 303ff., 547ff.

15. See Walter Goerlitz, ed., *Regierte der Kaiser? Kriegstagebuecher, Aufzeichnungen, und Briefe des . . . Admiral Georg Alexander von Mueller 1914–1918* (Göttingen: Musterschmidt Verlag, 1959), 51–52.

16. See *Weltkrieg,* 3:7ff.

17. See ibid., 40–54, 73–104, 263–75.

18. See *Weltkrieg,* 4:6ff., 105ff., 300ff.

19. See ibid., chap. 9; and Oberst Max Bauer, *Der grosse Krieg in Feld und Heimat* (Tübingen: Osiander, 1921), 57–58.

20. See Hermann Cron, *Geschichte des deutschen Heeres im Weltkriege* (Berlin: Siegismund, 1937), 43–44.

21. During the first half of the war, all three Armee-Abteilungen were actually named after their commanders: Col.-Gen. Ludwig Baron von Falkenhausen (born in 1844), Gen. Hans Gaede (1852), and Gen. Hermann von Strantz (1853). The latter commanded the sector next to the Fifth Army, and several of his divisions would play an active role in the Verdun offensive in 1916.

22. All of them were at least ten years younger than von Knobelsdorf and held a rank of colonel or lower. One of them, Col. Wilhelm Wild of Armee-Abteilung Strantz, was Wilhelm Groener's best friend since their common days at the War Academy. Thus Groener, one of the key figures at OHL, was particularly well informed about developments in the Kronprinz's army group.

23. The arrangement of having command of one army and of the army group combined in one hand (and one staff) remained in effect until 25 November 1916, when the Fifth Army finally received a commander and a general staff completely separated from the army group headquarters. See Cron, *Geschichte*, 44–45.

24. Attacking with thirty-nine divisions against only seventeen on the German side, the French army would never again "find itself in a more favorable position," but in the end the hoped-for breakthrough did not materialize. See Pierre Miquel, *La Grande Guerre* (Paris: 1983), 350ff. In the midst of the crisis, the Prussian war minister reminded OHL that the Kronprinz was too young to handle his increased responsibilities, and that von Knobelsdorf should not be expected to look after a front stretching "from Reims to Basel all by himself." See BA/MA, *Wild Papers*, diary, 1 November 1915.

25. Cf. *Weltkrieg*, 10:1–41; Karl-Heinz Janssen, *Der Kanzler und der General* (Göttingen: Musterschmidt Verlag, 1967), 175ff.; Holger Afflerbach, *Falkenhayn* (Munich: Oldenbourg, 1994), 360ff., 543ff., and passim; and Gerd Krumeich, "Saigner la France?" in *Guerres mondiales et conflits contemporains*, no. 182 (April 1996): 17–29. See also BA/MA, *Tappen Papers*, "Besprechung mit dem Generalleutnant a.D. Tappen im Reichsarchiv am 6.9.1932."

26. See *Weltkrieg*, 10:56–67, 204. In the trenches, the mood seems to have been quite optimistic, though. See, e.g., Major K.A. von Laffert to Generalmajor von Unger, 13 February 1916, BA/MA, *Nachlass Fritz von Unger*, N83/2.

27. The postponements were demanded by the heavy artillery specialist at Fifth Army headquarters, Generalmajor Schabel, who reminded von Knobelsdorf that in rain and mist it was impossible to assess the effectiveness of German shelling. See *Weltkrieg*, 10:61ff. According to Guy Pedroncini, "La bataille de Verdun," *Guerres mondiales et conflits contemporains*, no. 182 (April 1996): 7–15, Joffre was well aware of Germany's intentions and preparations since the beginning of the year and reinforced Verdun's defenses accordingly. (Most older studies suggest that the French were ill prepared for the German onslaught.)

28. See *Weltkrieg*, 10:72ff.; and *Tappen Papers*, Diary, 21–27 February 1916.

29. See *Weltkrieg*, 10:203ff.

30. Mudra, ennobled in 1913, was a military engineer by training and had distinguished himself as a corps commander in the Argonne sector. Kewisch earned a Pour le Mérite

in 1918 and was recalled to active duty in the Second World War, serving as a staff officer in occupied Yugoslavia.

31. Like Mudra and many other senior commanders, Gallwitz was a commoner by birth. He was also a devout Roman Catholic and regarded by some as a potential candidate for the chancellorship of the Reich.

32. See *Weltkrieg*, 10:140–75, 223–53.

33. Retired since 1910 Eugen von Falkenhayn had been given the newly formed XXII Reserve Corps in September 1914. He retained that command until December 1918, the only three-star general in the German army to hold the same post for such a long period.

34. See Max von Gallwitz, *Erleben im Westen, 1916–1918* (Berlin: E. S. Mittler, 1932), 1ff.

35. General Ludendorff was so impressed by Wetzell's record that he made the major his own chief of operations as soon as he and Field Marshal von Hindenburg had taken charge at OHL in August 1916. Upon his retirement in 1927, General Wetzell became the editor of several military journals and spent four years in China as an advisor to the Kuomindang.

36. Cf. *Weltkrieg*, 10:260–70; Afflerbach, *Falkenhayn*, 370ff.; Groener, *Lebenserinnerungen*, 305 6, 549; and *Wild Papers*, diary, 27 March and 7 April 1916.

37. See Gallwitz, *Erleben im Westen*, 10, 19, 23–24, 31, 35, 42. Count von der Schulenburg, who had replaced Lieutenant Colonel von Heymann on 21 April (see n. 7 above), became chief of staff of the Kronprinz's army group seven months later. During the Third Reich, the count attained the rank of SS-Obergruppenführer and was even considered for the position of war minister in 1938.

38. See *Wild Papers*, diary, 5 and 8 May 1915.

39. See *Weltkrieg*, 10:176ff., 253ff.

40. Ibid., 389ff., 418ff.; Gallwitz, *Erleben in Westen*, 45, 54–55, 90.

41. After the war, Baron von Luettwitz played a major role in the events leading to the Kapp Putsch. See F. L. Carsten, *The Reichswehr and Politics, 1918–1933* (Berkeley: University of California Press, 1973), 45ff., 76ff.

42. See Ritter, *Staatskunst*, vol. 3, chap. 6; Janssen, *Der Kanzler*, chap. 24, and Afflerbach, *Falkenhayn*, chap. 23.

43. See *Weltkrieg*, 11:117–73. Also sacked were the commander of the VII Reserve Corps, Gen. Hans von Zwehl; his chief of staff, Lt. Col. Hans von Loesecke; and the commander of the Bavarian 39th Reserve Division (which had been stripped of most of its younger soldiers a few months earlier). On the low morale of many German units on the East Bank see William Hermanns, *The Holocaust: From a Survivor of Verdun* (New York: Harper and Row, 1972).

44. Alistair Horne, *The Price of Glory: Verdun 1916* (London: Macmillan, 1962), 221–22 and passim.

45. One of the exceptions was Col. Max Bauer, but then he was highly critical of just about everyone. See his *Der grosse Krieg*, 58, 66, 101, 106, and passim.

46. Kronprinz Wilhelm, *Meine Erinnerungen*, 201, 227ff.

CHRONOLOGY OF FRITZ VON LOSSBERG

30 Apr 1868	Born, Bad Homberg.
13 Jan 1886	Appointed Fahnenjunker, 2nd Foot Guard Regiment.
13 Nov 1886	Promoted to Fähnrich.
17 Aug 1887	Promoted to lieutenant.
1 Oct 1894	Entered Kriegsakademie.
17 Aug 1895	Promoted to first lieutenant.
15 Mar 1898	Candidate, Great General Staff.
29 Mar 1900	Promoted to captain.
18 Aug 1900	Assigned to XIV Army Corps, General Staff.
17 Feb 1903	Assigned as company commander, 114th Infantry Regiment.
22 Apr 1905	Assigned to 19th Division, General Staff.
27 Jan 1907	Promoted to major.
1 Oct 1907	Assigned as instructor, Kriegsakademie.
1 Oct 1910	Assigned to XVII Army Corps, General Staff.
1 Oct 1912	Assigned as battalion commander, 2nd Battalion, 94th Infantry Regiment.
16 Jun 1913	Promoted to lieutenant colonel.
1 Oct 1913	Assigned to XIII Army Corps, chief of the General Staff.
23 Jan 1915	Assigned as deputy chief, Operations Division, OHL.
24 Jul 1915	Promoted to colonel.
26 Sep 1915	Assigned to Third Army, chief of the General Staff.
2 Jul 1916	Assigned to Second Army, chief of the General Staff.
19 Jul 1916	Assigned to First Army, chief of the General Staff.
21 Sep 1916	Awarded Pour le Mérite.
11 Apr 1917	Assigned to Sixth Army, chief of the General Staff.
24 April 1917	Oak Leaves added to the Pour le Mérite.
23 Jun 1917	Assigned to Fourth Army, chief of the General Staff.
3 Aug 1917	Promoted to major general.
6 Aug 1918	Assigned to Army Group Boehn, chief of the General Staff.
31 Oct 1918	Assigned to Army Herzog Albrecht von Württemberg, chief of the General Staff.

10 Jan 1919	Assigned to Border Defense Army Corps South, chief of the General Staff.
27 Jul 1919	Assigned as commander, 26th Reichswehr Brigade.
31 Aug 1919	Assigned to General Kommando II, chief of the General Staff.
1 Aug 1920	Assigned as commander, 6th Division and Wehrkreis VI.
1 Oct 1920	Promoted to lieutenant general.
1 Jan 1925	Assigned as commander, General Kommando I.
1 Oct 1926	Promoted to general of infantry.
31 Jan 1927	Retired.
14 May 1942	Died, Lübeck.

Fritz von Lossberg

David T. Zabecki

Fritz von Lossberg was one of the most important tacticians of the twentieth century. He played an instrumental role in developing most of the principles and techniques we still associate with modern defensive tactics. As the chief of staff of five different field armies, he directed virtually all the major German defensive battles on the western front from the autumn of 1915 until the end of 1917. He became known in the German army as "der Abwehrlöwe"—the Lion of the Defensive.

Lossberg was born at Bad Homberg in 1868 to an old Thürungian military family. At the age of nineteen he joined the elite 2nd Foot Guards Regiment as an officer candidate. He was the third member of his family to serve in that regiment. His talents were recognized early. In 1894 he entered the Kriegsakademie while still a second lieutenant. Following his qualification as a General Staff officer in 1900, his career followed the usual pattern of alternating between General Staff and line assignments, including company and battalion command. From 1907 to 1910 he served as an instructor at the Kriegsakademie.

At the start of World War I, von Lossberg was the chief of staff of XIII Corps. Lossberg's unit took part in the early fighting around Ypres and then moved to the eastern front. In January 1915 von Lossberg became the deputy chief of the operations section at Oberste Heeresleitung (OHL), the German army's general headquarters in the field. The chief of the German General Staff at the time was Gen. Erich von Falkenhayn, and von Lossberg's immediate superior as chief of the operations section was Col. Gerhard Tappen. Lossberg and Tappen had known each other during peacetime service and were not on the best of terms. When von Falkenhayn moved OHL main headquarters to Pless, to be closer to the eastern front, he took Tappen with him. Lossberg and a small group of liaison officers remained at the OHL forward command post at Mézières on the western front. The Pless headquarters, however, retained the authority to move and deploy units.[1]

Falkenhayn pursued a ruthless strategy of exploiting the Allies' tactical doctrine of conducting rigid defenses with the bulk of their forces packed into the forward trenches. In those positions they became just so many targets for German firepower. Oddly enough, von Falkenhayn followed the same defensive doctrine, insisting that German commanders hold the frontline trace at all costs. There were two schools of thought among the staff officers at OHL, however. The debate revolved around where the defensive battle should actually be fought, at the front line or behind it. Many of the junior officers at OHL, including Lt. Col. Max Bauer and Capt. Hermann Geyer, favored a flexible defense fought behind the front line. Lossberg, at first, favored the rigid defense fought at the front line.[2] As one of the few officers at OHL with direct combat experience, he felt his colleagues were too prone to overestimate the capabilities of combat units and underestimate the problems of frontline combat.[3]

Lossberg believed that staff officers should have frontline combat experience. He often sent junior staff officers from OHL to the XVI Corps sector to gain combat experience. When Tappen found out about it, he ordered von Lossberg to stop the practice immediately.[4] On 5 May 1915 the entire main operations section of OHL was on a train and out of communications with the forward headquarters. On his own authority, von Lossberg issued operational orders to western front units in order to deal with an emergency situation. Technically, von Lossberg overstepped his authority by not going through the operations chief first. When Tappen found out, he restricted von Lossberg from directly communicating with western front units, even only to request information. Falkenhayn, who also knew von Lossberg well from peacetime service, later overturned Tappen's order. Lossberg later wrote in his memoirs, "Colonel Tappen and I had completely different natures. For me, pure and simple practical action was the most important thing. This has been the basis for good understanding with my superiors and my subordinates all my life."[5]

On 25 September 1915 the French launched a major offensive in Champaign. Lieutenant General Maximillian von Höhn, the chief of staff of the Third Army, immediately requested permission to pull back. On that same day, von Lossberg was with von Falkenhayn at a meeting with the kaiser at Mézières. When asked his opinion on the situation, von Lossberg was very critical of the Third Army course of action. After a private talk between von Falkenhayn and the kaiser, von Lossberg was told he was being sent to the Third Army as chief of staff. Lossberg had wanted to return to a field unit. All other army chiefs of staff at the time, however, were at least major generals. Lossberg was a new colonel with just two months time in grade.[6]

Lossberg wasted no time getting to his new assignment. En route he developed an operational plan based on holding the present positions and fighting for every inch of ground. When he arrived at Third Army headquarters the VIII Reserve Corps had just requested permission to initiate a night withdrawal previously approved by von Höhn. On his own authority, and prior to consulting with the army commander, von Lossberg canceled the move. The commander of the VIII Reserve Corps accepted the decision, even though he was a lieutenant general and the new army chief of staff was only a colonel.[7]

The commander of the Third Army, Gen. Karl von Einem, confirmed von Lossberg's order to the VIII Reserve Corps. Lossberg then asked for and received Vollmacht, the authority to issue orders and shift units without consulting first with the commander. Armed with that power, von Lossberg immediately headed for the front to assess the situation.[8]

Lossberg reached the front late on the afternoon of 25 September. The French already had taken most of the German forward line, which lay along the forward slope of a ridge. Eighteen French divisions were attacking five German, and the French had a three-to-one superiority in artillery. The Germans still held their second trench lines, which lay behind the crest of the ridge. Lossberg decided to anchor the defense on this second line along the reverse slope. From that position the Germans were masked from French artillery fire, but German artillery observers still had clear fields of observation to call fire down on the French attackers as they cleared the crest of the ridge. If the French managed to gain a foothold in the German second line, they were to be ejected with immediately launched counterattacks. Lossberg intended to hold the line at all costs, but he did not pack the leading trenches with his forces. The immediate counterattacks would maintain the integrity of the position.

In effect, von Lossberg's defensive scheme ensured that German infantry and artillery supported each other, while forcing the French infantry to fight separated from its own artillery. French artillery firing blind ran the risk of hitting their own troops.[9] By the end of that first day von Lossberg was so confident that the line would hold that he ordered the start of construction for billeting for the coming winter. The French attacks continued throughout the winter, but Lossberg's combination of reverse slope defense and immediate counterattacks held. While at the Third Army, Lossberg also revised the staff working procedures, giving all staff officers direct access to the chief of staff without having to go through the quartermaster general.[10]

Lossberg remained at the Third Army through the early summer of 1916. The Allies started telegraphing their next major offensive push in late June, when British artillery began massive shelling in the German Second Army sector, along the Somme. When the attack jumped off on 1 July, the Germans inflicted 60,000 casualties on the British. It was the bloodiest single day in British history. But the Germans took heavy losses too. On 2 July the chief of staff of the Second Army, Major General Grünert, recommended a pull-back along the line. Falkenhayn disagreed, after seeing the Second Army positions for himself.[11] At 11:30 that day, von Lossberg received a call from OHL telling him that he had just been appointed the chief of staff of the Second Army.

Lossberg arrived at Second Army headquarters at 05:00 on 3 July. Grünert was already gone and the Ia gave Lossberg the situation briefing. Within an hour of his arrival, von Lossberg met with the commander of the Second Army, Gen. Fritz von Below, who immediately gave his new chief of staff Vollmacht. Lossberg then headed for the front lines to make a personal reconnaissance. He identified a series of high points that had great tactical value as artillery observation posts. He made the control of those positions the center of gravity of his scheme of defense. Conferring at the end of the day, von Lossberg and von Below agreed that the current line could be held. They also started planning a large-scale, deliberate counterattack to retake the ground lost during the first two days of the battle. They never got the chance to execute that plan, however, because the necessary forces were drawn into the battle for Verdun, raging to the south.[12]

During the Somme campaign von Lossberg and von Below visited the front together almost every day. They normally left their headquarters about 07:30, by which time von Lossberg had been up for several hours already working on reports to OHL. Their first destination always was the point of the previous day's heaviest fighting. After talking to the commanders on the ground, they formulated the army order for the day, which they communicated to their headquarters by telephone. During this same period on the Allies' side of no-man's-land, British and French soldiers almost never saw a general officer or a General Staff officer at the front.[13]

On 19 July OHL split von Below's command into the First and Second armies. Lossberg and von Below stayed with the half that became the First Army, in which sector the heaviest fighting of the long and bitter Somme campaign continued. On 28 August von Falkenhayn was sacked as chief of the General Staff and replaced by Field Marshal Paul von Hindenburg. Transferring from the eastern front with his own chief of staff, Gen. Erich Ludendorff, Hindenburg assumed actual command of OHL, with Ludendorff assuming the position of first quartermaster general. In theory, Ludendorff was to continue functioning as the field marshal's chief of staff, but in practice Ludendorff became the de facto commander in all but name.

Almost immediately, Hindenburg and Ludendorff suspended the German attack at Verdun, put all German forces on the western front on a defensive posture, and concentrated on knocking Russia out of the war in the east. In the west Ludendorff initiated a complete review and overhaul of German tactics, both offensive and defensive. Lossberg came to play a key role in that process.

During his time on the Somme, von Lossberg determined that it took anywhere between eight and ten hours for a message to travel one way in either direction between a divisional headquarters and the front line. The tactical situation usually changed drastically in the time that it took information to flow up and the corresponding orders to flow back down. Lossberg concluded that the only way to improve tactical responsiveness was to give the frontline battalion commanders total control of their own sectors. The higher head-quarters, then, had the obligation to support the frontline commanders' decisions. The battalion commander also would have operational control of any reinforcements committed to his sector, regardless of the size of the reinforcing unit or its commander's rank. This approach ensured continuity of command and exploited the frontline battalion commander's superior knowledge of the terrain and the situation.[14]

Lossberg's innovations effectively shortened the chain of command. Under this system, the regimental commander became a manager of reinforcements and logistical support. At the next higher levels the role of the divisional commanders mirrored that of the frontline battalion commanders. The divisions controlled everything in their sectors without having to get permission from the corps. When a reinforcing division was committed, it came under the operational control of the commander of the reinforced division.[15]

As part of Ludendorff's tactical reforms the German army adopted von Lossberg's innovations and incorporated them into a new doctrinal manual, published by OHL on 1 December 1916. *Principles of Command in the Defensive Battle in Position Warfare* was written primarily by OHL staff officers Bauer and Geyer.[16] Despite his own influence over the new doctrine, von Lossberg believed that the *Principles* were far too liberal in allowing frontline units to yield ground in the face of a strong attack. He still believed that a ridged forward defense was the best defensive tactic, with the flexible defense in depth reserved for special situations only. Lossberg rebutted much of what was in *Principles* with his own analysis, *Experiences of the First Army in the Somme Battles*. Despite all the criticism that historians have leveled against Ludendorff, the first quartermaster general must be given credit for encouraging healthy professional debate over tactical doctrine in the best traditions of the German General Staff. Ludendorff had OHL reprint and widely distribute von Lossberg's pamphlet. When the British captured a copy, they translated it and distributed 2,800 copies.[17]

On 21 September 1916 von Lossberg was awarded the Pour le Mérite. The following spring OHL began to detect indicators of a large British buildup in the Arras area. The attack commenced against the Sixth Army sector on 9 April. Supposedly operating under the new principles of flexible defense, the Sixth Army committed its reserves too late, allowing the British to break into the German front on a wide sector and to capture Vimy Ridge. Late on the morning of 11 April, Ludendorff called von Lossberg to tell him he was being transferred to the Sixth Army as chief of staff.

Immediately upon hearing the news von Lossberg asked Ludendorff for Vollmacht. This was significant, because instead of asking the Sixth Army or even the army group commander for Vollmacht, von Lossberg asked OHL. This amounted to de facto command of the Sixth Army, and von Lossberg believed he needed that much authority because he still did not trust the new flexible defense doctrine. Ludendorff gave von Lossberg Vollmacht without hesitation, and then passed the information to the Sixth Army commander, Col. Gen. Ludwig von Falkenhausen; the army group commander, Crown Prince Rupprecht of Bavaria; and his chief of staff, Gen. Hermann von Kuhl.[18] Upon hearing the news von Kuhl remarked, "If anyone can straighten out this tangle, he will."[19]

Despite von Lossberg's determined opposition to the new defensive doctrine, Ludendorff had total confidence in his ability to stabilize the situation on the ground. Before he even reported to Sixth Army headquarters, von Lossberg visited the front lines to assess the situation. He immediately saw that the British control of Vimy Ridge gave the British an overwhelming advantage in artillery observation that made a rigid forward defense all but impossible. Lossberg thus opted for a flexible defense in depth, lightly manning the forward positions, allowing them to give ground under heavy pressure, and then counterattacking with strong reserves. Lossberg readily admitted that his defensive scheme ran counter to almost everything he had written in his pamphlet.

Within two days of his arrival at the Sixth Army von Lossberg had organized a flexible defense of fifteen divisions and 150,000 troops, eighteen miles long and ten miles in depth. He estimated quite accurately that it would take the British artillery at least three days to displace forward over the newly captured ground to extend their range. The British would not be able to launch any new attacks in that period. Lossberg used that time to reorganize and reinforce the Sixth Army's new rearward main position. On 14 April the British launched a limited-objective attack to expand the salients they created five days earlier. British VII Corps jumped off at 05:30. By 08:00 they were back at their own line of departure, having taken over 60 percent casualties in their lead units.[20]

Thus, one of the German army's strongest opponents of flexible defense in depth became the first to make it work in a large-scale battle.[21] The heavy German losses on the first day at Arras caused Ludendorff and others at OHL to question the efficacy of the new defensive doctrine. Once von Lossberg was on the scene and in control, it became obvious that the doctrine was sound, but that errors in its application had been the problem.[22] An after-action analysis of the battle of Arras issued by OHL in January 1918 credited the outcome to "the prodigious creative mental energy of this exceptional man."[23] On 24 April 1917 von Lossberg received the Oak Leaves to the Pour le Mérite, awarded only 122 times during World War I.

By May 1917 the British had started shifting their forces northward, to the sector of the German Fourth Army. Sensing another major offensive coming in the Passchandaele sector, Ludendorff on 8 June asked von Lossberg and the chief of staff of the Fourth Army to exchange jobs. Lossberg arrived at Fourth Army headquarters on 13 June, reporting to the army commander, Gen. Friedrich Sixt von Armin. Lossberg had worked with Sixt von Armin when the latter was a corps commander in the First Army. This was the first time that von Lossberg had the opportunity to organize a defense before the start of a battle.[24]

Lossberg issued the Fourth Army defense order on 27 July, establishing what was called the Flandern Line. It was a flexible defense in depth, whose key feature was a line of counterattack divisions ten to fifteen kilometers behind the front line. The position extended the entire forty-kilometer length of the Fourth Army's three corps. The British attack came on 31 July. Despite the tremendous slaughter on both sides, the German line held. The British finally broke off the Battle of Passchendaele (also known as Third Ypres) on

17 November after suffering 324,000 casualties. Total German casualties were about 200,000.

Passchendaele finally resolved the debate within OHL about whether the main defensive battle should be conducted in or behind the front line. The answer was both. The frontline divisions fought in and for the front line; the counterattack divisions fought behind the front line. The OHL after-action report later stated that Lossberg deserved "the credit for having given practical shape to the organization of the new defensive battle in all its details."[25] Not all at OHL were von Lossberg admirers, however. Lieutenant Colonel Georg Wetzell, Ludendorff's operations chief, said that von Lossberg's transfer to the Fourth Army made it look as if he was the only General Staff officer who could conduct a defensive battle.[26]

After Russia collapsed and withdrew from the war at the end of 1917, the Germans shifted to the strategic offensive on the western front. The series of five German offensives launched between March and July 1918 produced the most stunning tactical successes of the war. Strategically, however, they led nowhere. All of the attacks also were deeply flawed on the operational level. Writing in his memoirs after the war, von Lossberg criticized Ludendorff for pursuing operational breakthroughs where only tactical breakthroughs had been achieved.[27]

On the extreme north flank of the German line, the Fourth Army played no role in the massive Operation Michael launched on 21 March. When Michael failed, the Germans immediately followed up with Operation Georgette, farther to the north. On 9 April the Sixth Army launched the main attack in the direction of the key British rail center at Hazebrouck. The following day the Fourth Army launched the supporting attack toward Messenes Ridge, and then to the critical high ground at Mount Kemmel. The problem with Georgette was that it was too small to achieve decisive results, because far too many German forces had been expended in Michael.

The Sixth Army attack quickly ground to a halt and the main effort of Georgette shifted to the Fourth Army. By 17 April von Lossberg had to report to von Kuhl that seven divisions of the Fourth Army were burned out and that the continuation of the attack against Mount Kemmel was not possible without at least five fresh divisions.[28] On 23 April the Fourth Army renewed the attack against Mount Kemmel, eventually taking it. On 29 April, however, von Lossberg recommended to Ludendorff that the offensive should be suspended. The Germans held Mount Kemmel, but they failed to take the operationally decisive heights of Cassel and Mount des Chats, which would have forced the British to abandon the blood-soaked Ypres salient, if not all of Flanders.[29]

The Fourth Army played no role in the subsequent three German offensives, Blücher, Gniesenau, and Marneschutz-Reims. Following Marneschutz-Reims, which was launched on 15 July, the Fourth Army was supposed to follow through with the long-planned and frequently postponed Operation Hagen, the final blow against the Allies that would push the British off the Continent. The plan called for the Fourth Army to deliver the main effort with five corps and twenty-nine divisions, supported on the left by the Sixth Army with two corps and seven divisions.[30]

The attack date for Hagen was set for 1 August. But Marneschutz-Reims failed and the Allies launched a robust counterattack into the German positions west of Rheims on 18 July. On 19 July von Lossberg strongly recommended to Ludendorff that the Germans withdraw immediately to the Siegfried Line, their starting line for the offensives in March. A dispirited Ludendorff refused to consider it, blaming all the past failures on his operations chief, Wetzell.[31]

On 20 July Ludendorff summoned von Lossberg to OHL. Shattered, Ludendorff talked about resigning. Lossberg talked him out of it, but later regretted doing so. Ludendorff then sent the German army's defensive expert to the Soissons area to assess the situation. Lossberg left under the mistaken belief that Ludendorff would act on his recommendations. By the time von Lossberg returned to OHL on 25 July, the overall situation had further deteriorated, and he was shocked to find that Ludendorff had not yet acted on any of his recommendations.[32]

On 8 August OHL established a new army group, with Gen. Hans von Boehn as commander and Lossberg as chief of staff. That same day the British Fourth Army counterattacked at Amiens with 456 tanks and 800 aircraft, caving in the German Second Army. Ludendorff would later dub 8 August as "the Black Day of the German Army." Writing in his postwar memoirs, von Lossberg said he would have placed the Black Day at 18 July.[33]

At a conference of the army group chiefs of staff at OHL on 6 September, Lossberg reported on the overall weakness of the Hindenburg defensive line, and the fact that work on the next successive position, the Hermann Line, had not yet begun. He thus recommended that when they were forced out of the Hindenburg position, the whole German line from Verdun to the sea should fall back beyond the planned Hermann Line to the Antwerp-Meuse line in one well-planned and organized bound. Construction on that line should start immediately. The resulting line would be forty-five miles shorter. Ludendorff rejected the proposal and stuck to his plan to construct the Hermann position. It was a major mistake. The Hindenburg position collapsed on 8 October, and the Germans were pushed back to the Meuse in chaos.[34]

After the Hindenburg position collapsed, just as von Lossberg predicted it would, Ludendorff fired Germany's defensive expert. Oddly enough, in his own postwar memoirs Ludendorff commented how von Lossberg's confidence in *him* had been a great source of satisfaction throughout the war.[35] When Ludendorff resigned on 26 October, British and German press reports initially predicted that he would be replaced by von Lossberg.[36] Five days after Ludendorff's resignation, von Lossberg was appointed chief of staff of the army of Duke Albrecht of Württemberg.

Following World War I von Lossberg remained in the Reichswehr and contributed to the tactical and organizational reforms of Gen. Hans von Seeckt. Lossberg initially commanded a brigade; he then served as a corps chief of staff, commanded a division, and after that commanded a corps. He retired in January 1927 as a general of infantry.

Notes

Note: Information for the chronology is from "Chronologies of German General Officers," Bundesarchiv/Militärarchiv, Freiburg, Germany, File MSg 109/10849.

1. Graeme Wynne, *If Germany Attacks: The Battle in Depth in the West* (London: Faber and Faber, 1940), 84.
2. Ibid., 88–89.
3. Fritz von Lossberg, *Meine Tätigkeit im Weltkriege 1914–1918* (Berlin: Mittler and Sohn, 1939), 131.
4. Ibid., 131.
5. Ibid., 151–52.
6. Ibid., 166–67.
7. Wynne, *If Germany Attacks*, 91–92.
8. Lossberg, *Meine Tätigkeit*, 172.
9. Wynne, *If Germany Attacks*, 92–94.
10. Lossberg, *Meine Tätigkeit*, 174.
11. Oberkommando des Heeres, *Der Weltkrieg 1914 bis 1918*, vol. 10 (Berlin: Mittler und Sohn, 1936), 355.
12. Lossberg, *Meine Tätigkeit*, 220–22.
13. Wynne, *If Germany Attacks*, 127; Lossberg, *Meine Tätigkeit*, 224.
14. Timothy T. Lupfer, *The Dynamics of Doctrine: Changes in German Tactical Doctrine During the First World War*, Leavenworth Papers Nr. 4 (Ft. Leavenworth, Kan.: U.S. Army Combat Studies Institute, July 1981), 19.

15. Wynne, *If Germany Attacks*, 125, 160.
16. Erich Ludendorff, *My War Memories, 1914–1918* (London: Hutchinson, 1920), 386.
17. Wynne, *If Germany Attacks*, 131, 249; Lupfer, *Dynamics of Doctrine*, 9–11.
18. Lossberg, *Meine Tätigkeit*, 280–81.
19. Wynne, *If Germany Attacks*, 200.
20. Lupfer, *Dynamics of Doctrine*, 30, Wynne, *If Germany Attacks*, 203, 206.
21. Lossberg, *Meine Tätigkeit*, 283, Wynne, *If Germany Attacks*, 206.
22. Ludendorff, *My War Memories*, 422–27.
23. Wynne, *If Germany Attacks*, 213.
24. Lossberg, *Meine Tätigkeit*, 295.
25. Wynne, *If Germany Attacks*, 213.
26. Albrecht von Thaer, *Generalstabsdienst an der Front und in der O.H.L.* (Göttingen: Vandenhoeck and Ruprecht, 1958), 125–26.
27. Lossberg, *Meine Tätigkeit*, 321.
28. James E. Edmonds, *Military Operations, France and Belgium, 1918: March–April, Continuation of the German Offensives*, History of the Great War Based on Official Documents (London: Macmillan, 1937), 355.
29. Hermann von Kuhl, *Entstehung, Durchführung und Zusammenbruch der Offensive von 1918* (Berlin: Deutsche Verlaggesellschaft für Politik und Geschichte, 1927), 155. For a thorough analysis of the spring 1918 offensives see David T. Zabecki, *The German 1918 Offensives: A Case Study in the Operational Level of War* (London: Routledge, 2006).
30. Army Group Crown Prince Rupprecht, *Operations Order Ia 8082*, 1 July 1918, Bayersiche Kriegsarchiv, Munich, Germany, File Hgr. Rupprecht, Bd. 112. For a complete discussion of the plan for Operation Hagen see Zabecki, *The German 1918 Offensives*, chapter 11.
31. Lossberg, *Meine Tätigkeit*, 344.
32. Ibid., 345–49.
33. Ibid., 350, 354.
34. Ibid., 357.
35. Ludendorff, *My War Memories*, 21.
36. Wynne, *If Germany Attacks*, 340.

CHRONOLOGY OF MAXIME WEYGAND

21 Jan 1867	Born Brussels, Belgium.
1873	Arrived in France.
1887	Graduated from St. Cyr.
1888	Graduated from the Cavalry School at Saumur, and joined the 4th Regiment of Dragoons as sublieutenant and French citizen.
1906	Promoted to captain.
1907	Promoted to major.
1912	Promoted to lieutenant colonel; attended the Center des Hautes Etudes Militaires.
4 Aug 1914	Germany invaded France.
17 Aug 1914	Named chief of staff to Gen. Ferdinand Foch's new Ninth Army; continued as Foch's chief of staff for the remainder of the war.
1916	Promoted to brigadier general.
1918	Promoted to major general.
1920	Headed the French military mission to Poland; promoted to general of corps.
1923–24	Appointed high commissioner to the Levant.
1930–35	Chief of staff of French army.
31 Jan 1935	Retired from the army.
3 Sep 1939	France declared war on Germany; recalled to active duty as commander of French forces in the Near East.
19 May 1940	Replaced Maurice Gamelin as chief of the French General Staff.
22 Jun 1940	France surrendered; Vichy minister of defense.
Sep 1940	Appointed governor general of Algeria and delegate general in French North Africa.
Nov 1941	Recalled to metropolitan France and dismissed from his posts.
11 Nov 1942	Arrested by Germans and imprisoned.
May 1945	Released from prison by U.S. Army troops; arrested in Paris as a member of the Vichy government.
1946	Released from prison.
1948	Rehabilitated.
28 Jan 1965	Died, Paris.

Maxime Weygand

Spencer C. Tucker

Chief of Staff to Generalissimo Ferdinand Foch during World War I, Maxime Weygand was born in Brussels, Belgium, on 21 January 1867. The identity of his parents has never been established but there were persistent stories that he was the illegitimate son of Belgian royalty, possibly even King Leopold II himself, and that he was later educated in France at Belgian state expense. At age six, in mysterious circumstances, Maxime arrived in France, where he was given a tutor and the last name of de Nimal. If there was any royal support it was but slight, for Weygand remembered frugal surroundings while growing up.

In 1875 Maxime de Nimal entered a Paris lycée as a boarding pupil. Six years later he transferred to Louis-le-Grand, the nation's leading lycée. He had already decided to become an army officer. At Louis-le-Grand he took a leading role in the March 1883 revolt of boarding students against their masters that became something of a national event. Banished from the lycée, he was sent to the vicinity of Marseille. This experience jarred him, and he returned to Paris in the summer of 1884 to prepare for entrance to the French military academy a very different person.

In October 1885 the minister of war issued a special order admitting Belgian citizen Maxime de Nimal to the French military academy at St. Cyr. Stability, self-discipline, and academic success now replaced the turbulence of his earlier educational experience. After two years, de Nimal graduated in July 1887 in the top 10 percent of his class. He also had won acceptance into the upper echelon of the military elite. In the fall of 1887 he entered the French cavalry school at Saumur, where he graduated among the top ten in his class.

Two months later, in October 1888, he joined the 4th Regiment of Dragoons stationed at Chambéry as Sublieutenant Maxime Weygand, French citizen. He took the family name of François-Joseph Weygand of Arras near the Belgian border. He later confirmed that the elder Weygand was a father in name only, used so he could obtain French citizenship.

For the next twenty years Weygand worked hard to make a success of his chosen profession. Various cavalry postings followed, and he enjoyed rapid promotion, including a captaincy in 1906 at only twenty-nine. In 1900 he married Renée de Forsanz, daughter of one of his commanders in the 9th Dragoons.

Like most of his fellow officers, Weygand was conservative in outlook and Republican only by necessity. This is reflected in the fact that throughout his life he never believed Capt. Alfred Dreyfus to be innocent of treason. The Dreyfus Affair racked the French army, and Weygand joined others in contributing to a fund to aid the widow of Maj. Hubert Henry, who committed suicide after admitting to forgeries that implicated Dreyfus. Apparently Weygand did not suffer during the subsequent army purge of anti-Dreyfusards.

In 1907 Weygand won promotion to major, largely on the strength of his excellent record as an instructor at Saumur. This posting, beginning in 1902, was important in his career, for it enabled him largely to offset the fact that he did not attend the École de Guerre, held to be a prerequisite to high army command. Weygand had earned high praise as chief of the training division of the cavalry school for his new teaching methods.

In 1912 Weygand was promoted to lieutenant colonel and began to attract the attention of the highest army authorities in Paris. That same year he was selected to attend the Centre des Hautes Etudes Militaires in the capital, the so-called apprentice-marshals' school. There he performed brilliantly, winning the attention of Gen. Joseph J. C. Joffre, who kept a record of those officers he thought worthy of advancement.

At the beginning of World War I, Weygand was serving as a staff officer with the 5th Hussars Regiment in Foch's XX Corps and close to his headquarters. When French army commander in chief General Joffre named Foch to command the new Ninth Army on 17 August 1914, he assigned Weygand and Lieutenant Colonel Devaux to Foch's staff. Weygand would be chief of staff, Devaux assistant chief. Weygand had met Foch only three times before and then only on formal occasions. He remained Foch's chief of staff for the next nine years, accompanying the future marshal as he steadily advanced in responsibility.

The Foch-Weygand relationship did not get off to the best of starts. Foch was not an individual to give his trust easily, and at one point Weygand is said to have criticized one of Foch's orders to his face as "stupid" and, in return, he received a severe public tongue lashing. Foch forgave Weygand for his outburst, which probably resulted from his youthful inability to control himself under pressure. The event was important, however, for, as Philip Bankwitz has noted, "The Marshal thus immediately earned Weygand's undying respect and affection as a *maître* who exercised authority over him and yet accepted him at the same time. One of Weygand's psychological needs was thereby fulfilled and he repaid Foch's faith in himself a hundredfold in devotion and service."[1]

The relationship between the two men was cemented in the September Battle of the Marne, where Foch gave considerable latitude to Weygand in carrying out his decisions. Foch then commanded the Northern Army Group (January 1915 to December 1916). During January–March 1917 Foch became temporary commander of the Seventh and Eighth Armies. In May 1917 he was named chief of the War Ministry General Staff, in which post he served until March 1918, and Weygand followed him to Paris and experienced the world of politicians. Promoted to general of brigade at the end of 1916, Weygand fought hard for Foch's objectives. On 21 January 1918 Weygand submitted Foch's plan for operations in 1918 to the other Allied commanders, but they concluded that neither the Allies nor Central Powers could secure advantage on the western front in 1918 and that the Allies should therefore concentrate on driving Turkey from the war. As Foch noted in his memoirs, "General Weygand's influence and sagacity fortunately brought his collaborators back to a more opportune examination of the situation on the west, and secured their adherence to General Foch's point of view."[2] But neither Foch nor Weygand was able to convince the other Allied leaders of the need for a supreme Allied commander or for the creation of a general reserve. A day later, on 22 January, Weygand wrote to French premier Georges Clemenceau, presumably at Foch's behest: "While we stand under the menace—and perhaps on the eve—of the most powerful effort which the enemy has so far attempted against us, there exists no general plan for the operations of the Coalition in 1918." Foch was deeply concerned about the lack even of preparations for mutual support. Finally in the midst of the sledgehammer blows of the spring 1918 Ludendorff Offensive the Allies at last adopted unitary command. On 26 March 1918 Clemenceau secured agreement for Foch as Allied commander in chief; General of Division Weygand was his chief of staff.

Foch and Weygand worked extraordinarily well together and became one of the most famous military leadership combinations in history. Foch was a man of action and also a brilliant military thinker, but he had difficulties communicating his thoughts to others. Weygand understood Foch's mental processes absolutely and was able to communicate his chief's thoughts quickly and in clear and precise terms.

Foch's ideas tended to come to him early in the morning, and he made it his practice to meet first with Weygand to share these with him. Weygand then took Foch's general, cryptic, even fragmentary ideas and translated them into definite, practical instructions, never troubling his chief over details, for which he alone took responsibility. This was in fact what Foch wanted most in a staff officer.

As Foch noted, some men had superior intelligence that enabled them to see solutions to problems, but they did not know how to choose one, let alone accomplish it. Others were incapable of showing initiative. To Foch, the power to get things done called for intelligence, imagination, judgment, and decision. Weygand seems to have had all four of these qualities. Foch wrote of Weygand, "With his astonishing intelligence, memory, and power of work, at the end of three months he knew all of my views . . . and we were never apart. That is not the usual method of work for a Chief of the General Staff, but it is the best. He can express my views as well as I should have done myself."[3]

Weygand in effect became the marshal's second self, although always suppressing his own individuality. One French staff officer remarked that it was this utter forgetfulness of self that enabled Weygand to serve his chief so well. He had no other ambition apart from serving Foch to the best of his ability.

Sometimes when Foch did not have time to talk to someone he would simply tell the individual to see Weygand: "Weygand c'est moi," he liked to say.[4] Foch also referred to Weygand as "mon encyclopédie."

Weygand shared his chief's ups and downs. When Foch was removed from his command of the Northern Army Group following the heavy casualties of 1916 (which also cost Joffre his position as commander in chief of the army), it had almost a traumatic effect on Weygand, who regarded it as a classic case of civilian interference in military affairs. Weygand retained this distrust of the civilian leadership, and he did not hesitate on a number of occasions to stand up to Premier Clemenceau, who distrusted his military chiefs as illustrated by his well-known remark, "War is too important a business to be left to the generals." This was particularly evident in the last months of the war, when Clemenceau increasingly interfered in military matters.

Foch and Weygand were virtually inseparable, being apart during the war on few occasions. One of these came in the spring of 1917 when Weygand went to Berne, Switzerland, to consult with the Swiss General Staff over steps to be taken to counter a possible German move through that country. Weygand also occasionally represented his chief at important meetings if Foch could not attend. When he was chief of the French General Staff, Foch should have been the French military representative to the Supreme War Council, established in 1917, but he arranged to have Weygand take his place.

Foch did not like to have ideas thrust upon him. If Weygand took the initiative in suggesting things to his chief, he never admitted it. His task was simply to carry out Foch's will. Many who believed at first that Weygand was Foch's éminence gris, a kind of French Erich Ludendorff to a Paul von Hindenburg, soon discovered their mistake. Weygand never violated the role of the chief of staff by imposing himself between Foch and the men he commanded. One historian has noted that Weygand "was simply a translator and chief of staff of unrivaled exactitude and technical polish, performing an absolutely essential function for Foch."[5] This implies that Weygand was a "clerk" such as Louis-Alexandre Berthier to Napoleon Bonaparte. In fact he was much more. American colonel T. Bentley Moss, liaison officer between Foch and American Expeditionary Force commander Gen. John J. Pershing and also the translator into English of Foch's memoirs, said that Weygand described his relationship to Foch in these words: "The Marshal is the locomotive; I am the tender that furnishes him with coal and water." In fact, Moss thought Weygand was much greater than this; he described the relationship between Weygand and his chief as "a chemical union, whereby two distinct elements produce a substance having characteristic qualities of its own."[6] One senior British officer noted that the two men suited one another perfectly and thought exactly alike, although Foch was the deeper thinker of the two. Weygand may have been more intelligent, arriving at conclusions before Foch. The fact is that the two worked extraordinarily well together. Weygand has been described as very active and, like his chief, of tireless energy. He had great military knowledge, much of it learned from Foch, and a precise memory.

Although he was passionately devoted to his profession and to the French army, Weygand was not one-dimensional in the sense of his German counterpart Ludendorff. He was a consummate horseman who liked the outdoor life. But when he was in Paris he also liked to visit book, art, and antique shops. He had a wide circle of friends and was a man of considerable warmth and charm, and a delightful person in company.

Weygand's self-effacement was aided by his physique, for although Foch was short in stature he was sturdy; Weygand was both small and slight. Foch was animated in both speech and manner, whereas Weygand was restrained. In work Weygand was all business. Weygand's office was next to his chief and held the situation map. Foch, who did not like to be alone, was often in his chief of staff's office, contemplating the map and smoking.

Important for coalition warfare, Weygand got along well with foreign officers and always seemed to have the time to listen to their opinions and explanations. Those who knew him described him as tactful yet open and frank, always honestly expressing his own views. One of his important qualities was the ability to see the whole picture clearly and not be obsessed by some local aspect. Of strong character, he did have a violent temper, which on occasion he vented on others. Although he could say things quickly that would wound others, he was just as quick to ask forgiveness for these remarks. Weygand drove himself hard and expected the same of the rest of the staff. Complete loyalty to their chief characterized all of Foch's staff. If Weygand had any ambition for himself, it was to hold an independent command, which was, however, denied him during World War I.

Weygand worked well under pressure and is said to have been at his best in difficult circumstances, such as the German spring 1918 offensives. Then he managed to get Foch's orders carried out quickly and smoothly, with a minimum of friction when cooperation within the Allies was vital to survival.

As the German offensives ground to a halt, Weygand repeatedly pressed Foch to produce a definite plan for a general Allied offensive. Foch resisted but finally authorized Weygand to do so. The result was Weygand's 24 July memorandum that pointed out that the German offensive had failed and that the defeat "must first of all be exploited on the field of battle itself." The balance of numbers was tilting to the Allied side, which had already gained superiority in tanks and aircraft. The Allied armies had thus reached the turning point; "their numbers permit and the principles of war compel them to keep this initiative. The moment has come to abandon the general defensive attitude forced upon us till now by numerical inferiority and to pass to the offensive." The memorandum then went on to list a detailed program of offensive operations.[7] As Foch himself later recounted, "The memorandum of July 24 was entirely his composition, but it reflects my views exactly."[8]

At the end of the war on 8 November at Compiègne, Foch had Weygand read the armistice terms to the German delegation, and after the war, he was again at the marshal's side when Foch appeared at the Paris Peace Conference and when he clashed with Premier Clemenceau over what he regarded as far-too-lenient peace terms for Germany. Clemenceau and others found it convenient to attack Weygand for this, rather than Foch, and painted him as having put the ideas in Foch's mind. Nothing can be further from the truth, although Weygand certainly shared his chief's misgivings over the peace settlement and he did not hesitate to vent his misgivings publicly. He continued to blame the Versailles Treaty for French national apathy in the 1920s regarding defense matters and for World War II.

Weygand's association with Foch did result in keeping him in the public eye and did much to advance his military career, as he himself admitted.[9] Weygand's view was that without him Foch would still be Foch, whereas without Foch Weygand would not have reached the standard he attained. But this admiration was quite mutual. Some years after the war, Foch said of him, "Weygand! He is a paragon."[10]

In July 1920 British and French leaders met over the situation in Poland, which was then at war with Russia and showing every sign of being on the verge of defeat at the hands of invading Bolshevik armies. Prime Minister David Lloyd George asked Foch to go to Warsaw and study the situation. Foch was reluctant to do so unless he had a free hand and assurances that the Polish government would fulfill his conditions. He thought it would be useless to pour French arms into Poland otherwise. But there was also concern among Allied leaders that Foch's reputation would be at risk in such an operation. In the end Foch went in proxy when Premier Alexandre Millerand appointed Weygand to head up the military mission. Foch had urged Weygand's appointment: "He will do everything that I should do. . . . And later, if that is not enough, there will still be time for me to go myself."[11]

There would not have been time for Foch to have gone later, because the situation in Poland was by then desperate. By mid-August Russian armies were at the gates of Warsaw and the fall of the city seemed certain. Weygand arrived to a chilly reception from the Poles. His skill and tact succeeded in breaking down the resistance of most of the Polish leaders, save Chief of State Jósef Pilsudski, who wanted only French military equipment, not advice. It was Pilsudski who developed in secret the brilliant plan that lulled the Russians into complacency and brought victory in the Battle of Warsaw. Weygand quite correctly credited the Poles rather than himself for the victory, but Foch said, "Results alone count. I said, 'Send him and you will see!' And you have seen. We were the emergency repairers."[12]

Weygand was received back in France as a national hero and promoted to general of corps. Following the war Weygand spent a few years as Foch's peacetime chief of staff, during which time he was sent into the Ruhr with French troops to break German resistance in the matter of reparations payments. Again Foch commented, "Good! Once more we are sent to patch up things."[13]

Foch was wrong, for the Ruhr occupation was not successful in the long run. France's last independent action between the wars drew the condemnation of Britain and the United States, and its high financial cost brought a political shift to the left in France.

During 1923–24 Weygand was French high commissioner to the Levant (Syria and Lebanon), where he again gave proof of his administrative talents. Removed from this post following the left victory in the 1924 French national elections, Weygand found himself classified as "a general of the right" and identified with an aggressive foreign policy. Appointed head of the Centre des Hautes Etudes Militaires, he also became a member of the nation's highest defense body, the Conseil Supérieur de la Guerre. His retirement age was also prolonged.

In January 1930 Weygand succeeded Marshal Henri Philippe Pétain as chief of staff of the French army, which post he held until 1935. An early advocate of mechanized warfare, Weygand pushed through motorization of seven of the twenty peacetime divisions; in 1933 he secured formation of the Divisions Légère Méchanique (DLM) with 240 armored vehicles each.

On 31 January 1935, his sixty-eighth birthday, Weygand at last retired from active duty. In consideration of his service to the nation, a law was passed that kept him on the active list for life, without however specifying duties. Recalled at the start of World War II, Weygand served as commander of French forces in the Near East. In May 1940 he was recalled to France, and on 19 May replaced ineffective Chief of the French General Staff General Maurice Gamelin. As commander of the French army Weygand displayed energy far greater than his years, but he also inherited an impossible situation. Unsuccessful in his efforts to get the British Expeditionary Force to join in a combined effort to pinch off the German race to the sea, Weygand counseled capitulation. France surrendered a month later, on 22 June.

Weygand briefly served the government of Vichy France as minister of defense (1940) but was distrusted by Pétain's premier, Pierre Laval, who in September sent him to North Africa as governor general of Algeria and delegate general in French North Africa. Too openly, perhaps, Weygand talked of reversing the verdict of 1940. He opposed Vichy's collaboration with the Germans and granting them bases. While in the Vichy government, Weygand had also worked to develop ties with the United States. French admiral Jean François Darlan, then Pétain's chief minister, sought active collaboration with the Germans. As proof of French goodwill, in November 1941 Darlan summoned Weygand home to metropolitan France and removed him from his posts. Weygand then went into enforced retirement at his home in Grasse, near Cannes.

In November 1942, after the Allied invasion of North Africa, Pétain called on Weygand for advice. He stayed three days at Vichy trying to stiffen Pétain's resolve and secure an order for the fleet to leave Toulon. On 11 November the Germans arrested Weygand, and he spent the rest of the war years in prison. Released by U.S. troops in May 1945, Weygand flew to Paris where, on the orders of Charles De Gaulle, he was arrested as a member of the Vichy government. Released from prison the next year, he was rehabilitated in 1948.

Weygand lived quietly in retirement. The author of numerous books, including biographies of marshals Turenne and Foch and three volumes of memoirs, he was elected to the French Academy. Weygand died in Paris shortly after his ninety-eighth birthday, on 28 January 1965.

Notes

1. Philip Charles Farwell Bankwitz, *Maxime Weygand and Civil-Military Relations in Modern France* (Cambridge, Mass.: Harvard University Press, 1967), 14.
2. Ferdinand Foch, *The Memoirs of Ferdinand Foch*, trans. Col. T. Bentley Mott (Garden City, N.Y.: Doubleday, Doran, 1931), 238.
3. Major-General Sir George Aston, *The Biography of the Late Marshal Foch* (New York: Macmillan, 1929), 153.
4. Ibid., 192.
5. Bankwitz, *Maxime Weygand*, 13.
6. T. Bentley Mott, introductory note in Foch, *The Memoirs of Ferdinand Foch*, xxiv.
7. B. H. Liddell-Hart, *Foch, The Man of Orléans* (Boston: Little, Brown, 1932), 342–43.
8. Ibid., 341.
9. Maxime Weygand, *The Role of General Weygand; Conversations with His Son, Commandant J. Weygand*, trans. J. H. F. McEwen (London: Eyre and Spottiswoode, 1948), 20.
10. Aston, *Biography of the Late Marshal Foch*, 297.
11. Liddell-Hart, *Foch*, 433.
12. Ibid., 434.
13. Ibid., 439–40.

2 Oct 1862	Born in County Limerick, Ireland.
1882	Appointed second lieutenant, Royal Warwickshire Regiment.
1886–90	Assigned as adjutant, 2nd Battalion Royal Warwickshire Regiment.
1894	Graduated from the Staff College.
1895–97	Assigned as instructor, Royal Military College Sandhurst.
1897–99	Assigned as deputy assistant adjutant general, South-Eastern District.
1899–1902	South African War. Assigned as staff officer to Sir Redvers Buller; staff officer, HQ Pretoria; assistant adjutant general, Harrismith District; assistant adjutant general, Natal, brevet lieutenant colonel.
1904	Assigned as deputy assistant adjutant general, Staff College.
1907	Assigned as general staff officer 1, Headquarters of the Army.
Mar 1909	Promoted to brigadier-general. Assigned as brigadier-general, general staff, Scottish Command.
1909–13	Assigned as director of Staff Duties, War Office.
1913–14	Assigned as commandant of Staff College.
1914	Promoted to major-general. Assigned as director of Military Training.
1914	Assigned as director of Home Defence, War Office.
Nov 1915	Assigned as assistant to the chief of the Imperial General Staff, War Office.
22 Dec 1915	Promoted to lieutenant-general. Assigned as chief of the general staff, General Headquarters, British Expeditionary Force.
1918	Assigned as general officer commanding and lieutenant governor of Guernsey.
1954	Died.

CHRONOLOGY OF HERBERT LAWRENCE

8 Aug 1861	Born, Southgate, England.
1882	Appointed second lieutenant, 17th Lancers, India.
1896	Passed out of Staff College. Assigned to the German Section of the Intelligence Division, War Office.
1898	Assigned as deputy assistant adjutant general.
1899	Staff Officer, Cavalry Division, South Africa.
By 1902	Promoted to brevet lieutenant colonel. Assigned as commander, 16th Lancers.
1903	Retired and entered The City.
1904–9	Served as commander, King Edward's Horse.
1914	Rejoined the active army.
8 Sep 1914	Promoted to colonel. Assigned as general staff officer 1, 2nd Mounted Division.
Jun 1915	Promoted to brigadier-general.
21 Jun 1915	Assigned as general officer commanding, 127th Brigade, 42nd Division.
Jul 1915	Deputy inspector general of communications, Mudros.
19 Aug 1915	Assigned as general officer commanding, 53rd Division (temporary).
17 Sep 1915	Promoted to major-general. Assigned as general officer commanding, 2nd Division and general officer commanding, Number 3 (Northern) Section, Suez Canal Defences.
6 Nov 1916	Assigned as general officer commanding, 71st Division.
12 Feb 1917	Assigned as general officer commanding, 66th Division, Knighted, KCB.
Jan 1918	Assigned as brigadier-general, general staff (Intelligence), GHQ.
24 Jan 1918	Promoted to lieutenant-general. Chief of the General Staff, General Headquarters, British Expeditionary Force.
Late 1918	Promoted to general.
1943	Died.

Launcelot Kiggell and Herbert Lawrence

Andy Simpson

Sir Launcelot Kiggell, as Sir Douglas Haig's chief of staff for the most controversial part of his career (from early 1916 to late 1917), has attracted only censure. Even Haig's apologists stress Kiggell's limitations and especially the temperamental unfitness for the job. However, though his tactical views have been almost invariably represented as the epitome of the blinkered attitudes of chateau generals, this was not the case.

Launcelot Edward Kiggell was born in County Limerick, in 1862, into an Anglo-Irish gentry family of such modest means that he was not educated at an English public school, a rarity among officers of his generation. Nevertheless, he attended the Royal Military College, Sandhurst, and was commissioned into the Royal Warwickshire Regiment in 1882. His rise thereafter was steady and unspectacular, as might have been expected from a socially unconnected soldier in a line regiment. He acted as adjutant of the Warwicks' 2nd Battalion from 1886 to 1890, passed out from the Staff College in 1894, and was an instructor at Sandhurst from 1895 to 1897. At this point he took on his first staff job and remained a staff officer for the rest of his career. In the South African War he was initially a staff officer to Sir Redvers Buller, then at British headquarters in Pretoria, and he went on to two appointments as assistant adjutant general. In 1904 Kiggell returned to the Staff College, by now a lieutenant colonel, and remained there until 1907.

Lt. Gen. Sir Herbert Lawrence in the front row, second from right.
(Lt. Gen. Sir Launcelot Kiggell is not pictured.)

Since his was not a strong personality, it was only at this time that he seems first to have made any mark on contemporaries. Unfortunately, the impression he made was not a good one. In 1905 he gave a paper to the Aldershot Military Society on the future shape of battle. Despite the events in South Africa (in which he had, after all, been involved) and those going on in Manchuria at the time, his model for wars to come was derived entirely from the Napoleonic and Franco-Prussian wars, stressing that battles would be localized with reserves conveniently placed within a few hours' march. Unsurprisingly, his audience was critical of this view.

Nevertheless, Kiggell was considered a safe pair of hands, and his career continued to prosper. Appointed a brigadier-general in 1909, he took up the post of director of staff duties (DSD) at the War Office. He was the immediate successor of Sir Douglas Haig, who had left to take up the post of chief of the General Staff in India. Haig had delayed his own departure until he found the right man to replace him. This meant, obviously, that the most reliable candidate would be one whose ideas were similar to his own, and as Haig's protégé Kiggell was ideal. Indeed, Haig's most recent biographer rather waspishly—although completely inaccurately given Kiggell's infantry background— remarked that a man who was "conveniently, a traditional cavalryman" was the obvious choice. And it does seem that Haig did his best to control Kiggell by means of fortnightly letters from India, more or less telling him what to do on a variety of matters. A man of low self-esteem, Kiggell had not considered himself up to the job in the first place and had to be persuaded by Haig to take it, so he was in no position to resist pressure from Haig later.[1] In any case, he and Haig enjoyed a relationship in which his admiration for Haig was met with a kind of jovial affection from the latter, who would begin letters "My Dear Old Kigge."[2] Haig, however, did not entirely dominate Kiggell, since he also wrote to consult him on appointments to important posts in India.[3]

Indeed, Kiggell accepted the appointment of commandant of the Staff College in October 1913, despite earlier opposition from Haig.[4] In this capacity the impression Kiggell seems to have conveyed is of "a scholarly type, of a retiring nature, and content to leave well alone." Since his most notable achievement as commandant was to revise the standard text *Operations of War* by Sir Edward Hamley for a new edition, this was not an inaccurate description of him.[5] Kiggell, however, also had a role in the propagation of military thought in the army. The framework for the British army's operations was *Field Service Regulations* (1909), Part 1 (*Operations*), produced under Haig's auspices when

DSD, and at Staff College conferences Kiggell was prominent in explaining how *Field Service Regulations* were to be employed.

Promoted to major-general in 1914, Kiggell spent the first two years of World War I at the War Office, initially as director of Military Training, then as director of Home Defence, and finally as assistant to the chief of the Imperial General Staff. It may safely be assumed that, like most of his contemporaries, Kiggell wished to serve in France, and this duly came to pass when Haig became commander in chief of the BEF at the end of 1915. Haig's first choice for his chief of the General Staff (CGS) was considered too junior, and so, on Lord Horatio Kitchener's recommendation, the job went to Kiggell, of whom Haig wrote in his diary, "I have the greatest confidence in him as a soldier also as a gentleman."[6]

It appears that for much of his time as CGS Kiggell acted simply as Haig's mouthpiece, but he nevertheless made his own contribution to the conduct of operations. The most famous of these was a document entitled *Training of Divisions for Offensive Action*, written by Kiggell and issued in May 1916. This document is conventionally blamed for the disaster on the first day of the Battle of the Somme (1 July 1916) and has been criticized for reflecting prewar thought and especially *Field Service Regulations*.[7] Kiggell, however, has been maligned in this respect. First, *Field Service Regulations* were applicable throughout the war. They were designed as a loose conceptual framework, adaptable to any of the potentially manifold fighting situations in which the British army might find itself. They were supposed to be supplemented by training and manuals, such as that written by Kiggell, which were more specific. Therefore, references in *Training of Divisions* to *Field Service Regulations* did not necessarily reflect a viewpoint divorced from the reality of the western front. Second, *Training of Divisions* has been criticized especially for forcing the attackers on 1 July to advance slowly across no-man's-land in waves, maximizing the casualties suffered. Though Kiggell does seem to have advised that the troops advance in lines, he also acknowledged that it was not possible to lay down definite rules for the attack, since divisional objectives necessarily varied, and in fact the infantry on 1 July did not all adopt a linear formation.[8]

The bulk of the document consisted of a distillation of the lessons of previous attacks, such as the need to train troops on scale models of their objectives, that fresh troops should be passed through the first wave to go on to the farther objectives, and so on. The principal reasons for the failure on 1 July 1916 were the ineffectiveness of the preliminary British bombardment of the German positions and of British counterbattery fire. Where the attack did succeed, on the southern flank, there was less German artillery, the British infantry had enjoyed the protection of a creeping barrage, and they employed troops specifically to mop up the German soldiers who had survived the bombardment in deep dugouts. It should be noted that *Training of Divisions* specifically mentioned that troops should be allocated to clean up captured positions.[9]

For most of the Battle of the Somme, Kiggell remained firmly in the background, apart from being sent on errands by Haig. He acted as a middleman in the discussions between Haig and Sir Henry Rawlinson, general officer commanding of the Fourth Army, regarding the latter's proposal for a night attack on 14 July, conveying messages in both directions and being consulted by the commander in chief.[10] Kiggell was later sent by Haig to admonish Rawlinson for his poor tactics and piecemeal attacks in August. Similarly, during the planning for the Battle of Flers-Courcelette (15 September 1916), Kiggell on Haig's instructions wrote to tell Rawlinson that his plan for the use of tanks in the forthcoming attack lacked boldness. Both Kiggell and Haig believed a breakthrough was possible, while Rawlinson did not. Kiggell, however, demonstrated a better grasp of reality in a note on the use of tanks he wrote a few weeks later, stressing the limitations of the Mark I tank and the need to use it as an adjunct to the artillery-infantry attack, not its driving force. He also noted that he considered that "the utility of the tanks has been proved."[11] Given the slowness and unreliability of the tanks of 1916 this was eminently reasonable and, whatever Kiggell's shortcomings as a chief of staff, in no way reveals him to have been a cavalry-fixated technological illiterate—the stereotype of World War I British staff officers.

Kiggell continued to function in his usual, almost invisible, way during the Battle of Arras. His unwillingness or inability to convey army commanders' concerns to Haig was notable during the Battles of Bullecourt (subsidiary to the Arras offensive) and can only have hindered communications within the army. This also proved to be a problem during the Third Battle of Ypres (July–November 1917), when Haig failed to coordinate properly his army commanders (Gough of Fifth and Plumer of Second Army), and Kiggell was unwilling or unable to press him to do it.[12] Gough was firmly of the opinion that Kiggell was simply a yes-man, weak in character and susceptible to pressure from Haig to conform to his ideas. Another officer, however, took the view that Kiggell was simply worn out, and Gough may have had a rather jaundiced view of him. Kiggell had joined Haig in criticizing Gough's tactics of ineffective small attacks in August and early September 1917, and then carried out further investigations. He reported to Haig that Gough's subordinates were reluctant to represent their real views regarding operations to Fifth Army headquarters, and later that divisions were unwilling to serve in the Fifth Army at all.[13] This led ultimately to the sacking of Gough's chief of staff.

At the end of 1917 Kiggell's own dismissal took place. Ironically, it was prefaced by another example of his telling tales to another's detriment, this time, on 9 December 1917, when he informed Haig that his army and corps commanders had no confidence in his chief of intelligence, Brig.-Gen. John Charteris, who subsequently lost his job. After the Third Battle of Ypres and the disappointment at Cambrai, dissatisfaction in London with Haig and BEF GHQ was running high, and more sacrifices were required. As a result, on 20 December Kiggell left GHQ to return to Britain, ostensibly because his health had broken down. He did not return, taking the post of lieutenant-governor of Guernsey until his retirement in 1920.[14] He died in 1954.

There seems no doubt that Kiggell was a poor chief of staff. He left a revealing comment on Sir Henry Wilson in his papers: "the only V.I.P. I ever felt completely at ease with."[15] This lack of self-confidence when dealing with other senior officers was a grave disadvantage to Kiggell and badly hampered communications between GHQ and its subordinate formations. It also left him more or less unable to act independently of Haig, instead functioning only as his messenger and mouthpiece. It seems likely, however, that Kiggell has been underrated as a tactician, and given his realistic ideas on tanks, for example, he was not the red-tabbed reactionary some historians have portrayed.[16]

The Honourable Sir Herbert Lawrence, Haig's second chief of staff, was a more substantial personality than Kiggell. Lawrence's military career progressed rapidly in World War I, a success matched by his prewar achievements in business. A resourceful man, he was far better equipped to deal with the personalities he would encounter as chief of staff than was the insecure, stressed Kiggell. Like Kiggell, Lawrence has been characterized as a tactical traditionalist, but this was no more true for Lawrence than for his predecessor.

The contrast between the two men's backgrounds was substantial. Herbert Alexander Lawrence was born at Southgate (now part of London) on 8 August 1861, the son of Sir John Lawrence of the Punjab, later baron and viceroy of India. Educated at Harrow and Sandhurst, Herbert Lawrence was commissioned into the 17th Lancers in 1882. He was based in India until 1891, during which time he spent a period as the regiment's adjutant. Passing out of the Staff College in 1896, he moved to the Intelligence Division at the War Office in the German Section. Promoted to deputy assistant adjutant general in 1898, he went to South Africa the following year when the war broke out, serving as a senior staff officer of the Cavalry Division under Sir John French. Also on the divisional staff was Douglas Haig, with whom Lawrence appears not to have worked well. By the end of the war, Lawrence was commanding officer of the 16th Lancers and a brevet lieutenant colonel.

Despite the promise of his career, Lawrence left the army in 1903, partly because Haig had been preferred over him to the command of the 17th Lancers and partly because he needed more money to support his family. His business career prospered, assisted by his and his wife's connections, but he did not sever all his connections with the army. At the request of King Edward VII, Lawrence commanded King Edward's Horse (King's Colonials) from 1904 to 1909. At the outbreak of World War I, Lawrence was appointed a general staff officer grade I to the 2nd Yeomanry Division and he went to Egypt with that unit. During the Gallipoli campaign he rose to brigade and then divisional command. The summer of 1916 saw him in command of a corps-sized force, with which he defeated a German-Turkish force, capturing the Sinai Desert. In the autumn of 1916 Lawrence returned to Britain, apparently because he opposed the invasion of Palestine. After commanding the 71st Division (Home Forces) in February 1917, he commanded the 66th Division on the western front with some success during the Third Battle of Ypres.

When Brig. Gen. John Charteris was sacked as Haig's chief of intelligence in December 1917, he was replaced by Lawrence. And with the departure of Kiggell, Lawrence became CGS in January 1918. In this capacity, he acted as "a 'right arm' that he [Haig] had always lacked."[17] Lawrence, however, was not without his critics, notably Gen. Hubert Gough of the Fifth Army, who was sacked in March 1918 after his army was severely mauled in the German Michael offensive of that month. (Interestingly, in late 1917 Gough's chief of staff was dismissed and then given command of Lawrence's old 66th Division.) Gough felt that Lawrence, like Haig, had been complacent before the German attack. On 19 March Gough had requested two divisions from the meager general reserve, but was, he claimed, patronized by Lawrence, who in refusing gave him a lecture on the military unsoundness of committing reserves before the situation was clear.[18] Arguably, Lawrence was right. He and Haig were far more concerned with preserving the British position near the Channel ports, and felt that ground could be given up on the Somme (Gough's) sector if necessary. Lawrence has also been criticized for expecting the German attack to take a conventional form—that they would launch a number of small assaults to wear the British down and pull in their reserves, before the main attack.[19] But it was not unreasonable of Lawrence to expect the Germans to follow sound principles, rather than risk all on one throw of the dice, which in the event cost them the war.

Perhaps Lawrence's main contribution at this time was in liaison with the French. On 24 March he visited the headquarters of both the Fifth Army and the French Group of the Armies of Reserve. In order to encourage the French to counterattack, he agreed that British forces in the area would come under their command. It is hard to imagine Kiggell doing this.[20] In fact, Lawrence was in meetings with various French commanders for three days, including the crucial Doullens Conference on 26 March (at which it was decided to appoint General Ferdinand Foch Allied generalissimo).

Lawrence's independence of judgment was further demonstrated in July. Haig was in London when Foch summoned Lawrence to his headquarters on the eleventh. Foch explained that he expected a German attack in the Champagne sector and ordered four British divisions and a corps headquarters to move there. Lawrence (wrongly, in the event) did not believe that such an attack was likely, and that it was more probable that the next blow would fall on the British. Rather than disobey, Lawrence temporized, sending two divisions but holding the others back until Haig's return.[21] Given the paucity of the British reserves at this time, it was a decision requiring more than a little moral courage, and again contrasts with Kiggell's performance as chief of staff.

Lawrence's ability to deal effectively with the army commanders was also much greater than Kiggell's. On his way back to GHQ after seeing Foch, Lawrence went on his own initiative on 13 July to the Fourth Army headquarters and instructed its commander, Sir Henry Rawlinson, to prepare at once plans for an attack east of Amiens.[22] This set in motion the preparations for the Battle of Amiens in August. And on 22 August, General Sir Julian Byng, commander of the Third Army, went to Advanced GHQ to submit his plans for a forthcoming attack to Lawrence, who approved them. Haig had rejected the first draft.[23]

In August Lawrence also issued a memorandum to the army commanders, pointing out that they should be using advanced guards to get through the German outpost zone, with an infantry-artillery-tank assault to break the main line of resistance. This would be followed by a swift move to points of strategic interest. This has been denounced as an example of Lawrence (and Haig and others at GHQ) having a traditional mindset, since they still thought primarily in terms of artillery, infantry, and cavalry.[24] However, even without tanks (which Lawrence clearly favored), the infantry-artillery attacks of 1918, using predicted fire and new small-unit tactics, were anything but traditional. That Lawrence and others viewed the tank as an adjunct to the attack simply reflects the mechanical unreliability of the models in use in 1918 and the logistic difficulties of moving them around the front.[25]

Historian C. R. M. F. Cruttwell rated highly Lawrence's contribution to victory in August and after, suggesting that his policy of keeping divisions in sectors with which they were familiar "both economized men and promoted a smooth business-like progress."[26] Lawrence continued to act as Haig's right arm to the end of the war, discussing the prospects of an armistice that year in October (at which point Lawrence was pessimistic) and agreeing with him in criticizing Foch and Weygand's armistice proposals in November.[27]

After the war, Lawrence returned to The City (though he was only just passed over at various times for the posts of viceroy of India and chief of the Imperial General Staff) where his business prospered and his influence both in and outside the financial community grew. He died in 1943.

Herbert Lawrence was a considerable figure and, as a result, a far more effective chief of staff than his predecessor. In a year when the fortunes of the British Expeditionary Force were at both their highest and lowest in the war, his coolness and ability to take responsibility and use his initiative—to understand and work with Haig but, unlike Kiggell, to act effectively in his absence—were a great asset. Like Kiggell, Lawrence has been described as a tactical traditionalist, but this is even less fair of him than of Kiggell, given that he held field commands from 1915 to the end of 1917 with no little degree of success, and his efficient handling of divisional moves in the last three months of the war made a significant contribution to victory.

Notes

1. Gerard De Groot, *Douglas Haig, 1861–1928* (London: Unwin Hyman, 1988), 134, 135.
2. Letter from Haig to Kiggell, 27 April 1909. Kiggell Papers, 1/2, LHCMA. In an army addicted to nicknames, "Kigge" (pronounced "Kidge") was Kiggell's.
3. Brian Bond, *The Victorian Army and the Staff College, 1854–1914* (London: Eyre Methuen, 1972), 288.
4. De Groot, *Douglas Haig,* 135.
5. Bond, *The Victorian Army,* 288.
6. Diary entry for 21 December 1915 in Robert Blake, ed., *The Private Papers of Douglas Haig, 1914–1919* (London: Eyre and Spottiswoode, 1952), 119.
7. See, for example, Kiggell's *DNB* entry. Regarding *Field Service Regulations* and prewar thought see T. H. E. Travers, *The Killing Ground: The British Army, the Western Front and the Emergence of Modern Warfare 1900–1918* (London: Allen and Unwin, 1987), 134.

8. Robin Prior and Trevor Wilson, *Command on the Western Front* (Oxford: Blackwell, 1992), 179.
9. Sir James E. Edmonds, *History of the Great War: Military Operations, France and Belgium, 1916*, vol. 1 (London: Macmillan, 1932), appendices, 125–30.
10. John Terraine, *Douglas Haig, The Educated Soldier* (London: Hutchinson, 1963), 211–12.
11. Prior and Wilson, *Command on the Western Front*, 221. 230, 234–35; J. P. Harris, *Men, Ideas and Tanks* (Manchester: Manchester University Press, 1995); 67.
12. Jonathan Walker, *The Blood Tub: General Gough and the Battle of Bullecourt* (Kent: Staplehurst, 1998), 70.
13. Terraine, *Douglas Haig*, 251.
14. Ibid., 385–88. It has famously been alleged that just before his departure, Kiggell saw the battlefield of Passchendaele for the first time, and burst into tears, exclaiming "Good God! Did we really send men to fight in that?" However, this appears to be a fiction. For a thorough demolition of the myth, see Frank Davies and Graham Maddocks, *Bloody Red Tabs* (London: Leo Cooper, 1995), 16–21.
15. Kiggell Papers, File 2, LHCMA.
16. See Travers, *The Killing Ground*, passim.
17. Terraine, *Douglas Haig*, 388.
18. De Groot, *Douglas Haig*, 375.
19. T. H. E. Travers, *How the War Was Won: Command and Technology in the British Army on the Western Front, 1917–1918* (London: Routledge, 1992), 53.
20. Sir James E. Edmonds, *History of the Great War: Military Operations, France and Belgium, 1918*, vol. 1 (London: Macmillan, 1935), 418; Major-General Sir John Davidson, *Haig: Master of the Field* (London: Peter Nevill, 1953), 85–86.
21. Terraine, *Douglas Haig*, 443.
22. Sir James E. Edmonds, *History of the Great War: Military Operations, France and Belgium, 1918*, vol. 3 (London: Macmillan, 1939), 311.
23. J. P. Harris, *Amiens to the Armistice: The BEF in the Hundred Days' Campaign, 8 August 11 November 1918* (London: Brassey's, 1998), 135.
24. Travers, *How the War Was Won*, 148.
25. D. J. Childs, "British Tanks 1915–18, Manufacture and Employment," Ph.D. thesis, Glasgow University, 1996, 177–190, 199.
26. C.R.M.F. Cruttwell, *A History of the Great War 1914–1918* (Oxford: Oxford University Press, 1934), 554.
27. Terraine, *Douglas Haig*, 474, 477.

CHRONOLOGY OF JAMES GUTHRIE HARBORD

21 Mar 1866	Born in Bloomington, Illinois.
1886	Graduated from Kansas Agricultural College.
1889	Enlisted U.S. Army.
1891	Commissioned second lieutenant, U.S. Army.
1895	Graduated from the Infantry and Cavalry School.
1899-1901	Served in Cuba.
1902-14	Served in the Philippines.
1917	Attended Army War College.
1917	Assigned as chief of staff, AEF.
May 1918	Assigned as commander, 2nd Brigade, 2nd Infantry Division.
Jul 1918	Assigned as commander, 2nd Infantry Division.
Aug 1918	Assigned as commander, Service of Supply.
1919	Assigned as chief, U.S. Military Mission to Armenia.
1919-21	Assigned as commander, 2nd Infantry Division.
1921	Assigned as deputy chief of staff, U.S. Army.
1922	Retired from U.S. Army and became president of RCA.
1930	Chairman of the Board of RCA.
1947	Retired from business life.
20 Aug 1947	Died at his home in Rye, New York.

James Guthrie Harbord

James J. Cooke

O n 6 April 1917, after bitter debate, the U.S. Congress declared war
on Germany. It was an unprepared America that entered the conflict
in Europe that had raged since 1914. Her army consisted of less than
200,000 men scattered over the United States and its empire, so the decision
to send combat forces to France meant a massive increase in the army, rapid
modernization, and an expansion of the officer corps,
which would have been unthinkable only a few
months before. By May 1917 the United States
had a commander for those troops going
"Over There" in the person of Gen. John
Joseph Pershing, the most experienced
officer in the army.

From 1916 into 1917, Pershing had
commanded the Punitive Expedition into
Mexico to chase down the Mexican leader
Pancho Villa. One of the things that "Black
Jack" Pershing learned while campaigning in
Mexico was the absolute necessity of an efficient
staff to support and advise the commander. The
commander did not have the time to supervise his staff
and he needed an intelligent, hard-driving, chief of staff. Of equal importance
for John J. Pershing, his chief of staff would have to be a man of personal loyalty,
a soldier in whom "Black Jack" could repose his most intimate thoughts.

Like John J. Pershing, James Guthrie Harbord was the American success
story, the young man from the heartland who rose from humble beginnings
to the pinnacle of power. Harbord was born in Bloomington, Illinois, on 21
March 1866 and migrated with his family to Kansas. Planning a career in
teaching, he graduated from Kansas State Agricultural College at the age
of twenty. Like his friend Pershing, he found teaching unrewarding and in
1889 enlisted in the army. In 1891 he was commissioned as a lieutenant.

Within three years Harbord had accomplished a great deal, having been the distinguished graduate at the army's School of Cavalry and Infantry at Fort Leavenworth, Kansas. During the Spanish American War he saw no battle action, despite being in a unit that styled itself as the Torrey Rough Riders (2nd U.S. Volunteer Cavalry). After a stint with the 10th Cavalry, Harbord served in Cuba from 1899 to 1901 under Gen. Leonard Wood. In 1902 Harbord went to the Philippines where he served with Pershing.[1]

Once given the assignment to command the American Expeditionary Forces (AEF), Pershing began to assemble the staff that would go with him to France. He asked Major Harbord, then a student at the Army War College in Washington, to become the chief of staff. As Harbord began to compile a list of potential staff officers, he began to manifest a very protective attitude toward Pershing. On the way to France he worried that Pres. Woodrow Wilson would have to give Pershing more rank than a major general or he would have difficulties with other general officers, such as Leonard Wood and Hunter Liggett.[2] This concern for Pershing's rank and position would be an important part of Harbord's tenure as AEF chief of staff.

Harbord and his boss had only the vaguest idea of what they were doing in creating a general headquarters and a staff for the AEF. There were only about 200 trained staff officers in the U.S. Army, and none of those had any real experience at the divisional, corps, or army level of command and staff. There were a School of the Line and a Staff College at Fort Leavenworth, and the graduates were in great demand in the AEF. By and large it was the younger majors and lieutenant colonels, those who had spent two years at Fort Leavenworth, who would become the chiefs of staff for the combat corps and divisions, but there were so few of them.[3] In creating a staff Harbord faced the daunting task of bringing together a group of soldiers who had almost no training and precious little experience.

To complicate the situation, during their transatlantic trip, Pershing and Harbord organized the staff into three functional areas, each presided over by a "chief of section." Those selected, no matter how motivated and eager, were not deputy chiefs of staff directly under the supervision of the chief of staff. Only because of willingness and dedication did those chiefs work with Harbord. In Washington bureau and section chiefs had stymied the purchase, storage, and flow of supplies.[4] Harbord was determined that that would not happen. Another problem that surfaced immediately was the serious underestimation of how many officers it would take to run the General Headquarters (GHQ), AEF. Brigadier General Dennis Nolan, Pershing's very effective intelligence chief, recalled, "The British staff seemed to be sort of stunned that we had so very few officers with us. They took it to mean that we had very little comprehension of what we were going up against."[5] The British, and later the French, were correct as far as size and understanding were concerned. Pershing's staff in the summer of 1917 resembled the size of a combat brigade's staff rather than one for an army.

Once Pershing's party arrived in England, and then in France, there were rounds of receptions, obligatory visits to royalty and dignitaries, and sightseeing. In Paris Pershing had had enough and strained at the bit to get to work. By the late summer Pershing and the GHQ moved to Chaumont, which would be the home of the staff for the next year and few months.[6] It was time for James Guthrie Harbord to go to work as the chief of staff. Pershing had a goal in mind, and that was to create an American army that would have its own commanders and its own sector of the battlefield. Also, Black Jack Pershing firmly believed that the war would be lost or would end in inglorious stalemate unless the troops got out of the trenches and faced the enemy using open or maneuver warfare. This was the Pershing Orthodoxy, and Harbord was a disciple. No one served at the GHQ unless they showed to Harbord that they too were devoted to the Pershing Orthodoxy and to Black Jack himself. Also, Pershing was focused on the western front. In Washington, Secretary of War Newton Baker and Pershing had agreed that everything else was a sideshow.[7]

One of the first orders of business for Pershing was to construct a staff by taking the best ideas the British and French had to offer. Harbord understood that those detailed to run the various sections would have to spend the first weeks away from Chaumont to see what the Allies were doing to keep large armies in the field. At Harbord's urging in July and August, Pershing requested that the War Department quickly send dozens of trained officers to be assigned to work in the various staff sections. These officers, including Robert Davis, Frank R. McCoy, George Van Horn Moseley, Malin Craig, Preston Brown, LeRoy Eltinge, and others, were known as some of the best and brightest in the army at the time, and Harbord knew exactly where he wanted them to be in the staff at Chaumont.

No sooner had Harbord allocated space for the various sections at Chaumont than he realized that something was wrong. Preconceived notions about a staff did not fit the current situation and were basically unworkable. The old system of three sections—combat (operations), administration, and intelligence—simply would not work, as the American forces in France grew in number. Harbord's view, as chief of staff, was basically, "No one working under my supervision was expected to take to a superior any matter that he was officially competent to settle for himself. Powers not specifically reserved to higher authority were vested in subordinates."[8] Harbord had two reasons for this: first, he jealously guarded his relationship with Pershing; and second, as a good chief of staff, he protected his commander's time. Pershing could be a micromanager if not controlled, and he would get into minutiae. Harbord was determined not to allow small things to come before Pershing. Harbord would never conceal anything from Black Jack Pershing, but on the other hand he had no intention of allowing majors or lieutenant colonels to take up the commander's valuable time.

While Harbord set a tone for the GHQ there was still something wrong, and the staff was not functioning as it should. To rectify this, Harbord suggested and Pershing agreed that Col. William D. Connor be made chief of the Coordination Section. Connor viewed coordination between the sections as if he had a team of very spirited horses making it necessary to yell, "Speed up, slow down, go right, go left."[9] The basic problem for Harbord, and now for W. D. Connor, was that there were too many officers at Chaumont doing every possible task for the AEF. In the fall and winter of 1917 the AEF could afford some time since the combat strength of the force was four infantry divisions. Part of the problem rested with the fact that Harbord had not been trained at the Staff College at Fort Leavenworth, and much of what he was trying to do at Chaumont was very new for him.[10]

For the first few months at Chaumont Harbord remained reactive, allowing subordinates to present ideas and programs. Connor, who had extensive staff experience, corrected this to a point. For all practical purposes, William D. Connor, soon to be promoted to brigadier general, was Harbord's assistant. The one staff officer whom neither Harbord nor Connor felt the need to coordinate was Brigadier General Nolan, chief of AEF's intelligence effort. Personally selected by Pershing on Harbord's recommendation, Nolan became one of the GHQ's most effective staff officers, building a military intelligence section from literally nothing.

Harbord's job became easier in August when Harold B. Fiske and Robert C. "Corky" Davis arrived at GHQ. In July Pershing had requested several dozen officers for staff work, and those two majors were on the list. Fiske was assigned to operations, but soon became associated with all AEF training activities. He needed very little supervision from Harbord, and he got along well with Brig. Gen. Fox Connor, who ran the operations section. Together Connor and Fiske could manage training and operational problems without involving

Harbord. Davis, a West Point graduate (1898), had served in Cuba during the Spanish-American War and was cited for gallantry in the Philippines. He was a brilliant organizer who understood the necessity to run the office almost as a business. Davis was assigned to be the assistant adjutant general of the AEF, which well suited his many talents. At first Corky Davis, who was obviously a favorite of Pershing and Harbord, served under Brig. Gen. Benjamin Alvord; but as Alvord's health deteriorated Davis became in fact the adjutant general. When Alvord was ordered home because of ill health in the early fall of 1917, Davis stepped into the job.

Pershing and Harbord recognized that there would never be enough staff officers to do what the AEF had to do if the Americans were to field an army that could fight. In late August 1917 Pershing authorized the opening of a General Staff College at Langres to train officers for three months. Harbord selected Brig. Gen. James "Dad" McAndrew as head of the staff school, which was scheduled to open in October.[11] The British and French opposed the opening of the AEF's staff school, arguing that potential staff officers should be sent to their headquarters for training. The emphasis, in this practical environment, would be on staff procedures and combined arms warfare.[12] Harbord continually protected the Langres concept and made it a special emphasis item. The French believed that they would provide a director for the Staff College as well as instructors. It took Harbord the month of October to convince the French that all the AEF required were some advisors and instructors.[13]

With the staff slowly taking shape at Chaumont, Harbord spent a great deal of time being Pershing's major domo. Frankly, the GHQ at that point had little to do. By Christmas 1917 the AEF had the 1st, 2nd, 26th, and 42nd Divisions in France with little prospect of seeing other divisional sized units until late February or March. From Harbord's records and published accounts it appears that he spent a great deal of time in travel or in advising Pershing. W. D. Connor did a good job at coordination, but with the small size of the AEF, the staff could do little as long as the AEF's combat divisions were in training with either the British or the French.

Harbord had an eye for talent and wisely used officers who showed promise. He was not an unreasonable man and would listen to requests and complaints from subordinate officers. If Harbord found that a request made sense he would make a decision quickly. For example, Harbord noticed the great talents of Hugh A. Drum, a captain who accompanied Pershing to France on the steamship *Baltic*. Assigned to work with GHQ operations chief Brigadier General Connor, Drum was given a number of critical tasks. He was part of a major study on the AEF and strategy on the western front, he worked with the French on transportation questions, and he observed British and French operations. At Harbord's urging Drum was promoted to brigadier general and was picked to become chief of staff of the U.S. First Army.

Harbord could make a decision, a critical trait for a chief of staff. In January and February 1918 the AEF was in the process of building various schools, from the General Staff School at Langres to corps and divisional schools. In January, II Corps schools tapped Maj. William J. "Wild Bill" Donovan to become an instructor. At that time Donovan commanded a battalion in the 165th Infantry, 42nd Division. Donovan resisted the transfer, and the 42nd Division chief of staff, Brig. Gen. Douglas MacArthur, went directly to Harbord asking that Donovan remain with his unit. In a fairly short period of time, Harbord agreed that Donovan remain with his men and allowed MacArthur to select another officer to go to II Corps.[14] Harbord believed that for the chief of staff and the group of officers he controlled the "greatest interest is to identify and secure the latest for war: its greatest problem is to find the right men."[15]

Harbord picked the right men for the staff, but still things did not seem to be going quite right at Chaumont. Harbord later pinpointed the basic problem, stating, "As long as we had no troops [the original staff structure] worked well. If the war had ended before we left Paris, the Staff would have gone into history as a success."[16] In consultation with Pershing, Harbord decided to convene a board of trained staff officers to reconstruct the GHQ. On 7 February 1918, Harbord brought Col. Johnson Hagood to Chaumont to preside over a meeting to redefine the staff.[17] What came out of the meeting was a complete change in the way GHQ did business. The primary staff was divided into five sections, each headed by an assistant chief of staff. The G system—G-1 Personnel, G-2 Intelligence, G-3 Operations, G-4 Logistics, and G-5 Training—was put into place. Harbord would have control of the staff, with W. D. Connor continuing to coordinate efforts. Corky Davis would remain the adjutant general at Chaumont, freeing Harbord from the day-to-day concern over such things as writing orders and interpreting both army and AEF regulations and directives.

Of equal importance, the personnel and logistics functions would be moved out of Chaumont to Tours, creating a slimmed-down "battle staff" for Pershing. Harbord would then supervise this staff, advise the commander, arrange meetings for Pershing, and help oversee units in training.[18] The support Harbord gave to soon-to-be brigadier general Johnson Hagood and his board was one of Harbord's most important contributions as AEF chief of staff. What this reform did was to organize the staff and designate staff functions while at the same time plan for the battle staff that would carry on the two great campaigns during the fall of 1918. Harbord's concepts were repeated almost verbatim in 1919 when the U.S. First Army defined the chief of staff's role by saying, "The successful commander receives the advice from a staff, especially from his chief of staff. After coming to a definite decision as to a plan of action, he turns it over to such a staff."[19]

With the staff now functioning well, despite some grumbling from personnel and logistics officers who disliked being far removed from the seat of AEF power, Harbord was tasked by Pershing to take over a number of important duties. In late March he accompanied Secretary of War Baker on a tour of the front. Baker, who had been selected by Wilson in 1916 because of his well-known pacifist tendencies, enjoyed his relations with the AEF, and he found in Harbord a man with whom he could discuss issues of the greatest political importance.[20]

Harbord had the personal friendship of Pershing, and Harbord took for himself the personal mission of protecting and advising his general and his friend. He never tired of sending lengthy memoranda to Pershing about everything from promotions, to Pershing's relationship with his subordinate generals, to warnings about those in the War Department who might wish to do Black Jack Pershing some harm. This is a key in understanding Harbord as the first modern American chief of staff. Only one other man in the AEF could so approach Pershing, and that was Brig. Gen. Charles Gates Dawes. At first Harbord resented Dawes, who had been one of Pershing's closest friends since they both attended law school at the University of Nebraska. Pershing made Dawes the head of the Purchasing Board in August 1917, and Harbord quickly recognized the influence this man of business and banking had at Chaumont.[21] When Harbord later became the head of the AEF Service of Supply (SOS) in the late summer 1918, he relied heavily on Dawes and on Johnson, much to the aggravation of George Van Horn Moseley, the G-4 at Chaumont. Van Horn Moseley felt that Harbord had violated the system that he helped to create by bypassing the head of logistics at Chaumont.[22]

How far should a chief of staff go to influence his commander? In Harbord's case, given the deep friendship between the two and given the fact that Harbord was plowing new ground, it appears that he became an alter ego. Harbord was constantly advising Pershing about everything from his relations with U.S. Army chief of staff Peyton March, the War Department, and senior

AEF generals. What Harbord did went way beyond just advice. Prior to the Baker visit in early 1918, Harbord told Pershing that when he discussed army matters with the secretary he should insist that Black Jack have a deciding voice in selecting who commanded the new divisions being formed in the United States for service in France. In other words, according to Harbord, Pershing should usurp the prerogatives of the Army chief of staff.[23]

When General March suggested a reasonable plan to rotate experienced AEF staff officers to the United States and replace them with good officers, sent to France to learn the system, Harbord told Pershing, "This is war and you can not in justice to your command or yourself, rob it of officers you have selected and trained in order to provide General March with an efficient staff."[24] Pershing killed the plan, and much of his opposition was based on Harbord's ideas. This is a case of Harbord's focusing on the AEF and not looking at total army requirements, and a good opportunity to train and professionalize staff officers was lost. The unwillingness of Pershing to take qualified and energetic officers from the General Staff in Washington created a good deal of animosity between those who served in France and those who remained in Washington.

On the other hand, Harbord's considerable organizational ability had given form and structure to the evolving AEF staff. The five G-level staff sections ran well, and work was done promptly, taking a great burden from Pershing's shoulders. Curiously, Harbord never saw fit to institute a formalized briefing program for Pershing, where each staff officer would present the current situation to the commanding general. Pershing was fed bits and pieces of what the staff was doing, and that was all filtered through Harbord. Only Dennis Nolan, the G2, had immediate access to Pershing when intelligence information became available, and Nolan updated Pershing's situation map. Certainly Harbord was guarding Pershing's time by controlling access to the general, and Pershing did have a bad tendency to take too much time with those who came into his office. But one must wonder how much Pershing knew about the interrelationship of the various staff sections.

In April 1918 Harbord expressed a great desire for a combat command, which Pershing had promised him. What Harbord wanted was the 1st Brigade of the 1st Infantry Division, a highly prized assignment.[25] On 30 April 1918 Harbord was sent to command the 2nd Brigade, the Marine Brigade, of the 2nd Infantry Division, and he eventually rose to command the division in the July fighting.[26] The communications between Harbord and Pershing never slowed down, and when Harbord became head of the SOS in August 1918, he continued as Pershing's adviser. After the war Harbord took it upon himself to advise Newton Baker on what to do with Pershing as the AEF was coming home to the United States.[27] Harbord also handpicked his successor at AEF GHQ. Brigadier General James "Dad" McAndrew was brought from Langres to Chaumont and served as Pershing's chief of staff until the end of the war.[28]

What did Harbord, with no staff education prior to the war, accomplish as Pershing's chief of staff? When Pershing, Harbord, and the small contingent of American soldiers boarded the ship *Baltic* in 1917 they had no idea of what constituted a modern warfighting staff. The concept of three functional areas was faulty and unworkable. It is to Harbord's credit that this was recognized and corrected with the Hagood Board in 1918. Before Johnson Hagood went to Chaumont, Harbord had taken major steps forward. On 21 September 1917 he standardized the staff sections' reports, instituted a message log system, and established a centralized message distribution system. By October the staff was working on established time lines, and in January 1918 Harbord designated an assistant chief of staff to manage the staff when he was away from Chaumont. Also by January he had put in place a procedure for staff visit reports whereby a staff officer would share his impressions with all other members of the GHQ staff. McAndrew inherited a well-organized five-section staff with five solid section chiefs.

On the other hand, Harbord was too involved with questions that were better left to Pershing. Nowhere is this more evident than in Harbord's constant campaigns against the War Department and Army chief of staff March. Harbord's personal commitment to Pershing often worked to the detriment of the army as a whole. Pershing guarded his own rights and responsibilities as commander of the AEF, but Harbord, because of their personal relationship, reinforced and pushed Pershing to even more antagonism toward Washington. As head of the SOS Harbord often ignored the system he had set up and clashed with George Van Horn Moseley over supply–G-4 issues. Harbord's support for and reliance on Dawes and Hagood created a gulf between the SOS and the G-4 at Chaumont at a time when supply matters were at their most critical in the fall of 1918.

Harbord, however, must be seen in the context of where the AEF staff began and where it ended. As the first American operational-level chief of staff in a modern war, Harbord created a system that worked. He had an eye for talent, as shown by his selection of Dennis Nolan as G-2 and his support for making Hugh Drum chief of staff for the First Army. Pershing was his friend; and his loyalty to Black Jack never wavered; but it did cloud his vision for the army as a whole. He knew what he had done in the Great War. In February 1929 Harbord addressed the Army War College about his time as chief of staff, and he said, "As [the AEF staff] was organized and it was operated, it should form the model for any future war in which our country may engage if under circumstance . . . similar to those which confronted us in France."[29] James Guthrie Harbord had his share of faults, but as chief of Staff of the AEF during a critical period he set a tone for the rest of the war and for future chiefs of staff who served in the field.

Notes

1. James G. Harbord, *The American Expeditionary Forces: Its Organization and Accomplishments* (Evanston, Ill.: Evanston Publishing, 1929), 12.
2. James G. Harbord, *Leaves from a War Diary* (New York: Dodd, Mead and Co., 1925), 8.
3. Edward M. Coffman, "The AEF Leaders' Education for War," in *The Great War, 1914–1918*, ed. R. J. Q. Adams (College Station: Texas A&M Press, 1990), 139–59. Of critical importance is the first-rate Timothy K. Nenninger, *The Leavenworth Schools and the Old Army: Education and Professionalism and the Officer Corps of the United States Army, 1881–1918* (Westport, Conn.: Greenwood, 1978). Also see James J. Cooke, *Pershing and His Generals: Command and Staff in the AEF* (Westport, Conn.: Praeger, 1997).
4. For a detailed study of the confusion and chaos in Washington see Phyllis A. Zimmerman, *The Neck of the Bottle: George Washington Goethals and the Reorganization of the U.S. Army Supply System, 1917–1919* (College Station: Texas A&M Press, 1992).
5. Dennis Nolan's typed memoir on Pershing's memoirs, completed between 1931 and 1932 is in the Nolan Papers, U.S. Army Military History Institute Archives, Carlisle Barracks, Pennsylvania (hereafter MHI with appropriate collection noted).
6. John J. Pershing, *My Experiences in the World War*, vol. 1 (New York, 1931), 100–104.
7. Baker to Peyton March, 7 September 1927, in the Peyton Conway March Papers, Library of Congress (LOC), Washington, D.C.
8. Harbord, *American Expeditionary Forces*, 23–24.
9. Interview with Maj. Gen. W. D. Connor, Washington, D.C., 21 October 1947, in Army General Staff Interviews Collection, MHI.
10. These comments appear between 9 and 31 August 1917 in the Hugh Drum Diary, Hugh Drum Papers, MHI.
11. Memo by Colonel Paul Malone, 27 August 1917, in Records Group 120, Carton 1608, Records of the General Headquarters, National Archives, Washington, D.C.
12. Memorandum by Col. Briant Harris Wells, c. June 1918, in the Maj. Gen.M Briant Harris Wells Papers, MHI.
13. Harbord, *Leaves from a War Diary*, 206–7.
14. Diary entry, 3 February 1918, in the William J. Donovan Diary, 1917–18, William J. Donovan Papers, MHI.

15. Harbord, *American Expeditionary Forces*, 73.
16. James G. Harbord, *The American Army in France, 1917–1919* (Boston: Little, Brown, 1936), 211.
17. Diary entries for 8 and 9 February 1918 in the Johnson Hagood Diary, Hagood Family Papers, MHI.
18. Harbord, *American Expeditionary Forces*, 25–27. Harbord, *The American Army in France*, 213–17.
19. First U.S. Army Definition of the Chief of Staff, 1919, in the Hugh Drum Papers, MHI.
20. Harbord, *Leaves from a War Diary*, 241–52.
21. Ibid., 353–56.
22. Van Horn Moseley to March, 21 December 1931, in Peyton March Papers, LOC.
23. Harbord to Pershing, 8 March 1918, in the James G. Harbord Papers, LOC.
24. Harbord to Pershing, 16 March 1918 and 28 March 1918, ibid.
25. Harbord to Pershing, 13 April 1918, ibid.
26. Harbord, *American Expeditionary Forces*, 6–7.
27. Harbord to Pershing, 30 April 1919, in Harbord Papers.
28. Harbord to Pershing, 30 March 1918, in ibid.; Harbord, *The American Army in France*, 263–64.
29. Harbord, *American Expeditionary Forces*, 26–27.

Contributors

James J. Cooke is professor emeritus of history at the University of Mississippi. He is the author of five books on World War I, including *All-Americans at War*; *Pershing and His Generals*; *The U.S. Air Service in the Great War*; *The Rainbow Division in the Great War, 1917–1919*, and *Billy Mitchell*. His academic honors include Chevalier, Ordre des Palmes Académique (France); Fellow, The Royal Historical Society (United Kingdom); and Honorary Fellow of the Second World War Experience Centre (United Kingdom). His military experience includes extensive service with the Mississippi Army National Guard. During the Gulf War he served as a liaison officer from the U.S. XVIII Airborne Corps to the French 6th Light Tank Division. He was placed on the retired list as a brigadier general in 1995. His military decorations include the Bronze Star medal.

Samuel J. Doss served in the U.S. Army as a field artillery officer and an Army historian. He holds a BS in political science from James Madison University and an MA in history from George Mason University. He is currently vice president of Operational Support and Services (formerly REEP, Inc.), a provider of battlefield staff rides, language services, and special forces training to the U.S. military. He has personally led more than seventy battlefield staff rides for U.S. Army officers and noncommissioned officers on European and American battlefields, and covering all periods of military history. He is the editor of three book-length projects, a contributor to *World War II in Europe: An Encyclopedia*, *Military History* magazine, and the *International Journal of Naval History*.

Dr. Antulio J. Echevarria II is currently assigned as the director of research at the Strategic Studies Institute at the U.S. Army War College in Carlisle Barracks, Pennsylvania. A retired U.S. Army officer, he graduated from the U.S. Military Academy in 1981, was commissioned as an armor officer, and has held a variety of command and staff assignments in Germany and in the

United States. He has also served as an assistant professor of European history at the U.S. Military Academy, as the Squadron S-3 (Operations Officer) of 3-16th Cavalry, as chief of Battalion/Task Force and Brigade Doctrine at the U.S. Army Armor Center at Fort Knox, as a researcher and writer on the Army After Next project, as a speechwriter for the U.S. Army chief of staff, and as the director of National Security Affairs at the Strategic Studies Institute. He is a graduate of the U.S. Army's Command and General Staff College and U.S. Army War College, and holds MA and PhD degrees in history from Princeton University. He has published three books: *Clausewitz and Contemporary War*; *Imagining Future Wars*; and *After Clausewitz: German Military Thinkers before the Great War*. He also published articles in a number of scholarly and professional military journals.

Dr. Robert T. Foley is senior lecturer in modern military history at the University of Liverpool. Before joining the University of Liverpool, he taught for five years at the Joint Services Command and Staff College. A specialist in German military thought, he has published extensively on the subject. His *German Strategy and the Path to Verdun* won the Royal Historical Society's Gladstone Prize in 2005. He has also published an annotated translation, *Alfred von Schlieffen's Military Writings*, and has published numerous articles in academic and military journals. Dr. Foley is currently working on two major projects: The first, "Quest for Decisive Victory in the First World War," will provide a re-examination of Ludendorff's strategic thought during World War I. The second, "Making Strategy: Studies in Decisionmaking During Wartime," will use a series of case studies to analyze successes and failures in the formulation of strategy during a number of twentieth-century conflicts.

Norbert H. Gaworek taught German, Russian, and Soviet history at the University of Wisconsin–Green Bay after earning a PhD in history and a certificate in Russian studies from the University of Wisconsin–Madison. In 1999 he retired from teaching and the chairmanship of the history department. He served on active duty with the 3rd Armored Division (Spearhead) from 1959 to 1962; he headed the legal section of Division Artillery and the Hanau Area Command in Germany. Gaworek has published in regional, national, and international publications on military history, economic warfare, and international affairs. He produced twenty-four one-hour public television programs for the annual Great Decisions series, which were broadcast throughout Wisconsin. He also founded *Voyageur: Historical*

Journal of Northeast Wisconsin. Until his retirement he was a fellow in the Seminar on Armed Forces and Society and taught an on-line graduate course in Russian military history for American Military University. Gaworek now lives in St. Paul, Minnesota, with his wife and youngest son.

David S. Heidler and **Jeanne T. Heidler,** natives of Georgia, met and married in graduate school. They have taught at the university level for almost two decades. David is currently associated with Colorado State University–Pueblo, and Jeanne is professor of history at the U.S. Air Force Academy, where she also serves as deputy of American history. They have collaborated on numerous articles on the early American republic and antebellum periods as well as several books, including *Old Hickory's War: Andrew Jackson and the Quest for Empire; Encyclopedia of the War of 1812;* the five-volume *Encyclopedia of the American Civil War; Daily Life in the Early American Republic, 1790–1820; Manifest Destiny; The War of 1812;* and *The Mexican War.* They are currently writing a biography of Henry Clay that will be published by Random House in 2009.

Steven B. Rogers is a historian who has been based in Washington, D.C., for the past thirty years. He holds a BA in German and English from Florida Southern College, an MA in German literature from the University of Arizona, and a PhD in German studies from the University of Maryland. He served as a contributing editor for *World War II in Europe: An Encyclopedia.* He is also the editor of *A Gradual Twilight: An Appreciation of John Haines.* He has written and lectured extensively on a variety of historical and cultural topics and is currently working on a book about Frank Lloyd Wright's designs for Florida Southern College. He resides with his wife in Mount Rainier, Maryland.

Paul J. Rose is a professor emeritus with the European Division of the University of Maryland. He has a BA from the University of Maryland, an MA from the University of Arkansas, an MS from Troy University, and a DEA from the Sorbonne. He was a contributor and assistant editor for *World War II Europe: An Encyclopedia.* He is retired from the Air Force and is a certified on-line teacher who taught both distant education and traditional classroom courses for the University of Maryland in the fields of history and political science until his recent retirement. He lives with his wife, Yvette, on the French Riviera.

Andy Simpson is a software testing consultant by profession. He was born in North Shields, United Kingdom, and educated at the University of London, where he received a BA (Hons.) in history and a PhD. His books include *Hot Blood and Cold Steel: Life and Death in the Trenches of the Great War*; *The Evolution of Victory: British Battles on the Western Front, 1914–18*; and *Directing Operations: British Corps Command on the Western Front, 1914–18*. He contributed to the new *Oxford DNB*; *The Reader's Guide to Military History* (ed. C. Messenger); and *Command and Control on the Western Front: The British Army's Experience, 1914–1918* (ed. G. D. Sheffield and D. Todman). He is a member of the Centre for First World War Studies at the University of Birmingham and the British Commission for Military History.

Ulrich Trumpener is an emeritus professor of history at the University of Alberta, Canada. His many publications deal mostly with military and diplomatic developments in Europe and the Middle East in the last century. He is the author of *Germany and the Ottoman Empire, 1914–1918*.

Spencer C. Tucker retired from teaching in 2003 as holder of the John Biggs Chair of Military History at the Virginia Military Institute. He is the author or editor of twenty-seven books and encyclopedias on military and naval history, including *The Great War, 1914–18*; *The European Powers in the First World War: An Encyclopedia*; and the award-winning five-volume *Encyclopedia of World War I: A Political, Social, and Military History*.

Steven E. Woodworth is the author of *Jefferson Davis and His Generals: The Failure of Confederate Command in the West*; *Davis and Lee at War*; *Six Armies in Tennessee: The Chickamauga and Chattanooga Campaigns*; *While God Is Marching On: The Religious World of Civil War Soldiers*; and *Beneath a Northern Sky: A Short History of the Gettysburg Campaign*. He is the editor of *Grant's Lieutenants: From Cairo to Vicksburg*; *Civil War Generals in Defeat*; and *The American Civil War: A Handbook of Literature and Research*. He received his BA from Southern Illinois University in 1982 and his PhD from Rice University in 1987, and he has taught at Texas Christian University since 1997.

David T. Zabecki is the author of *Steel Wind: Colonel Georg Bruchmüller and the Birth of Modern Artillery* and *The German 1918 Offensives: A Case Study in the Operational Level of War*; the editor of *World War Two in Europe: An Encyclopedia*; *Vietnam: A Reader*; and the editor and co-translator of *On the*

German Art of War: Truppenführung. He is also the editor of *Vietnam* magazine, the only regularly published periodical devoted to the military history of the Vietnam War. He enlisted in the U.S. Army in 1966 and served as an infantry rifleman in Vietnam in 1967 and 1968. He continued serving in the regular Army, the Army National Guard, and the Army Reserve until his retirement in 2007. He is a 1988 graduate of the U.S. Army Command and General Staff College and a 1995 graduate of the U.S. Army War College. He has commanded as a captain, lieutenant colonel, colonel, brigadier general, and major general. From 1998 to 2000 he was the chief of staff of the 7th Army Reserve Command in Germany. From 2000 to 2002 he was one of the deputy chiefs of the U.S. Army Reserve. In 2002 and 2003 he was the commanding general of the 7th Army Reserve Command, and during the buildup and first months of the war with Iraq he served simultaneously as the director of the U.S. Army Europe Deployment Operations Center, which moved 33,000 soldiers and their equipment from Europe to the Middle East. During the last half of 2003 he served in Israel as the senior security advisor to the multi-agency U.S. Coordinating and Monitoring Mission, also known as the Roadmap to Peace in the Middle East. In 2004 he commanded all U.S. forces in Normandy, France, committed to supporting the observances of the sixtieth anniversary of the D-day landings. In 2005 and 2006 he commanded the U.S. Southern European Task Force Rear (Airborne) and served as the senior U.S. Army commander south of the Alps. He holds a PhD in military science, technology, and management from Britain's Royal Military College of Science.

Bibliography

Allen, Stacy D. "'If He Had Less Rank': Lewis Wallace." In *Grant's Lieutenants: From Cairo to Vicksburg*, ed. Steven E. Woodworth, 63–89. Lawrence: University Press of Kansas, 2001.

Anderson, Eugene. *Nationalism and the Cultural Crises in Prussia, 1806–1815*. London, 1967.

Asprey, Robert B. *The German High Command at War: Hindenburg and Ludendorff Conduct World War I*. New York: Morrow, 1991.

Aston, Major-General Sir George. *The Biography of the Late Marshal Foch*. New York: Macmillan, 1929.

Bankwitz, Philip C. F. *Maxime Weygand and Civil-Military Relations in Modern France*. Cambridge, Mass.: Harvard University Press, 1967.

Bauer, Max. *Der grosse Krieg in Feld und Heimat*. Tübingen: Osiander, 1921.

Baumgart, Winfried. *Deutsche Ostpolitik 1918*. Munich: Oldenbourg Verlag, 1966.

Blake, Robert, ed. *The Private Papers of Douglas Haig, 1914–1919*. London: Eyre and Spottiswoode, 1952.

Blond, Georges. *La Grande Armée*. Translated by Marshal May. Reprint. London: Arms and Armour Press, 1997.

Bond, Brian. *The Victorian Army and the Staff College, 1854–1914*. London: Eyre Methuen, 1972.

Bowden, Scott. *Napoleon at Austerlitz*. Chicago: Emperor's Press, 1997.

Braim, Paul F. *The Test of Battle: The American Expeditionary Forces in the Meuse-Argonne Campaign*. Shippensburg, Pa., 1987.

Broers, Michael. *Europe Under Napoleon, 1799–1815*. New York: Hodder Arnold, 1996.

Bucholz, Arden. *Moltke and the German Wars, 1864–1871*. New York: Palgrave, 2001.

———. *Moltke, Schlieffen and Prussian War Planning*. Oxford: Berg, 1991.

Carr, Caleb. "The Man of Silence." *Military History Quarterly* (Spring 1989): 104–5.

Carsten, F. L. *The Reichswehr and Politics, 1918–1933*. Berkeley: University of California Press, 1973.

Castle, Ian. *Aspern and Wagram 1809: Mighty Clash of Empires*. Osprey Military Campaign 33. London: Osprey Publishing, 1994; reprint, 1997.

Catton, Bruce. *Grant Moves South*. Indianapolis: Little, Brown, 1960.

Chandler, David. *Aspern and Wagram*. New York: Macmillan, 1994.

———. *Austerlitz 1805: Battle of the Three Emperors*. London, 1990.

————. *The Campaigns of Napoleon: The Mind and Method of History's Greatest Soldier.* New York, 1973.

————. *Jena 1806: Napoleon Destroys Prussia.* Osprey Military Campaign 20. London: Osprey Publishing, 1993.

————. *On the Napoleonic Wars.* Mechanicsburg, Pa. 1994.

————. *Waterloo.* Osprey Military Campaign 18. London: Osprey Publishing, 1993.

————, ed. *Napoleon's Marshals.* New York: Macmillan, 1987.

Chetlain, Augustus. *Recollections of Seventy Years.* Galena, Ill.: Gazette Publishing, 1899.

Coffman, Edward. *The Old Army: A Portrait of the American Army in Peacetime, 1784–1898.* Oxford: Oxford University Press, 1986.

Coignet, Jean-Roch. *The Note-Books of Captain Coignet: Soldier of the Empire, 1799–1816.* London, 1998.

Connelly, Owen. *Blundering to Glory: Napoleon's Military Campaigns.* Wilmington, Del.: Scholarly Resources, 1987.

Cooke, James J. *Pershing and His Generals: Command and Staff in the AEF.* Westport, Conn.: Praeger, 1997.

Corum, James S. *The Roots of Blitzkrieg: Hans von Seeckt and German Military Reform.* Lawrence: University Press of Kansas, 1992.

Craig, Gordon A. *The Politics of the Prussian Army, 1640–1945.* Oxford: Oxford University Press, 1956.

Cron, Hermann. *Geschichte des deutschen Heeres im Weltkriege.* Berlin: Siegismund, 1937.

Crosswell, D. K. R. *The Chief of Staff: The Military Career of General Walter Bedell Smith.* Contributions in Military Studies. New York: Greenwood, 1991.

Davidson, John. *Haig: Master of the Field.* London: Peter Nevill, 1953.

Davies, Frank, and Graham Maddocks. *Bloody Red Tabs.* London: Leo Cooper, 1995.

De Groot, Gerard. *Douglas Haig, 1861–1928.* London: Unwin Hyman, 1988.

Delderfield, R. F. *The March of the 26: Napoleon's Marshals.* London, 1962.

Derrecagaix, Victor Bernard. *Le Maréchal Berthier, Prince de Wagram et de Neuchatel.* Paris, 1905.

Destremau, Bernard. *Weygand.* Paris, 1989.

Douglas, Henry Kyd. *I Rode with Stonewall, Being Chiefly the War Experiences of the Youngest Member of Jackson's Staff from the John Brown Raid to the Hanging of Mrs. Surratt.* Chapel Hill: University of North Carolina Press, 1940.

Dupuy, Trevor N. *A Genius for War: The German Army and General Staff, 1807–1945.* Englewood Cliffs, N.J.: Prentice-Hall, 1977.

————. *The Military Lives of Hindenburg and Ludendorff of Imperial Germany.* New York: Watts, 1970.

Echevarria, Antulio J., II. "Moltke and the German Military Tradition: His Theories and Legacies." *Parameters* 26 (Spring 1996): 91–99.

Eckenrode, H. J., and Bryan Conrad. *George B. McClellan: The Man Who Saved the Union.* Chapel Hill: University of North Carolina Press, 1941.

Ehlert, Hans, Michael Epkenhans, and Gerhard P. Gross. *Der Schleiffenplan: Analysen und Dokumente*. Munich: Ferdinand Schöningh, 2006.

Elting, John. *Swords Around the Throne: Napoleon's Grand Armée*. Detroit, 1988.

Epstein, Klaus. *The Genesis of German Conservatism*. Princeton, N.J.: Princeton University Press, 1966.

Esposito, V. J., and John Elting. *A Military Atlas of the Napoleonic Wars*. New York, 1964.

Falkenhayn, Erich von. *General Headquarters 1914–1916 and Its Critical Decisions*. London: Hutchinson, 1919.

Fedyshyn, Oleh S. *Germany's Drive to the East and the Ukrainian Revolution, 1917–1918*. New Brunswick, N.J., 1971.

Fischer, Fritz. *Griff nach der Weltmacht: Die Kriegszielpolitik des kaiserlichen Deutschland, 1914–1918*. Düsseldorf: Droste Verlag, 1964.

Foch, Ferdinand. *The Memoirs of Ferdinand Foch*. Translated by T. Bentley Mott. Garden City, N.Y.: Doubleday, Doran, 1931.

Foerster, Roland G., ed. *Generalfeldmarschall von Moltke: Bedeutung und Wirkung*. Munich: R. Oldenburg, 1991.

Foerster, Roland, et al. *Operational Thinking in Clausewitz, Moltke, Schlieffen, and Manstein*. Bonn: E. S. Mittler, 1989.

Foerster, Wolfgang. *Ludendorff: Der Feldherr im Unglück*. Wiesbaden, 1952.

Foley, Robert T. *Alfred von Schlieffen's Military Writings*. London: Frank Cass, 2002.

Gallwitz, Max von. *Erleben im Westen, 1916–1918*. Berlin: E. S. Mittler, 1932.

———. *Meine Führertätigkeit im Weltkriege, 1914–1916: Belgien, Osten, Balkan*. Berlin: Verlag E. G. Mittler, 1929.

Gilbert, Martin. *The First World War: A Complete History*. Fort Leavenworth, Kan.: Command and General Staff School Press, 1996.

Goodspeed, D. J. *Ludendorff: Genius of World War I*. Boston: Houghton Mifflin, 1966.

Grant, Ulysses S. *Personal Memoirs of Ulysses S. Grant*. 2 vols. New York: Charles L. Webster and Company, 1885.

Great Britain, Foreign Office. *Treaty of Peace Between the Allied and Associated Powers and Germany and Other Treaty Engagements, Signed at Versailles, June 28, 1919*. London, HMSO, 1925.

Groener, Wilhelm. *Lebenserinnerungen: Jugend, Generalstab, Weltkrieg*. Edited by Friedrich Freiherr Hiller von Gaertringen. Göttingen: Vandenhoeck and Ruprecht, 1957.

Haeften, Hans von. *Hindenburg und Ludendorff als Feldherren*. Berlin, 1937.

Harbord, James G. *The American Army in France, 1917–1919*. Boston: Little, Brown, 1936.

———. *The American Expeditionary Forces: Its Organization and Accomplishments*. Evanston, Ill.: Evanston Publishing, 1929.

———. *Leaves from a War Diary*. New York: Dodd, Mead, and Co., 1925.

Harris, J. P. *Amiens to the Armistice. The BEF in the Hundred Days' Campaign, 8 August–11 November 1918*. London: Brassey's, 1998.

———. *Men, Ideas, and Tanks*. New York, 1995.

Hassler, Warren W., Jr. *General George B. McClellan: Shield of the Union*. Baton Rouge: Louisiana State University Press.

Haythornthwaite, P. J. *The Napoleonic Source Book*. New York, 1990.

———. *Napoleon's Military Machine*. London, 1988.

Hindenburg, Paul von. *Out of My Life*. New York: Harper and Bros., 1921.

Hittle, J. D. *The Military Staff: Its History and Development*. Harrisburg, Pa.: Military Service Publishing, 1949.

Hoffmann, Max. *Die Aufzeichnungen des Generalmajors Max Hoffmann*. 2 vols. Berlin: Karl Friedrich Nowak, 1929.

———. *War Diaries and Other Papers*. 2 vols. Translated by Eric Sutton. London: Martin Secker, 1929.

———. *The War of Lost Opportunities*. Reprint. Nashville, 1999.

Hofschröer, Peter. *1815: The Waterloo Campaign—Wellington, His German Allies, and the Battles of Ligny and Quatre Bras*. London: Greenhill Books, 1998.

Hollon, W. Eugene. *Beyond the Cross Timbers: The Travels of Randolph B. Marcy, 1812–1887*. Norman: University of Oklahoma Press, 1955.

Horne, Alistair. *How Far from Austerlitz? Napoleon 1805–1815*. New York, 1997.

———. *The Price of Glory: Verdun 1916*. New York, 1963.

Hourteoulle, F. G. *Jena, Auerstaedt: Triumph of the Eagle*. Translated by Alan McKay. Paris, 1998.

Howard, Michael. *The Franco-Prussian War: The German Invasion of France, 1870–1871*. London: Routledge, 1989.

Janssen, Karl-Heinz. *Der Kanzler und der General*. Göttingen: Musterschmidt Verlag, 1967.

Johnson, David. *Napoleon's Cavalry and Its Leaders*. New York: H&M Publishers, 1978.

Jonas, Klaus W. *The Life of Crown Prince Wilhelm*. London, 1961.

Jones, Archer. *Civil War Command and Strategy: The Process of Victory and Defeat*. New York: Free Press, 1992.

Jones, R. Steven. *The Right Hand of Command: Use and Disuse of Personal Staffs in the Civil War*. Mechanicsburg, Pa.: Stackpole Books, 2000.

Kaulbach, Eberhard. "The Prussians." In *Waterloo: Battle of Three Armies*, ed. Lord Chalfont, 52–56. New York: Knopf, 1980.

Kessel, Eberhard. *Moltke*. Stuttgart: K. F. Koehler, 1957.

———. *Moltkes erster Feldzug: Anlage und Durchführung des türkisch-ägyptischen Feldzuges 1839*. Berlin: Mittler, 1939.

Kitchen, Martin. *The Silent Dictatorship: The Politics of the German High Command under Hindenburg and Ludendorff, 1916–1918*. New York: Holmes and Meier, 1976.

Kluck, Alexander von. *The March on Paris and the Battle of the Marne 1914*. London: Edward Arnold, 1920.

Leggiere, Michael. *Napoleon and Berlin: The Franco-Prussian War in North Germany, 1813*. Norman, Okla., 2002.

Letow-Vorbeck, D. *Der Krieg von 1806 und 1807, # 1, Jena und Auerstaedt*. Berlin, 1892.

Liddell-Hart, B. H. *Foch, The Man of Orléans*. Boston: Little, Brown, 1932.

Long, E. B. "John A. Rawlins: Staff Officer Par Excellence." *Civil War Times Illustrated* 12, no. 9 (1974): 4–9, 43–49.

Ludendorff, Erich. *The General Staff and Its Problems*. London, 1921.

———. *Kriegsführung und Politik*. Berlin, 1922.

———. *My War Memories*. 2 vols. London: Hutchinson, 1919.

Ludendorff, Margarethe. *My Married Life with Ludendorff*. London: Hutchinson, 1929.

Lupfer, Timothy T. *The Dynamics of Doctrine: Changes in German Tactical Doctrine During the First World War*. Fort Leavenworth, Kan., 1981.

MacDonell, A. G. *Napoleon and His Marshalls*. New York: Macmillan, 1934; reprint, London: Prion, 1990.

Mackensen, August von. *Briefe und Aufzeichnungen des Generalfeldmarschalls aus Krieg und Frieden*. Edited by Wolfgang Foerster. Leipzig: Bibliographisches Institut, 1938.

Marcey, Randolph B. *Border Reminiscences*. New York, 1872.

———. *The Prairies Traveler*. New York, 1854.

———. *Thirty Years of Army Life on the Border*. New York, 1866.

McClellan, George B. *McClellan's Own Story: The War for the Union, the Soldiers Who Fought It, the Civilians Who Directed It, and His Relations to It and to Them*. New York: Charles L. Webster and Company, 1887.

Meier-Welcker, Hans. *Seeckt*. Frankfurt: Bernard und Graefe Verlag, 1967.

Möller-Witten, Hanns. *Festschrift zum 100.Geburtstag des Generals der Infanterie a.D. Dr. Phil. Hermann von Kuhl*. Frankfurt: E. S. Mittler, 1956.

———. "General der Infanterie v.Kuhl zum 95.Geburtstag." *Wehr-Wissenschaftliche Rundschau* (June–July 1951): 78.

Moltke, Helmuth von. *Briefe über Zustände und Begebenheiten in der Türkei aus den Jahren 1835 bis 1839* (Berlin: Mittler and Sohn, 1876).

———. *Gesammelte Schriften und Denkwürdigkeiten des General-Feldmarschalls Grafen Helmuth von Moltke*. 8 vols. Berlin: E. S. Mittler, 1892.

———. *Leben und Werk in Selbstzeugnissen, Briefe, Schriften, Reden*. Birsfelden bei Basel, Switzerland: Verlag Schibli-Doppler, 1966.

———. *Militärische Werke*. Berlin: Mittler and Sohn, 1896.

Morris, William O'Connor. *Moltke: A Biographical and Critical Study*. 2nd ed. London, 1894.

Muller, Georg von. *The Kaiser and His Court: The Diaries, Note Books and Letters of Admiral Georg Alexander von Muller, Chief of the Naval Cabinet, 1914–1918*. London: Macdonald, 1961.

Nenninger, Timothy K. *The Leavenworth Schools and the Old Army: Education and Professionalism and the Officer Corps of the United States Army, 1881–1918*. Westport, Conn., 1978.

Nowak, Karl Friedrich, ed. *Die Aufzeichnungen des Generalmajors Max Hoffmann*. 2 vols. Berlin: Verlag für Kulturpolitik, 1929.

Paoli, Françoise-André. *L'Armée Française de 1919 à 1939*. 4 vols. Vincennes, France, 1970–77.

Paret, Peter. *Clausewitz and the State*. Princeton, N.J.: Princeton University Press, 1976.

———. *Yorck and the Era of Prussian Reform, 1807–1815*. Princeton, N.J.: Princeton University Press, 1966.

Parkinson, Roger. *The Hussar General: The Life of Bluecher, Man of Waterloo*. London: P. Davies, 1975.

Pershing, John J. *My Experiences in the World War*. New York, 1931.

Pertz, G. H. *Das Leben des Feldmarschalls Grafen Neithardt von Gneisenaus*. Vols. 1–3. Berlin: Reimer, 1864–69.

Porter, Horace. *Campaigning with Grant*. New York: Bonanza Books, 1961.

Prior, Robin, and Trevor Wilson. *Command on the Western Front*. Oxford: Blackwell, 1992.

Putnam, Douglas, Jr. "Reminiscences of the Battle of Shiloh." In *Papers of the Military Order of the Loyal Legion of the United States*, 2:198–207. 56 vols. Wilmington, N.C.: Broadfoot, 1994.

Rapp, J. *The Memoirs of General Rapp*. London, 1840.

Ritter, Gerhard. *The Schlieffen Plan: Critique of a Myth*. New York, 1958.

———. *Staatskunst und Kriegshandwerk: Das Problem des Militarismus in Deutschland*. 4 vols. Munich: R. Oldenbourg, 1954–64.

———. *The Sword and the Scepter: The Problem of Militarism in Germany*. Coral Gables, Fla., 1969–73.

Rochs, Hugo. *Schlieffen*. Berlin: Vossische Buchhandlung Verlag, 1926.

Rupprecht, Kronprinz von Bayern. *Mein Kriegstagebuch*. 3 vols. Munich: Deutscher National Verlag, 1929.

Scott, Winfield. *Memoirs of Lieut.-General Scott, LL.D. Written by Himself*. 2 vols. New York: Sheldon and Company, 1864.

Sears, Stephen W. *George B. McClellan: The Young Napoleon*. New York: Ticknor and Fields, 1988.

———, ed. *The Civil War Papers of George B. McClellan: Selected Correspondence, 1860–1865*. New York: Da Capo, 1992.

Shanahan, William O. *Prussian Military Reforms, 1786–1813*. New York: AMS Press, 1966.

Sherman, William Tecumseh. *Memoirs of General W. T. Sherman*. New York: Library of America, 1990.

Showalter, Dennis E. *Tannenberg: Clash of Empires*. North Haven, Conn.: Archon Books, 1991.

Simon, John Y., ed. *The Papers of Ulysses S. Grant*. Carbondale: Southern Illinois University Press, 1969– .

Simon, Walter, *The Failure of the Prussian Reform Movement, 1807–1819*. Ithaca, N.Y., 1955.

Simpson, Brooks D. *Ulysses S. Grant: Triumph over Adversity, 1822–1865*. Boston: Houghton Mifflin, 2000.

Skelton, William B. *An American Profession of Arms: The Army Officer Corps, 1784–1861*. Lawrence: University Press of Kansas, 1992.

Smith, Digby. *1813: Leipzig—Napoleon and the Battle of the Nations*. London: Greenhill Books, 2001.

Smith, Jean Edward. *Grant*. New York: Simon and Schuster, 2002.

Smythe, Donald. *Pershing: General of the Armies*. Bloomington, Ind., 1986.

Stone, Norman. *The Eastern Front 1914–1917*. New York: Macmillan, 1975.

———. "General Erich Ludendorff." In *The War Lords: Military Commanders of the Twentieth Century*, ed. Field Marshal Sir Michael Carver, 73–83. London, 1976.

Terraine, John. *Douglas Haig, The Educated Soldier*. London: Hutchinson, 1963.

Thaer, Albrecht von. *Generalstabsdienst an der Front und in der O.H.L.* Göttingen, 1958.

Trask, David. *The AEF and Coalition Warmaking, 1917–1918*. Lawrence, Kan., 1993.

Travers, Tim. *How the War Was Won. Command and Technology in the British Army on the Western Front 1917–1918*. London: Routledge, 1992.

———. *The Killing Ground: The British Army, the Western Front and the Emergence of Modern Warfare, 1900–1918*. London: Allen and Unwin, 1987.

Tucker, Spencer C. *The Great War.* Bloomington: Indiana University Press, 1998.

Tyng, Sewell. *The Campaign of the Marne 1914*. London: Humphrey Milford, 1935.

Uhle-Wettler, Franz. *Erich Ludendorff in seiner Zeit*. Berg: Kurt Vowinckel-Verlag, 1995.

U.S. War Department. *The War of the Rebellion: Official Records of the Union and Confederate Armies*. 128 vols. Washington, D.C.: Government Printing Office, 1881–1901.

Venohr, Wolfgang. *Ludendorff: Legende und Wirklichkeit*. Berlin, 1993.

von Kuhl, Hermann. *Der deutsche Generalstab in Vorbereitung und Durchführung des Weltkrieges*, 2nd ed. Berlin: E. S. Mittler, 1920.

———. *Entstehung, Durchführung und Zusammenbruch der Offensive von 1918*. Berlin: Deutsche Verlaggesellschaft für Politik und Geschichte, 1927.

———. *Der Marnefeldzug 1914*. Berlin: E. S. Mittler, 1921.

———. *Der Weltkrieg 1914–1918*. Berlin: Verlag Tradition Wilhelm Kolk, 1929.

von Lossberg, Fritz. *Meine Tätigkeit im Weltkriege 1914–1918*. Berlin, 1939.

von Moltke, Helmuth Graf. *Essays, Speeches, and Memoirs of Field-Marshal Count Helmuth von Moltke*. 2 vols. New York, 1893.

———. *Extracts from Moltke's Correspondence Pertaining to the War of 1870–71*. Fort Leavenworth, Kan., 1911.

———. *The Franco-German War of 1870–71*. London, 1914.

———. *Moltke: His Life and Character, Sketched in Journals, Letters, Memoirs, A Novel, and Autobiographical Notes*. New York, 1892.

———. *Moltke on the Art of War: Selected Writings*. Translated and edited by Daniel Hughes. Novato, Calif., 1993.

———. *Moltke's Correspondence During the Campaign of 1866 Against Austria*. London, 1915.

———. *Moltke's Correspondence: War of 1864*. Berlin, 1892.

————. *Moltke's Military Correspondence, 1866.* Leavenworth, Kan., 1931.

————. *Moltke's Military Correspondence, 1870–71.* 2 vols. Oxford, 1923.

————. *Moltke's Tactical Problems from 1858 to 1882.* Edited by Prussian Grand General Staff. London, 1903.

————. *Strategy: Its Theory and Application: The Wars for German Unification, 1866–1871.* Reprint. Westport, Conn., 1971.

von Seeckt, Hans. *Aus meinem Leben, 1866–1917.* Edited by Friedrich von Rabenau. Leipzig, 1938.

————. *Gedanken eines Soldaten.* Berlin: Verlag fur Kulturpolitik, 1929.

Walker, Jonathan. *The Blood Tub: General Gough and the Battle of Bullecourt.* Kent: Staplehurst, 1998.

Wallace, Lew. *Smoke, Sound and Fury: The Civil War Memoirs of Major-General Lew Wallace, U.S. Volunteers.* Edited by Jim Leeke. Portland, Ore.: Strawberry Hill Press, 1998.

Wallach, Jehuda L. *The Dogma of the Battle of Annihilation: The Theories of Clausewitz and Schlieffen and Their Impact upon the German Conduct of Two World Wars.* Westport, Conn.: Praeger, 1986.

Wawro, Geoffrey. *The Austro-Prussian War: Austria's War with Prussia and Italy in 1866.* Cambridge: Cambridge University Press, 1995.

Wetzell, Georg. *Von Falkenhayn zu Hindenburg-Ludendorff.* Berlin, 1921.

Weygand, Maxime. *Foch.* Paris: Flammarion, 1947.

————. *Idéale Vécu.* Vol. 1 of *Mémoires.* Paris: Flammarion, 1950.

————. *Mirages et Réalité.* Vol. 2 of *Mémoires.* Paris: Flammarion, 1953.

————. *Rappelé au Service.* Vol. 3 of *Mémoires.* Paris: Flammarion, 1957.

————. *Recalled to Service: The Memoirs of General Maxime Weygand.* London, 1955.

————. *The Role of General Weygand; Conversations with His Son, Commandant J. Weygand.* Translated by J. H. F. McEwen. London: Eyre and Spottswoode, 1948.

Wheeler-Bennett, John W. *Brest-Litovsk: The Forgotten Peace.* London: Macmillan, 1963.

White, Charles E. *The Enlightened Soldier: Scharnhorst and the Militarische Gesellschaft in Berlin, 1801–1805.* Westport, Conn., 1989.

Whitton, F. E. *Moltke.* New York, 1921.

Wilhelm, Crown Prince of Germany. *My War Experiences.* New York: Robert M. McBride and Co., 1923.

Wilson, James Harrison. *The Life of John A. Rawlins.* New York: Neale, 1916.

Wynne, Graeme. *If Germany Attacks: The Battle in Depth in the West.* London, 1940.

Zabecki, David. *The German 1918 Offensives: A Case Study in the Operational Level of War.* London: Routledge, 2006.

————. ed. *World War II in Europe: An Encyclopedia.* 2 vols. New York: Garland, 1999.

Zimmerman, Phyllis A. *The Neck of the Bottle: George Washington Goethals and the Reorganization of the U.S. Army Supply System, 1917–1919.* College Station: Texas A&M Press, 1992.

Index

The Naval Institute Press is the book-publishing arm of the U.S. Naval Institute, a private, nonprofit, membership society for sea service professionals and others who share an interest in naval and maritime affairs. Established in 1873 at the U.S. Naval Academy in Annapolis, Maryland, where its offices remain today, the Naval Institute has members worldwide.

Members of the Naval Institute support the education programs of the society and receive the influential monthly magazine *Proceedings* or the colorful bimonthly magazine *Naval History* and discounts on fine nautical prints and on ship and aircraft photos. They also have access to the transcripts of the Institute's Oral History Program and get discounted admission to any of the Institute-sponsored seminars offered around the country.

The Naval Institute's book-publishing program, begun in 1898 with basic guides to naval practices, has broadened its scope to include books of more general interest. Now the Naval Institute Press publishes about seventy titles each year, ranging from how-to books on boating and navigation to battle histories, biographies, ship and aircraft guides, and novels. Institute members receive significant discounts on the Press's more than eight hundred books in print.

Full-time students are eligible for special half-price membership rates. Life memberships are also available.

For a free catalog describing Naval Institute Press books currently available, and for further information about joining the U.S. Naval Institute, please write to:

Member Services
U.S. Naval Institute
291 Wood Road
Annapolis, MD 21402-5034
Telephone: (800) 233-8764
Fax: (410) 571-1703
Web address: www.usni.org